NURTURING PEACE

NURTURING PEACE

WHY PEACE SETTLEMENTS SUCCEED OR FAIL

FEN OSLER HAMPSON

UNITED STATES INSTITUTE OF PEACE PRESS
WASHINGTON, D.C.

The views expressed in this book are those of the author alone. They do not necessarily reflect views of the United States Institute of Peace.

United States Institute of Peace
1550 M Street, N.W.
Washington, D.C. 20005

First published 1996

Printed in the United States of America

The paper used in this publication meets the minimum requirements of American National Standard for Information Sciences—Permanence of Paper for Printed Library Materials, ANSI Z39.48-1984.

Library of Congress Cataloging-in-Publication Data
Hampson, Fen Osler.
    Nuturing peace : why peace settlements succeed or fail / Fen Osler Hampson.
      p. cm.
    Includes bibliographical references and index.
    ISBN 1-878379-55-0 (hard). — ISBN 1-878379-57-7 (pbk.)
    1. Peace treaties. 2. Armistices. 3. Conflict management. 4. International police. I. Title.
JX1952.H28 1996
327.1'72—dc20   96-16488
                                            CIP

CONTENTS

FOREWORD

$\mathbf{W}$e have now seen enough of the post–Cold War era to begin systematically reviewing the conclusions and refining the lessons that can be drawn from numerous cases of contemporary conflict. Indeed, the effort is, if not already overdue, then extremely timely. In the first place, a significant degree of what might be called "strategic disorientation" continues to affect the thinking of political leaders, scholars, practitioners, pundits, and citizens. The search for new conceptual frameworks is still under way, and when it comes to describing the current transitional global system we are faced with many more questions than answers. In the second place—and paradoxically—this disorientation and uncertainty have not inhibited all sorts of people from making sweeping judgments about where we are headed, what works and does not work in post–Cold War conflict situations, and which conflict scenarios lend themselves to which forms of external action, if any. Characterized by an artificial aura of certainty, much of this discussion appears divorced from (and bereft of) in-depth analysis and comparison of specific cases.

In *Nurturing Peace,* Fen Osler Hampson remedies these deficiencies and brings impressive scholarly rigor to bear in a comparative study of five cases of negotiated settlement. This is a comprehensive attempt to identify, understand, and rank the factors that have made for success or failure in Angola, Cambodia, Cyprus, Namibia, and El Salvador. Seldom have students of conflict offered us such a rich, multifactoral analysis of the ingredients that shape the outcome of settlements. Serious students and practitioners alike will be gratified to encounter in these pages a nuanced and carefully developed account of the relevant global, regional, and domestic context of each case, as well as selective diplomatic histories to illustrate the path to settlement and beyond.

By zeroing in on the crucial but often neglected *implementation phase* of settlements, Hampson presents an overview not only of whether settlements were in fact carried out as planned, but also of the dynamics of implementation and the linkage between presettlement and postsettlement negotiation. In the process, Hampson charts fresh ground in extending the theory of third-party mediation into the postsettlement phase; he expands in provocative ways the powerful concept of conflict "ripeness," while making clear the still important role of unique, case-specific factors. This book provides solid contextual grounding for the notion (and limitations) of ripeness, while also addressing other significant variables such as global and regional factors and the quality of the settlement package itself.

For practitioners, the merits of this accessible volume include its relative absence of obfuscatory academic scaffolding and its clear outline of what "implementors" need to do to avoid losing control of a situation to the opposing side or sides. One only hopes that the Western allies will read this book as they seek to translate into practice the accords reached at Dayton among the Serbs, Muslims, and Croats.

As the title suggests, *Nurturing Peace* strongly reinforces the idea that settlements are not self-executing. Indeed, those that "work" are nurtured by a continuous element of sustained, third-party leadership, mediation, problem solving, and peace building. When those external actors who helped mediate a settlement remain engaged and continue to furnish diplomatic backing and political will, then a settlement has a chance of succeeding. This external element, Hampson argues, provides the cement to hold things together when it comes time to put a blueprint into action. It also provides the essential components of creativity, flexibility, pressure, and incentives to keep the parties themselves from running aground—just as outsiders often play a variety of such roles during the presettlement phase. Seen in this light, we should "nurture" peace settlements because their implementation is, in reality, but another phase of a continuous political process. After reviewing five distinct cases, we learn in the concluding chapter not only how third parties play vital roles in peacemaking but also why those roles are so important.

There are no easy panaceas or silver bullets in *Nurturing Peace*. The outright successes of peacemaking—if this sample of cases is at all representative—are outnumbered by partial successes and failures. That should surprise no student of international politics; similar ratios apply to most diplomatic endeavors. But readers also will find here solid refutation of a number of widespread but dubious nostrums. For instance, Hampson demolishes the simplistic notion that these regional conflicts were ripened and settled as a direct result of Mikhail Gorbachev's "new thinking" and the ensuing cooperative phase in U.S.-Soviet relations.

Nurturing Peace provides a sober basis for hope about the post–Cold War global arena. It graphically demonstrates that fruitful foreign policy options do exist between the extremes of doing nothing and intervening with aggressive military force. But these options have their costs and requirements. Those who would write off UN peacekeeping and U.S. leadership within multilateral peacemaking efforts in complex, intrastate conflicts will find little comfort here. By the same token, those seeking quick fixes for the Afghanistans, Burundis, and Bosnias of our world by means of nonofficial, "track-two" initiatives or entirely noncoercive techniques of engaging armed combatants will also be disappointed. *Nurturing Peace* reminds us yet again why peacemaking requires persistence, toughness, and a steady hand on the steering wheel of foreign policy.

Chester A. Crocker
Georgetown University

PREFACE

I first became interested in the subject of this book after participating in several workshops for practitioners on the implementation of the Namibia peace accords. These workshops were sponsored by the Canadian Institute of International Peace and Security, which had the foresight and wisdom to recognize the need to explore how the international community can play a more effective role in assisting with the implementation of negotiated peace settlements. Regrettably, the Canadian Institute of International Peace and Security no longer exists, having fallen victim to budget cuts and the shortsighted policies of the Mulroney government some years ago. But Canadians are indeed fortunate that the United States Institute of Peace continues to thrive and to support much-needed policy-oriented research on some of the most difficult international problems of our time. I am indebted to the United States Institute of Peace for supporting my own work through the Jennings Randolph Fellowship Program. The Institute has provided an intellectually rich and enormously stimulating environment that has greatly enhanced my own understanding about the difficulties of nurturing peace. I also wish to thank the Cooperative Security Programme of the Canadian Department of Foreign Affairs and International Trade for its support of my early work on this project.

Over the years, many colleagues, students, and friends have helped nurture my interest in the question of why some peace settlements appear to "stick" whereas others "come undone" during the course of their implementation. Although only some of these people can be mentioned here, I am grateful to all of them for their contributions, whether in the form of shared insights, comments on draft chapters, or intellectual and moral support. All errors of omission and commission are, of course, mine.

Chester Crocker, Douglas Anglin, and Donald Rothchild read and commented on my work on the Angola-Namibia peace accords. Their insights have proven invaluable in helping me develop a keener and subtler appreciation of the intricacies of that settlement and the challenges of making peace in a "rough neighborhood." I learned much about Cyprus from Brian Mandell, Ronald Fisher, Tozun Bahcheli, and Lou Klarevas. Alvaro de Soto and Patricia Weiss Fagen graciously provided detailed comments on early drafts of my chapter on El Salvador, for which I am most grateful. Richard Solomon, James Schear, and Barbara Shenstone provided constructive suggestions on successive drafts of the Cambodia chapter in this volume. Pamela Aall and Chester Crocker read the conclusion too many times to mention, providing helpful suggestions and commentary in the process. Several of the fellows in the Institute's class of 1993–94 also shared their critical insights on various chapters. I wish to thank Shaul Bakash, Denis McLean, Norma Kriger, Saadia Touval, and Anne Thurston, in particular, for their comments and support. Joe Klaits and Michael Lund provided a supportive and enriching research environment for the fellowship program, as did the members of their staff. Bill Zartman and Steve Stedman at the School of Advanced International Studies, Johns Hopkins University, were generous critics of early chapters of this work, and I have learned much from Zartman's own ground-breaking work on the issue of "ripeness" in making peace.

My own work on this project was assisted by several very able graduate students at the Norman Paterson School of International Affairs, Carleton University. I learned a great deal from Alexandra Bugaliskis, a former graduate student and Canadian foreign ministry official, who had firsthand experience with the settlement in Namibia and wrote a very good research essay on this topic. Natalie Mychajlyszn and Jonathan Perkins provided superb research assistance and helped assemble materials during the early phases of this project. Lou Klarevas, a doctoral student at American University, served ably as my research assistant at the Institute and helped bring the project to final completion. Nigel Quinney provided invaluable editorial guidance in turning the manuscript into a book, as did three anonymous reviewers for the Institute Press. My final word of thanks goes to Dan Snodderly and his staff in the Institute's Publications and Marketing Department, who have been supportive of this project from its early days.

NURTURING PEACE

1

WHAT MAKES A PEACE SETTLEMENT STICK?

Peace agreements sometimes contain the seeds of their own destruction. The most famous instance of this is the Versailles peace treaties that followed World War I. The harsh punitive terms of the settlement, which severed Prussia and demilitarized the Rhineland, helped pave the way for the rise of Adolf Hitler in the 1930s. But even a peace treaty with less exploitative terms than those of Versailles may still fail to establish a lasting and durable political order. As Kalevi Holsti argues in his monumental study, *Peace and War: Armed Conflicts and International Order, 1648–1989,* the success of peace settlements to a large extent depends upon their ability to "anticipate and devise means to cope with the issues of the future."[1] Failure to do so may "set the stage for future eras of conflict and war."[2]

Peace agreements can unravel for other reasons, however. The parties may simply come to the conclusion that it is no longer in their interest to abide by the agreements they have negotiated. Without proper monitoring and enforcement mechanisms, agreements negotiated in good faith can still self-destruct in an escalating spiral of *alleged* violations and counter-recriminations. Without the assistance of third parties who can do what adversaries are unwilling or unable to do themselves, the peace process can grind to a halt.[3] Ambiguities in the text of an agreement may also become major points of contention; these often cannot be resolved

3

in subsequent negotiations or by mediation and arbitration. Conversely, agreements may be too rigid in their initial formulation to adapt to changing circumstances and political forces. Clearly, there are many reasons peace treaties fail.

This study explores why peace agreements succeed or fail, emphasizing how the implementation process affects the possibilities of achieving a durable peace settlement. The focus is on peace settlements that have been negotiated to deal with substate or intercommunal conflicts where third parties, notably the United Nations, have been actively involved not only in peacemaking but also in what UN Secretary-General Boutros Boutros-Ghali calls "post-conflict peace building," that is to say, "action to identify and support structures which will tend to strengthen and solidify peace in order to avoid a relapse into conflict."[4]

We must note at the outset that, in addition to the enormous difficulties of bringing conflicting parties to the negotiating table in civil or intrastate conflicts, the problems of reaching a settlement and making sure the parties continue to abide by it are by no means less formidable. Why is this so? Part of the reason has to do with the nature of civil conflicts in today's world. Unlike the ideologically driven bloc-to-bloc struggles of the Cold War, these "protracted social conflicts" are characterized by intense factional struggles between rival groupings additionally motivated by non-ideological factors. Typically, these conflicts are rooted in a multiplicity of conflicting and overlapping tensions evolving from ethnicity, religion, nationalism, communal strife, socioeconomic problems, regional grievances, and so on. These conflicts are marked by self-sustaining patterns of hostility and violence. They usually involve fierce competition among differing factions for access to and control of the state's political institutions and/or the search for national autonomy and self-determination.[5]

The rejection of any sort of political authority is obviously one source of difficulty in these conflicts. Another is the tendency for these conflicts to spill across borders, drawing in outside actors intent on exploiting the internal situation for their own ends. The emergence of what Barry Buzan calls "regional security complexes," which are characterized by "intense and relatively durable patterns" of amity and enmity and reinforced by "the addition of resources and allies," makes it difficult for outside actors to "moderate or control the local security dynamic."[6] Indeed, one of the enduring legacies of the Cold War is that many internal and regional conflicts were exploited by the two superpowers in their quest for global influence. Furthermore, the arming of different factions by other outside interests has only served to deepen the level of hostility and violence at both the intrastate and regional level.[7]

For third parties intent on offering their mediation services and other "good offices," these conflicts are not easily split into manageable and negotiable components. Much of the literature on third-party intervention suggests that conflicts are most amenable to resolution when issues (and parties) are well defined and are structured in a way that permits a confidence-building process to emerge over time.[8] Nevertheless, in many protracted social conflicts it is often difficult to identify a formula or pattern in which issues can be resolved first so as to lend momentum to the peacemaking process.

Getting the parties to the negotiating table and building momentum toward an agreement are only part of the difficulty, however. If one is lucky enough to secure an agreement, an even greater challenge is to translate the agreement into a concrete package of mutual commitments and undertakings that will end violence once and for all while restoring political order. Here, too, the peacemaking/peace-building process can break down. Like sand castles in quicksand, peace agreements can easily dissolve as a result of a renewed outbreak of civil violence. In the hostile environment of protracted social conflicts, an [*leaders lack the incentive to cooperate*] There is no socially cohesive society within the bor[...] rather a multiplicity of different communal grouping[s ...] power. The difficulties of implementing a viable peace process are thus fundamentally linked to what Brian Job identifies as (1) the state's lack of "effective institutional capacities to provide peace and order, as well as the conditions for satisfactory physical existence, for the population"; and (2) the ongoing sense of "internal threats to and from the regime in power."[9] The goal of political elites under these conditions is political survival, not cooperation or power sharing with those who seek to overthrow them.

It should therefore come as no surprise that most civil wars in the twentieth century have ended, as Stephen Stedman notes, "in elimination or capitulation." In the period from 1900 to 1989, out of a total of sixty-five cases, only 15 percent were resolved through negotiation, and "of these eleven cases of negotiated settlement, six were terminated through international mediation." The figure is somewhat higher (twenty out of sixty-five cases) if one includes "colonial wars, cases formalized by one-sided agreements, and cases that ended in the negotiated partition of the country."[10] Furthermore, a growing body of evidence reveals that negotiated settlements of civil conflicts are more likely to collapse than "settlements" achieved when one side is victorious on the battlefield. According to Roy Licklider, only "one-third of the negotiated settlements of identity civil wars that last for five years 'stick.'" And those conflicts that end in military victory "may be more likely to result in genocide or politicide after the war."[11]

Success and Failure in Postconflict Peace Building

Given that negotiated settlements are difficult to achieve, and obviously somewhat rare, the question of what determines success in restoring domestic order and ending civil violence is a critical one. The recent history of international relations is marked by some notable successes and some conspicuous failures in postconflict, peace-building efforts directed at ending civil conflict. Whereas some peace settlements have proved durable and have succeeded in bringing about an end to military hostilities and violence, others failed to prevent a relapse into armed confrontation and violence or, at best, to transform a cease-fire into a genuine political settlement. In light of the fact that negotiated success is rare, but far more desirable than conflicts that end in "elimination" or "capitulation," it is vital to study why some settlements succeed and others fail. With such knowledge, we can reduce the probability of repeating past mistakes that result from ignoring the important lessons of history. In particular, this study will examine five cases of settlements that succeeded or failed.

- On August 16, 1960, the Republic of Cyprus became an independent state. The country's constitution, which had been negotiated between the governments of Greece, Turkey, and Great Britain in Zurich the preceding year, called for a constitution adapted to the ethnic composition of the island, which was 80 percent Greek Cypriot and 18 percent Turkish Cypriot. Following a series of constitutional crises, in 1963 Archbishop Makarios, president of Cyprus, unilaterally offered a series of amendments that were rejected by the Turkish Cypriot community. The situation continued to deteriorate; serious fighting eventually occurred on the island. On March 13, 1964, the UN Security Council adopted Resolution 187 establishing a UN force (UNFICYP) to be deployed on the island to help restore peace. Although UNFICYP succeeded in supervising a cease-fire, there were numerous crises over the years. The most serious came in 1974 when Turkey launched an extensive military invasion on the north coast of Cyprus following a staged coup d'état against Archbishop Makarios by the Cypriot National Guard, then under the heavy influence of the ruling junta in Greece. Fighting was eventually halted, but the result was a partition of the island into two separate ethnic communities. In 1983 the Turkish community declared its independence and created the Turkish Republic of Northern Cyprus. Amid the two Cypriot states, UNFICYP forces remain deployed in an effort to maintain intercommunal peace. To date, in spite of numerous attempts at mediation by the UN secretary-general and other third parties, a lasting political settlement between the two communities remains elusive.

- On December 22, 1988, representatives of Angola, Cuba, and South Africa formally signed an agreement calling for the implementation of UN Security Council Resolution 435 (1978), which set in motion concrete plans for peace building in Southern Africa—of which Namibian independence was a central element. In 1989 and 1990 the United Nations with its phalanx of soldiers, police, and administrators helped steer the former puppet state of South West Africa through its first elections as the fully independent and democratic country of Namibia. Although the road to independence and free elections was a rocky one, Namibia succeeded in making the transition, enabling its people to live in peace.

- The deployment of the United Nations Angola Verification Mission (UNAVEM) in Angola in January 1989 also resulted from the implementation of UN Security Council Resolution 435 (1978). The Gbadolite Accords of 1989 calling for a cease-fire and other measures broke down almost immediately, and fighting resumed sporadically throughout the country. The Bicesse Accords signed in 1991 called for a new cease-fire between the government and UNITA rebels, new electoral laws, demobilization of troops, and national elections no later than November 1992. However, war broke out again in Angola after UNITA rebels rejected the results of the UN-monitored election, and it was another three years before a new settlement was concluded.

- In 1989 the FMLN guerrilla movement and the government of El Salvador formally invited the United Nations to broker peace negotiations to end a civil war that had claimed 75,000 lives. Following several rounds of negotiations, a preliminary peace accord was signed in New York City on December 31, 1991, followed by a final peace agreement in Mexico City on January 16, 1992. The accords led to a cease-fire, demobilized the FMLN, and paved the way for legal reforms of the electoral system that would allow the FMLN to participate in future elections.

- On October 23, 1991, the Paris Peace Agreements were signed, calling for national reconciliation in Cambodia, self-determination, free and fair elections, the disarming of all factions including the rebel Khmer Rouge, the installation of a transitional authority in Phnom Penh, and elections for a new Cambodian government to be organized by a United Nations Transitional Authority in Cambodia (UNTAC). On October 16, 1991, the UN Security Council passed Resolution 717 providing for the establishment of a United Nations Advance Mission in Cambodia (UNAMIC) to prepare Cambodia for the deployment of UNTAC. Although the deployment of UNTAC proceeded on schedule, fighting between the Khmer Rouge and the government continued, with the Khmer Rouge refusing to cooperate and to fulfill its obligations under the peace settlement. The election campaign was conducted in an atmosphere that was threatened by repeated violations of the cease-fire and by the Khmer Rouge's refusal to allow UNTAC to register voters in locations under Khmer Rouge control. Nevertheless, almost 90 percent of eligible voters went to the polls in a fair and remarkably peaceful vote. The election was the culmination of the biggest effort in UN history. Approximately 20,000 personnel from more than a dozen countries effectively ran the country for two years, repatriated 700,000 refugees, monitored a cease-fire, and operated key government departments. However, UNTAC's failure to maintain the cease-fire in the run-up to the elections undermined its credibility with the Cambodian people, and the Khmer Rouge has continued to wage war against the government since the elections.

Alternative Explanations of Success and Failure

How do we account for these different outcomes that are marked by varying degrees of success and failure in bringing about an end to civil strife and to recurring patterns of violence? A number of hypotheses or analytic approaches are suggested in the conflict resolution literature centering on (1) the role of third-party intervenors in facilitating dispute resolution; (2) the structural characteristics of conflict processes; (3) the changing dynamics of regional and/or systemic power relationships; and (4) the range of issues covered by the peace settlement in question, all of which can potentially affect the prospects of its durability. Before we turn to these different explanations, we need to clarify what we mean by "success" in assessing the outcomes of a peace settlement.

Needless to say, the definition of a successful settlement is highly problematic in the conflict resolution literature. For some, the conflict termination process must produce some set of arrangements that lasts for generations or stands some other test of time, demonstrating robustness and permanence.[12] The problem with this definition is one of infinite regress—that is, exactly when do we conclude definitively that a peace settlement has succeeded? We cannot, because the prospect of failure may lie just around the corner. Alternatively, as Christopher Mitchell argues, the notion of success is inherently relative because "some processes never manage to get the parties into dialogue, let alone to agree to a cessation of fighting. Others reach dialogue but fail to find a possible agreement. Still others . . . achieve agreement only to see it repudiated. Still others break down at the implementation stage and the process ends in recrimination and accusation of bad faith."[13]

Linking the notion of success to different phases of the peace process avoids the problem of defining the concept in terms of an unrealized, and possibly unattainable, end point. However, the definitional problem is not fully resolved. Do we define success in minimalist terms, as associated with, for instance, the onset of negotiations, the conclusion of a formal agreement, or the maintenance of a cease-fire? Or should we associate it with more comprehensive criteria like the demobilization of forces, the laying down of arms, and the eventual restoration of political order? Furthermore, should we include the establishment and maintenance of participatory, democratic political institutions in our definition of political order and success?

While there are no easy answers to these questions, we obviously must consider first whether the signatories abided by the terms of the initial agreement. (Typically these include provisions for a cease-fire and the laying down of arms according to some predetermined schedule.) Because the renunciation of violence by warring factions is clearly a necessary precondition for the restoration of political order, our definition of success begins with the ending of civil violence and armed confrontation. But success, in this sense, is only partial. For a peace settlement to be durable, institutions and support structures must be put in place so that the parties are discouraged from taking up arms again. As Boutros-Ghali explains in his report, *Agenda for Peace*:

> Peacemaking and peace-keeping operations, to be truly successful, must come to include comprehensive efforts to identify and support structures which will tend to consolidate peace and advance a sense of confidence and well-being among people. Through agreements ending civil strife, these may include disarming the previously warring parties and the restoration of order, the custody and possible destruction of weapons, repatriating refugees, advisory and training support for security personnel, monitoring elections, advancing efforts to protect human rights, reforming or strengthening governmental institutions and promoting formal and informal processes of political participation.[14]

Greater levels of success are thus associated with the comprehensiveness and durability of the confidence-building measures that are put in place during the postsettlement or peace-building phase of an agreement. Beyond keeping the peace itself, the list of tasks includes (1) reconstructing civil society at both the national and local level, (2) reintegrating displaced populations into the society and economy, (3) redefining the role of the military and police forces in the maintenance of law and order, (4) building communities and allowing them to survive by bridging the gap between emergency assistance and development, and (5) addressing the needs of particularly vulnerable sectors and groups in society such as women and children.[15] The ultimate success of the peace-building process in situations of civil conflict is thus directly related to a society's ability to make an effective transition from a state of war to a state of peace marked by the restoration of civil order, the reemergence of civil society, and the establishment of participatory political institutions. However, in the short term, if societies are to make this transition, the key considerations are these: Did civil strife and violence end? And did the parties fulfill the commitments they agreed to under the settlement?

By these criteria, Cyprus was a failure because the main provisions of the London-Zurich Accords and the subsequent constitutional settlement were not implemented, and violence between the two communities on the island erupted into a full-scale civil war. Namibia is a success because the civil war did come to an end, and key provisions in the peace settlement calling for Namibian independence, free elections, and the establishment of a new Constituent Assembly (which drafted the country's constitution) were implemented. In contrast, the 1991–92 settlement in neighboring Angola was an abysmal failure. Successive cease-fires failed to hold and although elections were held, they were disputed by UNITA. This dispute led to the outbreak of a full-scale civil war shortly thereafter. Like Namibia, El Salvador is a remarkable success story. After more than ten years of a bloody civil war, the rebel FMLN forces agreed to negotiate with the government in order to bring the war to an end. Negotiations were assisted by the United Nations and the United States, and a negotiated cease-fire managed to hold. The resulting peace agreements launched a process of national reconciliation that shows good promise of restoring democracy to El Salvador. The outcome in Cambodia was mixed. On the one hand, against all odds, free elections for a new government were held; voter turnout was high throughout the country. On the other hand, the leading rebel faction, the Khmer Rouge, opted out of the peace process and continued its civil war against the newly established government of Cambodia.

How do we explain the wide variation in outcomes in these five cases? Why have disputants abided by the terms of peace settlements in some instances and not others? And why has the postconflict, peace-building process advanced further in some countries than in others? A number of hypotheses or potential explanations are discussed here and explored more fully in the case histories in subsequent chapters.

Third Parties and the Politics of Peace Building

Some would argue that whether or not a peace agreement stands up during the postsettlement phase depends upon the degree of political commitment of the disputing parties to the peace process itself. However, this truism belies the fact that there always remain incentives for parties to take up their first option, that is, to return to armed struggle if they cannot achieve their objectives through cooperative means. This incentive is usually quite high during the early phases of the peace process. Moreover, if during the course of implementation the conditions underlying the parties' decision to pursue a negotiated settlement are significantly altered, then no piece of paper will be able to prevent them from pursuing their self-interest. Thus, a central question is what keeps parties on track and otherwise dissuades or deters them from taking up the first option.

One hypothesis is that the successful implementation of peace agreements depends upon the presence or availability of third parties that can proffer carrots or wield sticks to ensure that the process does not become derailed.[16] This proposition follows from much of the literature on third-party mediation, which suggests that third parties can facilitate conflict resolution by restructuring issues, identifying alternatives, modifying adversaries' perspectives, packaging and sequencing issues, building trust, offering side payments, or threatening penalties and/or sanctions. Through their intervention in the peacemaking process, third parties can change disputants' perceptions of the costs, risks, and benefits associated with an agreement versus a no-agreement situation. Third parties therefore serve as a crucial catalyst in developing a supportive relationship between adversaries and establishing the conditions that lead to not only conflict deescalation but also a redefinition of the conflict "as a problem to be solved and not as a contest to be won."[17]

The intervention of the third party thus transforms a dyadic bargaining system into a three- or multicornered relationship in which the third party effectively becomes one of the negotiators in a now transformed multilateral negotiating system. The tasks of the third party can cover a wide range of functions throughout the prenegotiation, negotiation, and implementation phases of the peace settlement process. These tasks include meeting with stakeholders to assess their interests, helping choose spokespeople or team leaders, identifying missing groups or strategies for representing diffuse interests, offering guarantees, drafting protocols and setting agendas, suggesting options, identifying and testing possible tradeoffs, writing and ratifying agreements, serving as observers, and monitoring and facilitating implementation of agreements.

By being involved in the implementation phase of a peace settlement, third parties can help to restore confidence, build trust, and change the perceptions and behavior of disputing parties. These include otherwise technical activities ranging from peacekeeping and monitoring of cease-fires, which help reduce the likelihood of armed confrontation and "accidental" encounters,[18] to assisting with the establishment of participatory political institutions—for example, via externally supervised and monitored elections that channel the frustrations and aspirations of the politically mobilized elements of society, thus reducing the prospects of armed violence.[19] As Mandell notes, confidence-building measures are especially crucial in the early stages of a peace settlement because they can forestall a resort to the use of force by the disputants, generate additional confidence-building measures beyond those initially implemented, heighten the cost of returning to the status quo ante, and create additional incentives for collaboration.[20] Mediation, conciliation, and arbitration by third parties can also help to resolve outstanding or unanticipated issues that emerge during the postconflict, peace-building phase and that threaten to derail the peace process.

Who are these third parties? Typically they include international organizations like the United Nations and its associated relief and development agencies, regional organizations, great powers, regional powers, and even groupings of smaller states. By acting independently or in unison, these third parties can help to sustain the commitment and cooperation of the disputing parties in the overall peacemaking and peace-building process.[21] Skillful and properly executed third-party interventions can have important implications for the long-term management and resolution of the conflict. The converse is also true. Clumsy and poorly timed or badly executed interventions can raise tensions and undermine the goals and objectives of the peace agreement and peacemaking process.[22]

Effective intervention also requires a careful sequencing of strategies and approaches. As Keashly and Fisher observe, protracted conflicts contain a large number of different constituencies with different demands, interests, and belief systems. "With such a large number of elements, it seems unreasonable to expect that a single intervention strategy could deal fully with all of them. It seems more useful to envision intervention . . . as a *coordinated* series of concurrent and consecutive strategies directed towards the long-term goal of resolving the conflict."[23]

The role that third parties play in the full range of activities associated with the negotiation and implementation of peace agreements is therefore possibly a key element in explaining why some peace settlements succeed and others fail. Peace settlements that enjoy high levels of third-party assistance and support during the entire course of the peacemaking and peace-building process are arguably more likely to succeed than those that do not.[24] In the chapters that follow, we explore the roles third parties have played in the settlement of conflicts in Cyprus, Southern Africa (Namibia and Angola), El Salvador, and Cambodia in order to assess whether their involvement and performance had a positive or negative impact on the fate of the settlement in question.

The Role of Ripeness in Peace Building

In addressing the role of third parties in postconflict peace building, we should recognize that conflict resolution and settlement processes may well depend upon factors that are *intrinsic* to the conflict itself, such that the contributions of outside third parties are marginal, at best, to the achievement of a durable and lasting peace settlement. It is axiomatic in much of the burgeoning literature on international mediation and negotiation that many conflicts have a self-sustaining dynamic of their own. In order for third-party interventions to be effective, it is often argued, the conflict has to reach a plateau or the level of a "hurting stalemate," at which point the parties no longer feel they can use force to gain a unilateral advantage and become willing to consider other options. At this point, the conflict, to use Zartman's phrase, is "ripe for resolution"[25] insofar as the parties perceive the costs and prospects of continued confrontation to be more burdensome than the costs and prospects of a settlement.

There are, however, important differences in the way "ripeness" is defined by scholars. Zartman argues that there are four independent conditions for ripeness—a hurting stalemate to the conflict, a looming catastrophe, valid representatives, and a way out of the conflict—though not all conditions need be present for ripeness to occur.[26] In contrast, Haass defines ripeness in terms of "the prerequisites for diplomatic progress" or "the circumstances conducive for negotiated progress or even a solution." These prerequisites or circumstances are based on the following conditions: "a shared perception of the desirability of an accord," willingness to reach a compromise, compromises based on formulas in which national interests of the parties are protected, and approaches or processes of dispute resolution that are acceptable to the parties.[27]

Haass's "conditions" come perilously close to defining ripeness in terms of the willingness of the parties to seek a negotiated compromise to settle their differences—that is, equating parties' often difficult-to-discern motivations and interests in a settlement with the negotiated outcome. Furthermore, shifting power balances and the emergence of a hurting stalemate are not the only factors that may make resolution more attractive in certain conflicts. Additional requirements for ripeness include the following: (1) the parties have redefined their interests—because of changes in leadership or constituency pressures, for example—and are no longer content with the status quo; (2) old norms and patterns of behavior have been replaced with new norms facilitating the possibilities for compromise and the achievement of a durable settlement; (3) the parties share perceptions about the desirability of an accord; (4) the parties have agreed on a common bridging process to settle differences; and (5) a formula allowing for compromise and a negotiated end to hostilities is available.[28]

The central importance of ripeness underscores the fact that third parties are only one element, and possibly a minor one at that, in the overall peacemaking/peace-building process. Haass, for instance, makes the claim that the success or failure of diplomatic efforts depends almost exclusively upon ripeness: "Whether negotiation will succeed will hinge on the shared perception by the disputants that an accord is desirable." And he suggests that

> too much diplomacy or mediation in an unripe situation can be counterproductive. Such activism, no matter how well intentioned or politically useful as a demonstration of concern, can lead parties in a dispute to avoid facing reality and making tough, but necessary, decisions. Paradoxically, outside activism can actually discourage the emergence of a situation in which outside activism might be productive.[29]

What some conflicts lack, therefore, is not so much a shortage of skilled third parties as ripeness to the conflict itself. For example, the continuing division of Cyprus between the Turkish Cypriot and Greek Cypriot communities may have more to do with a lack of ripeness than a shortage of third-party mediators—of which there have been many. In this instance the lack of ripeness is due to a preference for the status quo over any of the possible alternatives—alternatives that would dilute the political authority and autonomy of the island's two communities. Furthermore, the long-standing presence of a UN peacekeeping force on Cyprus has kept violence to a minimum that is obviously tolerable to both sides.

The question arises whether success or failure in the postconflict, peace-building phase of the peace process is also associated with a lack of ripeness. It is entirely conceivable that peace settlements may fail because the conditions associated with ripeness were not met at the time they were negotiated; that is, the conflict had not reached the level of a plateau or hurting stalemate, but the parties decided to negotiate an agreement anyway, possibly as a delaying or regrouping tactic, because the agreement was forced on them or for some other reason.

The notion of ripeness implies, wrongly perhaps, that a conflict has reached a new, stable equilibrium. However, this equilibrium can be upset by the terms of the agreement itself or by the fact that the parties view their positions and interests differently following the signing of the agreement. Thus the parties may seek to regain unilateral advantage shortly thereafter by the use of force. Paradoxically, a peace settlement may set in motion political forces that lead to an "unripening" process in which forces upset the new equilibrium that facilitated the agreement in the first place. This equilibrium can also be destroyed by the actions of outside actors that do not want the agreement to succeed and therefore take active measures to undermine it, for example, by providing arms or other kinds of support to various factions that initially had strong incentives to lay down their arms and pursue a negotiated settlement.

The possibility of unripening—that is, of a peace process that turns rotten during the settlement phase—is a real risk in civil conflicts where the basic infrastructure of the conflict is marked by a shifting constellation of group loyalties and identities that are not necessarily eliminated or abated by formal attempts at cooperation.[30] The fact that these conflicts are rooted in an extraordinarily complex mix of factors (including multiethnic and communal cleavages and disintegrations, underdevelopment and poverty, and distributive justice) also complicates the task of identifying the ripe moment and ensuring that a negotiated agreement is not jeopardized by a renewed flare-up of violence.

The fundamental elusiveness of the ripe moment in protracted social conflicts suggests that some, though obviously not all, conflicts may *not* be amenable to peaceful intervention by *any* third party—be it a great, middle, or small power, or an international organization. And for those conflicts that *are* amenable to the good offices of intermediaries, the prospects for success may well depend more on the dynamics of the conflict itself and situational pressures (internal or external) than the presence or absence of skilled third parties. In other words, the actions and contributions of outside third parties to peace building may have less to do with the reasons a settlement succeeds or fails than the structural characteristics of the conflict itself and whether or not the hurting stalemate at the time of the negotiated settlement is durable enough to make the peace last.

Systemic and Regional Power Balances

At a systemic level, great-power relationships and the changing dynamics of the East-West competition have been identified as having a major impact on the possibilities for diplomacy and resolution of regional conflicts.[31] During the height of the Cold War when competition was viewed as a zero-sum game, the superpowers relied on military instruments to achieve their aims, limiting the prospects for achieving negotiated and durable settlements. Conversely, the end of the Cold War and collapse of the Soviet Union have been associated with the settlement of many disputes and the promotion of security cooperation in some regions, notably in the Middle East, Southeast Asia, Central America, and Southern Africa. Many see a strong link between improving East-West relations in the late 1980s and the negotiation of peace agreements in Angola and Namibia, El Salvador, and Cambodia.[32]

Systemic explanations suggest that great powers have been able to facilitate conflict resolution and settlement processes by bringing pressure to bear on client states and other parties to conflict, and by working toward joint solutions based on a non-zero-sum view of their respective interests. Thus, for example, the settlement of conflict in Southern Africa is arguably part of a more general trend in systemwide relations that culminated in the collapse of the Soviet Union (although the continuation of fighting in Angola is obviously not part of this trend).

The use of force and changing politicomilitary balances of power may explain bargaining outcomes and the durability of certain peace settlements. Realist and neorealist writers in international relations see military strength and diplomatic resolve as the crucial ingredients of state power.[33] In this view, victories and losses in international politics are determined by the relative power resources that state actors can bring to bear on particular issues and problem areas. Declining Soviet hegemony in the face of American resolve may, therefore, best explain outcomes in certain conflicts.

Underlying all systemic-level explanations—be they of the "superpower détente bringing peace" or the "United States prevailing" variety—is the assumption that East-West rivalries lay at the heart of many (though clearly not all) regional and intrastate conflicts. Thus, according to this assumption, systemic change brought about subsystemic change and a corresponding shift in the behavior of regional actors to shifting power balances at the geostrategic level.[34] This view sees regional and even intrastate conflicts (the line between these two is often blurry) as largely driven by external factors and forces. Internal or subregional forces will be refracted through the prism of great power competition and global politics. The prospects for conflict resolution thus depend significantly on the ability of great powers to accommodate their divergent preferences or one great power's ability to prevail over the other.

The assumption that political behavior has subsystemic versus systemic roots informs the recent work of a group of scholars writing about regional security politics in the Third World following the end of the Cold War. As superpower influence has waned, so the argument runs, the importance of subsystemic patterns of relations among states that are "locked into geographical proximity with each other" has correspond-ingly grown.[35] These relations are marked by what Buzan calls patterns of amity and enmity that are shaped not just by the regional distribution of power but "specific things such as border disputes, interests in ethni-cally related populations, ideological alignments . . . [and] long-standing historical links."[36] Anarchy thus interacts with geography to create a dis-tinct and unique set of regional political relations of which the actors may or may not be fully cognizant. "Like a balance of power," Buzan argues, "a security complex can exist and function regardless of whether or not the actors involved recognize it. They will, of course, recognize the particular lines of threat that bear on them, for if they did not, the whole idea of security complexes would be void. But they may well not see, or appreciate fully, the whole pattern of which they are a part."[37]

In spite of the importance of history, geography, and culture, Buzan still sees behaviors at the regional level as being "threat driven" and informed by the degree of anarchy that prevails at the regional level. For example, he argues, "Typically, states will be much more aware of the threats that others pose to them than they will be of the threat they pose to others."[38] He also notes, "The individual lines of security concern can be traced quite easily by observing how states' fears shape their foreign policy and military behavior."[39] However, the fundamental point is that geography and propinquity are crucial to the way states perceive their allies and enemies. "Security interdependencies will be more strongly focused among the members of the set than they are between members and outside states."[40]

Although Buzan does not directly address the implications of the exis-tence of "regional security complexes" for conflict resolution and settle-ment processes, other writers have. In exploring the origins and devel-opment of the Arab-Israeli conflict, Sandler argues that the conflict has evolved from a state-communal conflict to one that includes important interstate interactions (regulated by deterrence rationales, balance of power mechanisms, arms races, and so forth). The spatial expansion of the conflict introduced new parties and actors so that the linkage between "internal" conflict systems and regional, interstate, and even international conflict systems is increasingly pronounced. According to Sandler, understanding the pattern of spatial expansion and a conflict's "compound structure" is central to any attempt at conflict resolution. Not only does the compound structure require third parties to contain this process of expansion, but it also implies that a combination of international and intercommunal intervention strategies will be prerequisites for conflict termination.[41]

Different intervention strategies are also required for each of these levels. At the communal level, issues of group identity and political participation must be addressed in order for conflict termination to be effective. At the interstate level, Sandler suggests that more traditional, power-based approaches directed at meeting the security requirements of affected regional powers are in order. It may be necessary not only to persuade, but also to dissuade regional powers from interfering in the affairs of their neighbors. Security guarantees and other kinds of incentives may also have to be offered as part of the settlement package.

The notion that most civil conflicts are usually embedded in the politics of a "regional security complex" is an important insight with significant implications for both peacemaking and peace building. It suggests that the success of a peace settlement is inextricably tied to the interests of neighboring regional powers and their overall commitment to the peace process. Regional powers can stand in the way of the peace process if they feel their interests are threatened by a settlement. They can also reinforce or shore up the peacemaking/peace-building process if they feel it will advance their interests. Third-party interventions that fail to take into account the impact of interstate or regional interests at the intercommunal level of conflict, according to this point of view, are doomed to failure. The ultimate success of a peace settlement thus may well hinge on a stable regional environment in which key regional actors are interested in taking constructive measures that promote conflict resolution.

Settlement Provisions

How does the actual design of a peace settlement affect the prospects of achieving peace? Holsti argues that the success or failure of peacemaking efforts in international politics is determined by whether or not a peace settlement fulfills a number of separate but interrelated functions. These functions are intended to support a stable international order in which stability is defined in terms of the avoidance of "system-threatening wars" and the maintenance of "effective control over those who might seek to destroy the order."[42]

According to Holsti, the prerequisites for peace include:

1. the provision of a system of governance that embodies certain norms of what constitutes acceptable behavior;

2. legitimacy, based on shared principles of justice that are incorporated into the peace settlement;

3. assimilation, which demonstrates "that the gains of living within the system . . . outweigh the potential advantages of seeking to destroy or dominate it";

4. a deterrent system powerful enough to prevent defections;

5. conflict-resolving procedures and institutions that "include procedures and institutions for identifying, monitoring, managing, and resolving major conflicts between members of the system," including the capacity "to impose settlement terms where continuation of a conflict poses a threat to the system as a whole";

6. consensus on war, that is, the recognition that war is a fundamental problem so that the design of new orders develops and fosters explicit norms against the use of force;

7. procedures for peaceful change, including "methods and procedures for reviewing settlement terms, for raising grievances, in general for adjusting commitments and responsibilities to new social, economic, demographic, and diplomatic conditions"; and

8. anticipation of future issues, that is, a system for anticipating issues that are potential sources of new conflict and for monitoring and handling them before they erupt into violence.[43]

Peace settlements therefore should be judged according to whether or not they meet these criteria.[44]

Holsti's suggestion is that we should carefully scrutinize the terms of a peace settlement in order to assess whether it is sufficiently comprehensive and durable to prevent, or otherwise deter, new challenges to the order that has just been created. Holsti's eight criteria are intended to apply to peacemaking efforts at the interstate level, but there is no *a priori* reason to exclude them from peacemaking efforts at the intrastate level, particularly since many so-called intrastate conflicts have a significant regional or international dimension as noted earlier. Holsti makes an important point that is not addressed by structural or systemic theories, or by theories of third-party intervention. It is that some peace agreements are simply badly designed, and this is the main source of their failure.

One factor that Holsti does not mention, but which other analysts have identified as crucial to resolving the problems of ethnic division, is the inclusion of power-sharing provisions in any negotiated settlement. Arend Lijphart defines power sharing as the "participation of the representatives of all significant groups in the government of the country and a high degree of autonomy for these groups."[45] Additionally, power sharing can include proportionality in political representation and public service appointments and the minority veto. Other authors view political relations as "negotiable" through the party system and mechanisms such as vote pooling and the formation of multiethnic coalitions. Donald Horowitz argues that these kinds of institutional mechanisms have alleviated some of the strains in ethnically and religiously divided societies.[46]

To the extent that peace settlements include provisions for free elections and the establishment (or reinvigoration) of democratic political institutions, an important question is whether they also contain provisions (explicit or implicit) for power sharing—either along the lines suggested by Lijphart or according to some other formula or set of principles. The general hypothesis is that a settlement is more likely to fail if it does not include power-sharing provisions than if it does.

Overview of the Study

In the case studies of Cyprus, Namibia, Angola, El Salvador, and Cambodia that follow, I explore the conditions under which a negotiated peace settlement led to cooperative behavior among disputing parties and laid the foundations for an effective process of peace building, or otherwise failed to do so. The above discussion has suggested a rich array of variables to consider. One of the challenges is to assess the relative importance of these different factors to the overall peacemaking and peacebuilding process.

These cases have been chosen for historical study and comparison because (1) the peace settlement in each case was directed at not only ending military violence and conflict but also creating a new set of political institutions; (2) prima facie implementation appears to have been important to the settlement process of the conflict; (3) third parties were involved in the negotiations that led to the settlement; (4) third parties were active in performing a variety of roles and functions during the implementation phase of the settlement that went beyond traditional peacekeeping, including assistance with the demobilization of forces, resettlement of refugees, domestic rehabilitation and reconstruction, electoral monitoring and supervision, and, in some cases, civil administration; (5) all of these conflicts had the potential to escalate into regional or even international conflicts; and (6) all at some point captured the attention of the United Nations and therefore the international community.

All of the cases analyzed in this study, with the exception of the Cyprus conflict, meet all six of these criteria. In the case of Cyprus, third parties were not actively involved in the initial implementation of the London-Zurich Accords of 1959. Nevertheless, Cyprus is included as an example of the critical role of third-party involvement, or specifically the lack thereof, not in nurturing a viable settlement, but in bringing the provisions of such an agreement to fruition. Furthermore, it is arguable that Cyprus served as an exemplar to be avoided in subsequent international peacekeeping and peace-building efforts.

The following specific questions inform the case studies and delimit the general scope of the inquiry:

- When did the settlement phase of the peacemaking process begin? Was there a lag between the negotiation of a set of principles or an agreement and its actual implementation?

- What were the "terms of trade" in the peace agreement? Were the zones of "constructive ambiguity" and terms of trade in the agreement so broad that they created new conflicts? Were there unresolved or unanticipated issues that could not be avoided during the implementation phase of the settlement?

- Did the conditions or assumptions under which a negotiated settlement was reached reflect the actual situation on the ground? Was there any change in these assumptions or on the ground during the post-conflict, peace-building phase of the agreement?

- What was the relationship between the disputing parties at the time the peace accords were signed? Was the relationship characterized by what Zartman, Haass, and others have called a "hurting stalemate,"[47] or was the relationship asymmetrical? Was the degree of mistrust high or low?

- What were the apparent motivations of the parties for signing the peace accords when they did? Were the parties genuinely interested in moving the relationship to a more cooperative footing, or were they simply interested in using a lull in fighting to regroup and consolidate their forces for future armed confrontation? (Were there also differences of opinion among different factions as to what might be gained by a settlement?)

- Were regional actors supportive of the accords?
- What disputes, if any, emerged concerning the interpretation accorded to various aspects of the agreement and the manner of their implementation? Did perceptions of the costs and benefits of the agreement change during implementation?
- What role, if any, did third parties (including the United Nations, regional and subregional organizations, and outside powers) play in the negotiation and settlement process? Was agreement or compromise reached bilaterally or with the assistance of third parties?
- What functions were outside third parties called upon to perform to facilitate implementation, including mediation, conciliation, fact finding, verification, monitoring, observation, peacekeeping, humanitarian assistance, refugee relocation and assistance, and electoral supervision and monitoring? How well were these roles performed? Did they contribute to or detract from trust and confidence building between the parties to the dispute?

This study attempts to situate peacekeeping and other third-party initiatives within the broader context of general peace-building and dispute settlement processes. It asks when third-party initiatives are likely to be most effective and whether they can affect the long-term outcomes of a peace settlement. At the same time, this study relates the role of third parties in dispute resolution to the structural characteristics of conflict and regional and/or systemic power relationships that arguably play a greater role in determining whether a settlement lasts or not.

It is the argument of this book that for peace settlements to succeed third parties must entrench and institutionalize their role in the peacemaking and peace-building process. Third parties must also possess significant resources and staying power to remain fully engaged in the negotiations leading up to the settlement and subsequent peace-building process. Interventions that fail are associated with a lack of staying power or an inability to muster the resources that are needed to build a secure foundation for a settlement. Ripeness is an extremely elusive goal in situations of civil conflict. To the extent that ripeness exists at all, it must be cultivated through a combination of carrots and sticks that are brought to bear on the conflicting parties themselves. Moreover, the equilibrium of forces that is achieved at the time of a settlement is easily upset as different factions jockey for power in the postsettlement phase of an agreement. Regional interests can also overturn a settlement unless they too are brought into the peace process or, at the very least, dissuaded (or deterred) from interfering in the affairs of their neighbors. With the end of the Cold War, regional powers have acquired greater potential to affect the situational dynamics of these conflicts. Thus, peace-building efforts at the intercommunal or domestic level must be complemented by security measures and other initiatives at the regional level. Third-party interventions that focus exclusively on one level to the exclusion of the other are doomed to failure.

Given the potentially large number of activities and tasks associated with the peacemaking and peace-building process, it is unreasonable to assume that any single organization or country can perform them on its own or can shoulder the full responsibility of ensuring that a settlement succeeds. Major costs are attached to intervention. For example, costs may be incurred as a result of taking on the process of mediation or taking responsibility for implementation, regardless of whether or not the intervention is a success. For third parties with limited influence or an indirect stake in the conflict, the costs and risks of intervention will usually outweigh the foreign policy benefits to be gained by involvement. This argues for a multilateral approach to conflict resolution, whereby the costs and risks of intervention can be shared within a larger group. Of course, this is easier said than done, and the problems of coordination among third parties that may not share similar interests and/or resources remain.

In view of these constraints it is truly remarkable that the peace-building process has advanced as far as it has in some cases. The experience and understanding of the causes of this success can be applied to ongoing peacemaking efforts in other regional settings. The current confrontations in the Balkans and Nagorno-Karabakh region of the former Soviet Union (and elsewhere in East Europe and Eurasia) are ample testimony to the difficulties of bringing about an end to armed violence. And the success of the Dayton Peace Accords for Bosnia will depend significantly on the skill of outside third parties in helping with their implementation.

Past agreements provide strong evidence that negotiated agreements cannot be put on autopilot; they require skillful, committed people at the controls. Peace settlements, no matter how precisely worded, are not comprehensive instruction manuals providing specific (let alone wise) answers to hundreds of questions that arise each week. Rather, they set forth the expectations, goals, and compromises that the parties and mediators held or accepted at a given point in time. The successful implementation of peace accords thus demands the full-time and sustained engagement of outside implementing agents.

CYPRUS

$\mathbf{A}$ lack of ripeness is a frequent explanation of why diplomacy and third-party mediation efforts have failed to resolve the ongoing dispute in Cyprus. For instance, Richard Haass writes:

> Greeks and Turks, within Cyprus and without, remain unprepared for ambitious diplomacy. Something more ambitious ought to be contemplated only when Greeks and Turks, as well as Greek Cypriots and Turkish Cypriots, are prepared to make difficult compromises on issues of central importance. . . . No outside person can impose a settlement on the Cyprus problem (or for that matter the Aegean problem). Neither situation is yet ripe for negotiation, because the local leadership has not yet concluded that the *status quo* is less desirable than what could be agreed on through diplomacy, and that the political risk inherent in negotiation is either worth taking or unavoidable.[1]

Another thoughtful observer of the situation argues, "Above all other factors contributing to the current impasse, the greatest impediment to resolution is the absence of a hurting stalemate. Neither Cypriot community is sufficiently dissatisfied with the status quo to make the difficult compromises necessary for resolving the conflict."[2]

But failure to resolve the Cyprus dispute is not due simply to a lack of ripeness; it also stems from the failure of successive third parties to cultivate ripeness, or, at the very least to provide the kinds of inducements that would carry the peace process forward.[3] As a matter of fact, in some cases interventions by third parties have served to exacerbate tensions between the two communities. At a more fundamental level, the lack of ripeness or absence of a hurting stalemate is also due to third-party involvement in the form of peacekeeping that has kept tensions at a moderate level and reduced the incentive for the Turkish Cypriot and Greek Cypriot communities to seek a political settlement. In many respects, the Cyprus experience highlights the difficulties of moving the peace process forward from a workable cease-fire to a durable peace settlement once peacekeeping forces have been deployed.

An additional barrier to resolution has been the obvious reluctance of the United States and NATO to put real pressure on either Greece or Turkey to resolve their differences over Cyprus. During the Cold War the need to maintain unity on NATO's southern flank was paramount and superseded the objective of achieving a permanent solution to the Cyprus problem. With the end of the Cold War, however, the Soviet threat has been replaced by troubles in the Balkans, the Middle East, and the Persian Gulf. These crises have had a higher priority than Cyprus in the overall concerns of NATO and the United States.

Recent UN mediation efforts have focused on advancing intercommunal talks between the Greek Cypriot and Turkish Cypriot communities; only in the 1990s have Greece and Turkey been drawn directly into and consulted about the details of a settlement. Clearly, any sort of negotiated solution to the conflict will require these two countries to agree to a settlement that is negotiated by the leaders of the two Cypriot communities. The historical record of negotiations shows that, when a proposed settlement has not been to the liking of Greece or Turkey, neither country has hesitated to use its power to undermine the proposal.[4]

For the purposes of this study, Cyprus is also a good example of how an implementation fails and why a political settlement—even one including extensive power-sharing provisions—that is imposed on warring factions can exacerbate political relations. The London-Zurich Accords of 1959, which led to the Constitutional Accord of 1960, are a striking example of a political settlement that failed. The settlement failed because (1) it was imposed by third parties; (2) it was too rigid to address the needs and interests of the two ethnic groups on the island; and (3) there was minimal third-party involvement in implementation, particularly when disputes arose between the Greek and Cypriot communities over implementation of key provisions in the Constitution. In other words, the accords contributed to the outbreak of conflict in Cyprus; the legacy of that failure has yet to be overcome.

The Cyprus example also illustrates that third-party intervention—even sustained third-party intervention—may not be enough to resolve a conflict unless regional actors and interests are included in the peace process as well by having a seat at the table. The failure to reach a lasting political settlement to the Cyprus crisis underscores the importance of achieving unified political support for negotiations at *both* the regional and international levels. At the same time, the fact that the two Cypriot communities are not at war underscores the important role played by the UN peacekeeping forces on the island. The absence of violent conflict suggests that peacekeeping has been a success in this case. But failure to link peacekeeping operations to a broader political strategy, particularly when peacekeeping forces were first deployed on the island, has locked the United Nations into a situation with no viable exit strategy. If UN forces do leave, it will be because donor countries have become weary of contributing troops to an operation that has no end in sight. The consequences might well be tragic were political tensions to rise and fighting to resume.

The first section of this chapter traces the history of the conflict in Cyprus. Then the obstacles posed by regional and outside interests to the conflict are discussed. Next we explore the reasons successive third-party efforts to mediate a political settlement, following the catastrophic failure of the 1959 peace accords, have been fruitless and whether this is due to a lack of ripeness to the conflict or to other factors. In advancing the argument that Cyprus is an example of the failure of successive mediators to coordinate interests at the regional and international level in order to develop a *unified* intervention strategy, the chapter also considers the alternative explanation that this failure is due more to a lack of ripeness than to what mediators have or have not done.

History of the Conflict

Cyprus was transferred to the United Kingdom by the Congress of Berlin in 1878, although the island remained under nominal Turkish control.[5] Cyprus became a formal colony of Britain in 1925, but, given its large Greek Cypriot population, the desire among its people to become part of the Greek state was strong. After World War II, anti-colonial, independence sentiments grew. A terrorist group called EOKA

(National Organization of Cypriot Fighters) was formed in 1955 and launched a series of bombing campaigns against the British in an effort to end colonial rule and achieve *enosis,* or unification with Greece. The British response was to seek a consensus with Turkey and Greece on the future of Cyprus. The British eventually concluded that their interests could best be served by retaining the sovereignty of their military bases on the island and by achieving a political settlement that would satisfy the interests of the majority Greek community on the island while protecting the interests of the minority Turkish community.[6]

Turkey, prior to 1955, had not been actively involved in the governance of Cyprus since the island's annexation by Britain during World War I. The movement for *enosis* forced Turkish and Turkish Cypriot leaders to reexamine their interests in Cyprus. In particular, they found unacceptable the prospect of a Turkish minority within a larger Greek state. Turkey also had strategic concerns about the extension of Greek territory to the southern flank of Turkey. A solution was negotiated by Britain, Turkey, and Greece at meetings in Zurich and London in 1959. However, the Greek Cypriot leader, Archbishop Makarios, and the leader of the Turkish Cypriot community, Fazil Küchük, were limited to signing documents already approved by Britain, Turkey, and Greece. At the London conference Makarios expressed a number of major objections to the Zurich agreement. They included reservations about the stationing of Greek and Turkish troops on Cypriot soil; the 30 percent representation of Turkish Cypriots in the legislature, public service, and Council of Ministers (which he considered to be disproportionate to the size of the Turkish Cypriot community); the separate majority vote in the House of Representatives; and the final veto of the president and vice president. But because the Greek government had already signed on to the Zurich agreement, it rejected Makarios's objections, and the agreements moved forward.[7]

The Draft Treaty Concerning the Establishment of the Republic of Cyprus recognized the island's independence if British rights to military bases were safeguarded. The Treaty of Alliance between Greece, Turkey, and Cyprus provided for the stationing of Greek and Turkish troops on the island to guarantee the island's independence. The Treaty of Guarantee was a pact between Britain, Greece, and Turkey recognizing the independence and territorial integrity of Cyprus and prohibiting activities directed at partition of the island. The pact also called for direct consultations among the guarantor powers should any problems occur, and granted each party the right, as a guarantor power, to take action to restore the status quo if the accords were violated in the absence of consultation. The agreements also provided for the creation of a Joint Constitutional Commission, the members of which included representatives of the Greek and Turkish governments and the two Cypriot communities. The commission completed its work in less than a year, and the draft Constitution was accepted by Cyprus on April 6, 1960, at which point it received its independence from the United Kingdom.

The Republic of Cyprus that came into existence on August 16, 1960, had several limitations imposed on its sovereignty. However, the constitutional provisions in the accords proved cumbersome and politically unwieldy. Instead of bringing the island's two communities together, the Constitution drove a wedge that moved them further apart and eventually led to full-scale civil war in 1964.[8] On the one side, many Greek Cypriots deeply resented the preclusion of *enosis* in what they considered undemocratic constitutional provisions. On the other side, many Turkish Cypriots disliked the Constitution because it precluded *taksim* (partition of Cyprus into two states) and failed to address adequately their concerns about being dominated by the Greek Cypriot majority.

The Constitution contained 196 articles and 6 annexes, making it one of the most comprehensive and complex documents of its kind.[9] The key articles in the Constitution, and those that proved the most controversial, concerned the presidency (Part I). They provided for a Greek Cypriot president, a Turkish Cypriot vice president, and a council of ministers having seven Greek Cypriot and three Turkish Cypriot Ministers. Both the president and the vice president had a veto over council decisions. The 7:3 ratio was also reflected in the composition of the legislative branch of government, which was composed of a House of Representatives and two Communal Chambers. Although many of the decisions of the House of Representatives were by majority vote, a majority in both communities was required on matters pertaining to electoral law, municipalities, and taxes. Parts VI, VII, and VIII of the Constitution dealt with the public service and armed forces. Again a 7:3 ratio was required for public service matters. The judicial branch comprised a Supreme Constitutional Court, a High Court, and several subordinate courts. The Constitutional Court had a sitting judge from each community and a non-Cypriot judge chosen jointly by the president and vice president, who served as the ex officio president of the court. The High Court was composed of one Turkish Cypriot judge, two Greek Cypriot judges, and one non-Cypriot judge. The High Court had jurisdiction over civil and criminal disputes in the two communities. Legal disputes concerning personal status and religious matters were dealt with by separate communal courts established by each Communal Chamber.

Separate municipalities were to be maintained in Cyprus's five major cities—Nicosia, Limassol, Famagusta, Larnaca, and Paphos—at least until the president and vice president examined the problem of how the municipalities could be conjoined.

Despite the Constitution's detailed provisions, implementation proved to be controversial and difficult. The 7:3 ratio for jobs in the public service was a major point of contention, and ambiguities regarding implementation were subject to conflicting interpretations. Twenty-seven cases were referred to the Supreme Constitutional Court for adjudication, but no ruling was handed down on any of the cases. The two sides were also at loggerheads over the army, with President Makarios favoring complete integration of communal forces and Vice President Küchük favoring separate units. They were unable to reach a compromise on this matter. As Stanley Kyriakides observes:

> The disagreement on the validity of the basic provisions of the Constitution had negative results. There was no willingness on the part of the Greek Cypriot community to preserve the Constitution, which they felt did not reflect the composition of the Cypriot society. On the other hand, the Turkish Cypriots clung to the Constitution as the only means of preserving their distinct communal identity. The net result of this constitutional factionalism was to prevent the Constitution from becoming a common symbol. In addition, this bi-communal factionalism constantly threatened the Constitution's preservation.[10]

One of the most politically intractable problems was the municipalities issue. After the EOKA rebellion in 1959, Turkish Cypriot municipalities had had separate political and administrative status conferred on them by the British colonial authorities. In 1963, however, President Makarios tried to absorb these communities into a single administrative structure by taking control of basic services under so-called Improvement Boards. Turkish Cypriots resisted and challenged the action before the Supreme Constitutional Court. However, the court was unable to give a clear ruling on the matter because of its own internal ethnic divisions.

President Makarios emphasized that his aim was to draw the two communities together by eliminating the provisions that split government functions on ethnic grounds and by removing the veto provisions that had frustrated the process of government. Mutual suspicions had increased to the extent that both communities were creating or expanding clandestine paramilitary forces. The Turkish Cypriot community did not accept the proposals, which would have in effect reduced its role in the government from a protected community to that of a minority. Serious disturbances broke out between the two communities. Violent confrontations in the northern suburbs of Nicosia on December 21, 1963, led to the deployment of the Turkish national contingent to that area on December 24.[11]

The governments of Britain, Greece, and Turkey offered their good offices to restore peace and order. On December 24 they proposed a joint peacekeeping force, to be composed of troops already stationed on the island. The Cypriot government accepted the offer; by the end of December a truce had been arranged between the communal factions in and around Nicosia, and a cease-fire line, now known as the "green line," was established to separate the communal areas by a neutral zone patrolled by British forces. A conference of representatives from Britain, Greece, Turkey, and the two Cypriot ethnic communities was convened in London in January 1964.

The London conference took place against a background of increasing tensions and worsening intercommunal violence. The government of Cyprus rejected proposals to strengthen the existing peacekeeping force based on contingents of the three guaranteeing powers or possibly other NATO nations, in favor of a force under UN auspices. The continuing deterioration of the local situation and the growing possibility of military intervention in Cyprus by Greece or Turkey provided strong incentives for establishing a UN peacekeeping force.

On March 4 the UN Security Council unanimously approved Resolution 186 recommending the creation of the United Nations Force in Cyprus (UNFICYP) for the preservation of international peace and security.[12] UNFICYP was expected to prevent a recurrence of fighting and to contribute to the maintenance of law and order and the restoration of normalcy to the island. The government of Cyprus agreed to the establishment and deployment of the force, which was to be stationed for an initial period of three months. As the situation continued to deteriorate, it became imperative that peacekeeping forces be deployed as quickly as possible. An advance force of 1,100 Canadian peacekeepers arrived in Cyprus on March 15. They reinforced an existing British force, making UNFICYP operational on March 27. This action diminished the incentive for Turkey to intervene, and by the end of April other national contingent forces had arrived on the island. By August 1964 UNFICYP force levels were just over 6,200, with military contingents from Austria, Canada, Denmark, Finland, Ireland, Sweden, and the United Kingdom. Civilian police contingents from Australia, Austria, Denmark, New Zealand, and Sweden were also on the scene.[13]

The peacekeeping operation was funded by the troop-contributing nations. The government of Cyprus and the secretary-general were authorized to accept voluntary contributions for the maintenance of UNFICYP. However, the voluntary funding arrangement proved to be inequitable because, unlike the circumstances in other operations, troop-contributing nations had to provide the cost of the troops. Compensation for additional expenses of contingents and the central operating costs of UNFICYP could only keep balance with the inflow of voluntary contributions. From the beginning, UNFICYP was in a deficit position because of the general reluctance to support voluntary contributions.[14]

Acceptance of the voluntary funding formula was one of the compromises required to establish UNFICYP. Security Council members generally agreed that the threat of communal violence leading to civil war, and possibly war between Greece and Turkey, required intervention.[15] The Security Council itself was divided over how to deal with the problem. Some took the view that only the Cypriots themselves could resolve the problem of self-determination. Others felt that the Zurich and London agreements had been imposed on the people of Cyprus and therefore that the treaties had to be modified. A third view was that the existence of Cyprus could not be separated from the regional context. Two of the permanent members, France and the Soviet Union, opposed any arrangement that would extend peacekeeping mandates, give mediators more autonomy, or provide for long-term financial funding of the operation.

UNFICYP was guided by the principle of impartiality in its dealings with the Greek Cypriot and Turkish Cypriot communities. It could use only minimal force in its self-defense. Each community had a different view of UNFICYP's role: whereas the Greek Cypriots saw it as a way to suppress Turkish Cypriot rebellion and extend the authority of the government, the Turkish Cypriots saw it as a way to protect and restore their separate community status guaranteed under the 1960 Constitution.

UNFICYP successfully deterred major military operations and helped promote an uneasy truce between the two communities. Its three-month mandate was first extended to six months, and later extended indefinitely.

With the initial fighting, however, the communities on each side had congregated into enclaves, particularly on the Turkish side. These enclaves were protected by defensive fortifications, which were encircled and besieged by forces from the opposing side. One of UNFICYP's challenges was to dismantle these fortifications and persuade local forces to leave them unoccupied.

Between 1964 and 1967 UNFICYP was able to help restore government services and utilities and bring a measure of stability to economic life and activity. It escorted movements of food and merchandise and was responsible for civilian traffic, land maintenance arrangements, water and electrical utilities, and basic government services such as social security and postal service. Arrangements for these activities had to be negotiated with local authorities on an ad hoc basis in the absence of a political settlement. UNFICYP, however, was not able to disarm the rival factions completely, nor was it able to bring about an end to the fighting. Recurrent crises and occasional outbreaks of armed hostilities kept tensions high. This prompted various outside third parties to intervene in the conflict in the hope of mediating a negotiated settlement. But none has been successful. In the discussion that follows, we try to explain why.

Superpower and Regional Interests

At one level Cyprus is a communal conflict that began as a colonial struggle against British rule; at another level it is a regional conflict because of the relationship each community has with Greece and Turkey. Furthermore, conflicts between Greece and Turkey over territory and resources in the eastern Mediterranean have served to expand the interstate dimensions of this conflict.[16] The compound structure of the conflict and the dependency relationship of the island's two ethnic communities to their mainland supporters have posed major challenges to third-party efforts aimed at a lasting political settlement.

Greece and Turkey have played both direct and indirect roles in the conflict. The ethnic and intraethnic aspects of the conflict have been manipulated by outsiders looking to advance their own interests.[17] The conflict has been at the center of Greco-Turkish relations not only because of the cultural and social ties between these mainland states and the island's two ethnic communities, but also because of the respective security interests of Greece and Turkey in the Mediterranean. The Treaty of Lausanne, signed by Greece and Turkey in 1923, placed under Greek sovereignty many of the islands of the eastern Aegean. Several aspects of the conflict between Greece and Turkey stem from their incompatible interests in this area. The Lausanne treaty defined the boundaries between the two countries until 1947, when Italy ceded the Dodecanese islands to Greece. One of the most serious rifts in the relationship between the two countries took place in 1973, when Turkey challenged Greece over seabed rights in the Aegean. The Turkish intervention in Cyprus occurred shortly thereafter, and relations between the two countries reached one of their lowest points, culminating in Greece's withdrawal from NATO's integrated military command as a protest to a perceived pro-Turkish tilt during the 1974 crisis.

At a wider, systemic level the conflict in Cyprus became entangled in the politics of the Cold War. The conflict between Greece and Turkey over Cyprus and other areas was a potential source of weakness on NATO's southern flank.[18] During the Cold War NATO feared this rift might undermine the strategic objectives of the alliance and be exploited by the Soviet Union. Tensions in Cyprus, and the Greco-Turkish relationship generally, were of concern to NATO members and the principal reason the United States, Canada, and Britain became involved in mediating a political settlement to the conflict in Cyprus. Interventions by NATO and its members, especially Britain and the United States, attempted to resolve the conflict as a Greco-Turkish problem. When these efforts failed the United Nations appointed various mediators who tried to resolve the conflict as an intercommunal problem. Part of the reason for the focus on the intercommunal nature of the conflict was to avoid threatening the interests of Greece and Turkey or pressuring them in a way that would further disrupt NATO relationships. The end of the Cold War has brought more room for maneuver and leverage by the great powers, although Turkey's increasingly pivotal role in the Middle East (as witnessed during the Gulf War) places it in a strong position to resist outside pressure from the United States or NATO.[19]

The regional and extraregional dimensions of the conflict have thus been a key source of difficulty in reaching a political accommodation in Cyprus. Successive mediation efforts, with the exception perhaps of negotiations in the 1990s, have failed to take into account adequately the fact that the conflict is both an intranational and international conflict. The resistance to resolution in Cyprus is not due simply to the absence of a hurting stalemate or of ripeness, but to the inherent complexity of the conflict itself, which demands an approach that addresses communal and state interests at these different levels. As Raimo Väyrynen explains:

> Regional conflict formations are a complex mixture of intra-national, intra-regional and extra-regional conflicts of violent character. A novel feature of these conflict formations is that they have become more complex and more entangled in the sense that they cannot be easily decomposed into individual conflicts. Such an effort fails easily because of the pervasive linkages existing between different forms of conflict.[20]

Third Parties and Efforts to Negotiate a Political Settlement

None of the recurrent attempts by various third parties to mediate a comprehensive political settlement to the conflict in Cyprus has succeeded. The first efforts began in 1964 when the United States launched a number of initiatives that centered on securing an agreement between the Greeks and the Turks. The first of these was a direct appeal by President Lyndon B. Johnson to the Greek and Turkish prime ministers for settlement talks—an appeal that fell on deaf ears. Johnson's efforts were followed by UN-mediated talks between Greece and Turkey with the participation of a former U.S. secretary of state, Dean Acheson. Under the Acheson plan, a large portion of Cyprus would have been unified with Greece, and Turkey would have received a military base in the northeast corner of Cyprus in addition to the Greek island of Kastellorizo. Furthermore, a few Turkish Cypriot cantons with local autonomy were to be created. The plan was rejected by Archbishop Makarios, who regarded it as an attempt at double *enosis*.

The UN Galo Plaza Report of 1965 sought to accord recognition to an independent and sovereign Cyprus. The report rejected *enosis* and *taksim* and was critical of the 1960 Constitution, arguing that the status quo ante could not be restored. The report stressed that a settlement could come about only through direct discussions between the two Cypriot communities, without direct input from Greece and Turkey. Archbishop Makarios accepted the report as a basis for negotiation, but the report was rejected by Greece and Turkey, which disagreed with the premise that they should be excluded from the process. Turkey, in particular, objected to the report's suggestion that discussions not be based on the 1960 accords.

In 1967 direct, if inconclusive, discussions were held between the leaders of Greece and Turkey about the future of Cyprus. These talks were followed by direct shuttle diplomacy undertaken by President

Johnson's envoy, Cyrus Vance, in an attempt to prevent open conflict over the deployment of Greek troops in Cyprus in April 1967. Vance succeeded in securing the withdrawal of Greek forces and persuading the two countries to renew talks.[21] The two countries were brought together by NATO again in 1971, when they reaffirmed their commitment to the London-Zurich Accords, with Turkey agreeing not to invade Cyprus under the Treaty of Guarantee without first consulting Greece.

In 1968 intercommunal talks began under the auspices of the United Nations. It was agreed that once concurrence had been reached on constitutional matters, international issues such as the Treaties of Alliance and Guarantee would be discussed by interested parties. The talks deadlocked in 1971 over the introduction of a set of Greco-Turkish proposals that had been agreed to at a meeting held under NATO auspices in 1967. However, there was substantial progress toward agreement on a range of issues, including local government, the judiciary, the legislature, the executive, and the police. The major difference between the two sides was a Turkish Cypriot preference for the concept of local autonomy, which clashed with the Greek Cypriot preference for a unitary state—a difference that has persisted in every negotiation between the two sides.[22]

Nevertheless, in 1974 a political settlement to the Cyprus problem appeared to be in the offing. Intercommunal talks had produced agreement on principles providing for a balance of Turkish Cypriot autonomy along with some modifications to the 1960 Constitution. The provisions confirmed an independent Cyprus, short of *enosis* with Greece.

However, the military junta of Brigadier Dimitri Ioannidis in Greece, which was supportive of pro-*enosis* elements in Cyprus, conspired to overthrow Makarios in a bid to achieve *enosis*. On July 15, 1974, the Cypriot National Guard, led by Greek officers, attacked the presidential palace. Makarios escaped and fled the island to rally international support against the coup plotters. Fearing annexation of Cyprus by Greece, Turkey invaded the island with its own military forces, claiming that it had a right to do so under the 1960 Treaty of Guarantee. The coup quickly collapsed and the Speaker of the House, Glafcos Clerides, took the reins of power. Turkish forces moved quickly to consolidate their control over the northern part of the island.

UNFICYP forces were not equipped to deal with a full-scale military invasion of the island by Turkish troops. Between July 20 and July 25 Turkey used its position to secure the protection of the Turkish Cypriot population. Isolated Greek Cypriot communities were moved to safe havens, and foreign missions were evacuated from Nicosia to the British base at Dhekélia. Nicosia airport, the site of some of the heaviest fighting, was eventually occupied by UN forces and designated a protected area. The Security Council authorized UNFICYP to maintain a cease-fire, which was gradually achieved by July 24. UNFICYP troop strength was increased to 4,440 personnel by August 14. From July 25 to July 30, the foreign ministers of Greece, Turkey, and Britain met to try to negotiate an end to the conflict. At the first 1974 Geneva conference the three countries signed a peace declaration, which determined that the cease-fire should be observed and negotiations carried forward. The agreement also called for assistance to be offered to the Greek and Turkish Cypriot communities, with the lead being taken by Greece and Turkey.[23] At the second Geneva conference separate plans were put forward by Clerides, Turkish Cypriot leader Rauf Denktash, and Turkish foreign minister Turan Gunes. The proposal presented by Denktash was based on earlier discussions in which he and Clerides had reached agreement. However, when all the parties came together and Clerides was joined by Greek foreign minister Mavros, the negotiation dynamic changed.[24] Faced with the increased leverage of the Turkish Cypriots created by the presence of the Turkish army in Cyprus, as well as pressures from both the Greek and Greek Cypriot extremists, Clerides asked for time to consider the Turkish proposals. However, negotiations to define a security zone and bridgehead collapsed when the Turkish army tried to expand its zone of control. Fighting resumed; UNFICYP once again had to act to restore the cease-fire and protect civilians. Partial cease-fires were established in Nicosia on August 15, and a general cease-fire was agreed to on August 16, 1974. But by this time the Turkish army controlled almost 40 percent of the island of Cyprus.

Following the events in 1974 the United Nations repeatedly tried to bring the two communities together and launch a new round of negotiations. However, efforts to resolve the intercommunal dispute in Cyprus were complicated by the Turkish occupation force, refugees, property losses, and de facto partition of the island's two communities. A series of informal meetings led to formal intercommunal talks in Vienna and New York in 1975 and 1976. These talks led to an agreement allowing a transfer of populations so as to permit a consolidation of communities. The intent of the agreement was to reduce the likelihood of conflict between the two communities, but it effectively divided the island into two distinct ethnic zones. This had important implications for future negotiations on how to develop a federal, bicommunal structure that would address each ethnic group's special interests.

During the decade 1976–86 various low-level and high-level meetings, intercommunal talks, and talks were initiated by the secretary-general. The chief difficulty in achieving political reconciliation was the fact that the Turkish Cypriot community was content with its separate political status, which culminated in the establishment of the Turkish Republic of Northern Cyprus in 1983.[25] On the other side, the Greek Cypriot community saw political reconciliation as possible only in the context of a bicommunal solution that allowed for the "three freedoms": freedom of settlement, freedom of property ownership, and freedom of movement. The removal of Turkish forces from the island was another Greek Cypriot precondition for settlement. Furthermore, other issues had to be dealt with, such as the question of Turkish settlers on the island, economic reconstruction, exploitation of resources, and development of infrastructure on a joint rather than unitary basis.

The first major initiative was a collaborative effort in November 1978 led by Britain, Canada, and the United States known as the ABC proposals. This intervention treated the conflict as an intercommunal one and offered a new set of constitutional principles and the promise of economic assistance once an agreement was reached. The Greek Cypriots objected to the constitutional arrangements, while the Turkish Cypriots rejected the proposals regarding security and territory.[26] Both communities were suspicious of the origins of the proposals, perceiving the package as yet another attempt by an outside power, this time the United States, to impose a solution. The two communities also felt that the initiative circumvented the United Nations, which they viewed as a more impartial instrument to achieving a fair settlement.

In May 1979 a new round of talks began between Denktash and Greek Cypriot leader Spyros Kyprianou under UN auspices; the result was the Ten-Point Agreement. The agreement reaffirmed the Four Guidelines of 1977, but talks bogged down in procedural details and questions of security.[27] Although the two community leaders shared the view that the Ten-Point Agreement had considerable merit, they were extremely suspicious about the influence Greece and Turkey were having on the process. Negotiations ended without agreement.

The resumption of talks in August 1980 involved discussion of a four-fold agenda in which the two communities exchanged various proposals. The United Nations periodically evaluated the progress of the talks. Special precautions were taken in this round to prevent public disclosure of proposals put forward by the parties; such disclosure had proved counterproductive in previous negotiations.[28] In November 1981 Secretary-General Kurt Waldheim produced an evaluation paper based on the 1980 agenda discussions, outlining points of agreement and disagreement between the two communities. It offered a number of proposals based on compromise positions put forward by the delegations in previous rounds. The evaluation paper was accepted by the Greek Cypriots as a basis for further discussion. The Turkish Cypriots, however, accepted it only as a framework for further negotiation because of continuing fears that their security interests might be compromised.

Intercommunal talks continued intermittently until 1983. The impression grew among Greek Cypriots that the Turkish Cypriots were merely going through the motions and were not serious about reaching an agreement. The Greek Cypriots also suspected that Turkey had ulterior motives and was trying to consolidate its control over northern Cyprus. The Turkish Cypriots, for their part, were increasingly frustrated by the Greek Cypriot failure to recognize them as equals in the negotiating process. They also were worried about a revival of the *enosis* movement, especially after Greek prime minister Andreas Papandreou expressed his solidarity with the Greek Cypriot community in January 1982.

In 1983 the UN negotiator Javier Perez de Cuellar issued an aide-mémoire outlining points of convergence of the two Cypriot communities in an attempt to clarify their respective views and encourage concessions. It implicitly suggested that the Turkish Cypriots would give up territory in return for a federal authority with a restricted sphere of competence.[29] In spite of opposition from within his own party, Kyprianou notified Perez de Cuellar that he conditionally accepted the aide-mémoire's contents. However, Greek leader Papandreou made it clear that he opposed the suggested compromise. Kyprianou agreed, reneging on his previous conditional acceptance.[30] As a result of this situation, Turkish Cypriot leader Denktash rejected the initiative in September 1983, and in November, uncertain about Greek Cypriot intentions, Denktash issued a unilateral declaration of independence establishing the Turkish Republic of Northern Cyprus.[31]

In 1984 Perez de Cuellar sought a comprehensive approach to resolving the Cyprus problem. He proposed inserting all the elements of convergence from the years of negotiation into a draft agreement that would be considered as an integrated whole. Presented to the parties at a summit

meeting in New York on Janaury 17, 1985, the draft agreement was ultimately rejected. It was accepted by Turkey and the Turkish Cypriots;
Papandreou of Greece, however, found the agreement unacceptable and
stated his objections prior to a formal response from Greek Cypriot
leader Kyprianou. Initially, Kyprianou seemed "inclined to accept" the
agreement until his meetings with Papandreou, who felt that it did not
adequately address the problem of Turkish troops on the island, the
three freedoms, and international guarantees.[32]

Positions hardened even further when Turkish prime minister Turgut
Ozal visited Cyprus in July 1986. During the visit Ozal commented on
how similar northern Cyprus was to the Turkish homeland and encouraged the continued development of the Turkish Cypriot community's
independent status. These comments were not received favorably by the
Greek Cypriot community.

During meetings in January 1988 in Davos, Switzerland, between the
Greek and Turkish prime ministers over boundary disputes in the Aegean
Sea, the two sides agreed that negotiations over Cyprus should remain
within the purview of the United Nations. Moreover, they agreed that
Cyprus should become the centerpiece of the Greco-Turkish agenda. At
the intercommunal level, talks got a new lease on life with the election of
George Vassiliou to the Cypriot presidency in 1988. Immediately upon
taking office, Vassiliou agreed to talks, which began in August 1988 at
the residence of the UN secretary-general's special representative. In a
departure from the format of previous talks, the negotiators abandoned
the imposition of frameworks and draft agreements. Instead, Cypriot
leaders held informal discussions without a formal agenda. In January
1989 Vassiliou presented Denktash with a document entitled "Outline for
Proposals for the Establishment of a Federal Republic and for the Solution of the Cyprus Problem." The proposals covered such issues as
demilitarization and security matters, protection of the three freedoms,
constitutional arrangements, and territorial considerations. In general, the
proposal supported the creation of a bicommunal, demilitarized, federal republic.

Since 1990 successive rounds of talks have been held between the
two communities. While some progress has been made, setbacks have
also occurred. Although Rauf Denktash agreed to the idea of a single
federated state, he has continued his campaign to create what would in
essence be a federal state subordinated to a federated state system. In
discussions about the constitutional aspects of an agreement, Denktash

has sought a high level of decentralization to ensure that both communities enjoy equal powers.

Talks that ended on March 2, 1990, failed because of a dispute over the meaning of the word "communities" and whether or not these communities would have the right to self-determination. Later in March, the Security Council took an important step in delineating in Resolution 649 the principles upon which an agreement would have to be reached: (1) a new Cyprus would be a nation with a single sovereignty and international personality; (2) all aspects of the agreement would respect the political equality of the two communities; and (3) the settlement would have to exclude as an option secession in part or otherwise. Both leaders affirmed their commitment to the principles in Resolution 649, which proved to be an important foundation for all the talks that followed.[33]

By mid-1990 the secretary-general's frustration was evident in his letters both to the parties and to the Security Council. The two main obstacles were the issues of territorial adjustments and displaced persons.[34] After numerous trips to the island and to Greece and Turkey, the secretary-general's special representatives were able to gather enough consensus that by September 1991 both sides had agreed to begin working on the completion of an overall framework agreement. The extensive set of ideas they drafted met with the approval of both Greek and Turkish officials, and brought new rays of hope to the decades-long dispute.[35]

The year 1992 was full of high-level meetings and draft agreements.[36] In June, the new secretary-general, Boutros Boutros-Ghali, convened the first round of new high-level talks in New York. At the second round that took place from mid-July to mid-August, the secretary-general stated that the talks had to focus on resolving the problems of territorial adjustments and displaced persons.[37] Regarding the former, the main issue was where the new boundaries should be drawn. Regarding the latter, there was disagreement over whether ownership of personal property should be decided according to the pre-1974 owner or the post-1974 occupant. In spite of these impediments, the secretary-general was sufficiently satisfied to convene a joint meeting for August 12–14. By autumn, however, the fissures had widened. New disagreements surfaced, for the most part initiated by the Turkish Cypriot leadership over the constitutional aspects of the framework agreement. The secretary-general was forced to issue a warning to the Turkish Cypriots that some of their ambitions were contrary to the ideas in the agreed-upon framework, as well as the principles set forth in Resolution 649.[38]

A new chapter on the Cyprus question was opened in April and May 1993 with the agreement by the two sides to a new set of confidence-building measures—a number of initiatives that would act as a precursor to a longer and more stable peace.[39] Most notable were plans to reopen the fenced area of Varosha, as well as Nicosia International Airport. Though promising at first, problems arose when Denktash insisted that the Turkish Cypriots were having to concede too much, and therefore that the benefits accruing to the Turkish Cypriot people would not be balanced in terms of quantity and timing. As a result of constant exceptions being made by the Turkish Cypriots and Denktash's broken promise to return to New York to ratify the package of confidence-building measures, a different approach was required. It took the form of track-two diplomacy, with "proximity talks" being held with members of the Turkish Cypriot community. In July 1993 members of the business community, the media, academics, and party leaders met with UN representatives. The groups of Turkish Cypriots expressed their support for the proposed confidence-building measures. With Turkey also voicing its approval, Denktash clearly had to deal with deep divisions between the Turkish Cypriot community and the leadership.

In January 1994 negotiations were back on track, and a round of proximity talks was initiated to agree on the implementation of the confidence-building measures. Expecting that this could be accomplished within two months' time, the secretary-general was highly disappointed when in April and May Denktash raised opposition to the wording of the document that came out of the proximity talks. Once again, his chief concern was the schedule of benefits. It was not enough that the secretary-general offered to append a letter to the agreement clarifying several of the provisions; Denktash would not agree to the package if changes were not made to the agreement itself. The Greek Cypriots, for their part, would not have objected to an explanatory appendix, but they stated forthrightly that they would object to any changes to the agreement itself.[40] Thus, the catch-22 situation so characteristic of these talks had once again brought the negotiation to a deadlock.

The Role of Ripeness

As noted earlier, a lack of ripeness is often said to explain why, in spite of numerous mediation efforts over the years, no political settlement in the Cyprus dispute has been achieved. Brian Mandell, for instance, asserts:

Above all other factors contributing to the current impasse, the greatest impediment to resolution is the absence of a hurting stalemate. Neither Cypriot community is sufficiently dissatisfied with the status quo to make the difficult compromises necessary for resolving the conflict.[41]

This is certainly true in a general sense, but greater levels of ripeness may be present at some levels of the conflict than at others. At the inter-communal level, for instance, a greater convergence of interests between the two communities exists now than in the past. The Greek Cypriot community has grown accustomed to the ethnic division of the island. Robert McDonald notes that

the focus of their negotiating demands has narrowed. Initially, they sought reintegration under a unitary government. Today they accept the concept of bi-communal federation and their concentration is more on increasing the size of the southern sector in order that the maximum number of refugees can return to their homes.[42]

The Turkish Cypriots have a stronger attachment to the status quo because their security interests are looked after by the presence of Turkish troops, and they continue to harbor concerns about being a minority under any sort of plan for unification. Nonetheless, widespread economic disparities between north and south and the booming economy in the south are sources of envy. Economic unification would bring obvious benefits to the Turkish Cypriot community. At the same time, the receding threat of *enosis*, which has long since been abandoned as a goal by political elites in the south, has removed a major friction point for the Turkish Cypriot community.

But ripeness is also a matter of perceptions.[43] Political elites must seek and desire change. One of the problems, according to some analysts, is that Denktash, the long-standing leader of the Turkish Cypriot community, continues to believe (at least publicly) that the Greek Cypriots still seek *enosis*.[44] Denktash's refusal to recognize changing political realities is thus seen as a major obstacle to change. Former Cypriot president Vassiliou has expressed his own frustration with Denktash in the following manner:

The main constraint in solving the Cyprus problem has nothing to do with ethnic conflict, but it is simply the desire of Denktash and some people around him and of President Ozal of Turkey to maintain the status quo. . . . When I met Denktash in New York I went there with the intention of nego-tiating a settlement. You know what Denktash has said. "Let us consider," he said, "that a non-solution is another option. That an option is a non-solution," by which he means continued partition of the island.[45]

Rauf Denktash's own view is that the asymmetry in political strength and the majority-versus-minority view of the Greek Cypriot community lie at the core of the problem:

> People think that we are opposing the legitimate government of Cyprus. They don't realize that our fight is against a Greek Cypriot Republic which is trying to impose itself in place of the government of Cyprus which was bi-communal. They don't realize that this is what the fight is about. For 28 years august bodies have been deciding that in Cyprus the Greek Cypriots are our government. If Greek Cypriots are our government, then we are what the government says we are: a rebellious nuisance of a minority helping an enemy to divide Cyprus and keeping Cyprus occupied. How can we be treated like this?[46]

The lack of ripeness at the intercommunal level in Cyprus is thus due not only to the lack of a hurting stalemate, but also, as Reed Coughlan argues, to a political leadership that distrusts the motives and intentions of the other side. At the same time, each side has a different definition of the problem, as the above statements reveal. Coughlan further notes:

> Each side casts the problem as an exclusive matter; that is, the Greek Cypriots see it solely as a matter of foreign intervention, the Turkish Cypriots as a domestic/ethnic conflict. Any successful negotiation will need to address both dimensions of the problem, and it will be necessary for both sides to recognize the other's viewpoint.[47]

But ripeness has also proved to be elusive in the interstate dimension to the conflict—if for different reasons. The continuing rift between Greece and Turkey over boundary disputes in the Aegean Sea remains a sore point in relations between the two countries. Greece and Turkey have had, and will continue to have, a major impact on negotiations, and any successful resolution of the Cyprus problem will also have to address their respective interests. "The conclusion is inescapable," observes former U.S. ambassador to Greece Monteagle Stearns, "that a successful resolution of the Cyprus problem must await progress on bilateral Greek-Turkish problems and a definite improvement in Greek-Turkish relations."[48]

Greece and Turkey thus need to reassess their mutual relations not just on Cyprus, but on broader territorial and resource questions in the Aegean. Resolution of the Cyprus question clearly requires a combination of communal and international strategies to deal with the various communal, regional, and geopolitical dimensions of the conflict. Moreover, this history of failed third-party efforts to achieve a lasting political settlement demonstrates the futility of treating the conflict solely as a regional (Greece versus Turkey) or a communal (Greek Cypriot versus Turkish Cypriot) conflict. An effective intervention strategy must deal explicitly and directly with conflicting interests at all levels.

Settlement Proposals: Strengths, Weaknesses, and Ambiguities

Although there have been numerous proposals for a resolution of the political conflict in Cyprus, none has proved acceptable to the parties. The only settlement accords as such were the Zurich-London Agreements of 1959, which were signed by Britain, Turkey, and Greece, as well as Archbishop Makarios on behalf of the Greek Cypriot community and Fazil Küçük on behalf of the Turkish Cypriot community. This settlement failed because it was too rigid and led to a set of constitutional arrangements that were unacceptable to the Greek Cypriot community.

Since the Turkish intervention of 1974, many attempts have been made to negotiate, with the assistance of third parties, a new federal, bicommunal political structure. These efforts have included the 1978 ABC (American, British, Canadian) initiative, the 1979 Ten-Point Agreement, the communal talks in the early 1980s, and the 1986 draft framework agreement of the UN secretary-general. The draft framework agreement in some respects represented the most comprehensive set of recent proposals. It accepted the communal division of Cyprus and set out guarantees for each of the communities. In addition, it established new guarantor powers that would be designated by the Security Council to protect the interests of each community. Greece and Turkey would have the right to intervene only if the Security Council–designated powers failed to act.

The draft framework also offered a number of proposals concerning the three freedoms. Freedom of access and movement of peoples would be assured, although each community would have the right to bar individuals deemed a threat to local security. Territorial adjustments would allow displaced persons to return to their homes. Displaced persons would have their property and homes restored to them or, if that were not possible, would receive adequate compensation. Turkish nationals who have settled in northern Cyprus would also be repatriated following discussions with the Turkish government, although the right of appeal to remain would exist.

A draft resolution outlining the secretary-general's proposals was debated by the Security Council in April 1988. However, the resolution was never put to a vote because the Soviet Union threatened to veto it. Since then a new round of negotiations centered on proposals presented by former Cypriot president George Vassiliou have taken place in an effort to reach a comprehensive settlement. And at the end of February 1990, the secretary-general convened a high-level meeting in New York between the Turkish Cypriot and Greek Cypriot leadership to try to resume the intercommunal dialogue. But these and subsequent talks have collapsed over the fundamental question of the right of each community to self-determination.

Assessment and Conclusions

Peaceful modes of intervention by third parties in the Cyprus dispute have involved a combination of tactics and initiatives, including mediation, fact finding, good offices, direct negotiations, and shuttle diplomacy. Third-party efforts to resolve the Cyprus problem were initially led by Greece, Turkey, and Britain, and subsequently by the United States and NATO. NATO member countries feared that the Cyprus dispute between Greece and Turkey had the potential to disrupt the alliance and weaken NATO's southern flank, hence the need for some sort of settlement. These efforts focused on finding a compromise that was compatible with the interests of Greece and Turkey. They failed because they were insufficiently attentive to the intercommunal dimensions of the conflict and each community's security interests. Subsequent efforts led by the United Nations have tried to promote intercommunal talks and have brought about a convergence of positions on key issues, although mutual suspicion and mistrust between the two communities continue to stand in the way of a settlement. To a significant extent, however, Greek and Turkish interference has had a negative impact on achieving progress toward a settlement and has stymied progress in intercommunal negotiations.

The United Nations, through its secretary-general and special representatives, has been involved in successive efforts to negotiate a political settlement to the conflict. The first UN initiative was Security Council Resolution 186, which led to the establishment of UNFICYP. Subsequent UN resolutions have extended UNFICYP's mandate and sought to promote discussions that would lead to a negotiated settlement. Over the years the efforts have included the Galo Plaza Report (1965); intercommunal talks under auspices of the United Nations, which began in June 1968 and continued intermittently until July 1974; the resumption of intercommunal talks following the Turkish intervention in 1974 under UN Resolution 3212; the Ten-Point Agreement of 1979, also under UN auspices; the continuation of intercommunal talks from 1980 to 1983, chaired by UN representative Hugh Gobbie; Perez de Cuellar's aide-mémoire of 1983, which put forward proposals based on points of agreement between the two communities; UN-sponsored intercommunal talks in 1988 and 1989; UN Resolution 649 (1990); and UN-sponsored intercommunal talks, which began in the fall of 1992.

The failure of successive third parties to bring about a negotiated settlement to the conflict in Cyprus is testimony to the protracted nature of the dispute and its compound nature, which is marked not just by competing communal interests on the island but also by conflicting regional interests, namely, those of Greece and Turkey. Although the absence of a hurting stalemate is one possible impediment to resolution, third-party mediation efforts, especially by the United Nations, have been hampered by the United Nations' inability to exert pressure on Turkey to withdraw its forces from the island. An improvement in Greco-Turkish relations that could lead to such a withdrawal is clearly a precondition for a resolution to the Cyprus issue, although Turkey maintains that Cyprus is independent from the territorial and resource disputes between Greece and Turkey in the Aegean.

The more recent experience of third-party attempts at peaceful intervention in Cyprus stands in marked contrast to earlier mediation efforts in the late 1950s and 1960s, which centered on finding a settlement that would be acceptable to Greece and Turkey, even at the expense of the interests of the two Cypriot communities. One of the principal reasons the London-Zurich Accords and the subsequent Constitutional Accord failed was that the settlement was imposed on the two ethnic Cypriot communities and was seen by the Greek Cypriot community as being inimical to its interests. In this respect, third-party efforts contributed to the escalation of the conflict by failing to strike the right balance in negotiations and the subsequent "settlement" between regional and intercommunal interests in Cyprus.

The demilitarization of Cyprus is a precondition for political reconciliation, but it remains difficult to negotiate. For the Greek community, the Turkish military and settler presence on the island is a threat to the island's security and stands in the way of a political settlement. Conversely, the

military buildup of the Cypriot National Guard is seen as a threat by the
Turkish Cypriot community. Demilitarization of both northern and southern Cyprus is ultimately crucial to the achievement of a long-term, comprehensive settlement. UNFICYP forces clearly have a major role to play
in the verification and monitoring of the military demobilization, should
that day arrive. As McDonald indicates:

> The principal matter which must be resolved is the presence of Turkish
> troops on Cyprus. The Turkish-Cypriots feel that a protective force must
> remain and there must be some form of guarantee whereby Turkey has a
> legal right of future military intervention. . . .
>   While the Greek junta of 1967–74 was intent on enosis, the civilian gov-
> ernments which have succeeded the dictatorship have repeatedly asserted
> that Greece has abandoned any unionist designs on the island and favours
> its continued independence. There are thus neither sound political nor legal
> reasons for the continued presence of Turkish troops on the territory of the
> sovereign state of Cyprus. Their presence serves only to secure Turkey's
> interest in maintaining a buffer state between the mainland and what was
> once the largest Hellenic island off its long and vulnerable coastline. Agree-
> ment to the withdrawal of these forces, or at very least, to a timetable under
> which this is to be effected, is the key to resolution of the Cyprus problem.[49]

Maintenance of the buffer zone is central to keeping the peace. As
such, it represents an important confidence-building measure. The likelihood of confrontation is diminished if UNFICYP can successfully demonstrate that it can prevent incursions into the zone. As a result of decisions
by troop-contributing governments to withdraw or substantially reduce
their contingents, the strength of UNFICYP since 1990 has fallen from
2,132 to 1,203, a reduction of 43.6 percent of the total force.[50] Given the
small and shrinking size of the UNFICYP force, it has had to rely on the
continued and sustained cooperation of both sides to maintain the cease-
fire and avoid accidental confrontations. Arguably, though, UNFICYP is
also part of the current problem in Cyprus and the conflict's resistance to
resolution. As Mandell and others note, the presence of the UN force in
Cyprus has reduced the prospect of violence and served to formalize the
division of the island through the maintenance of an effective cease-fire
along the "green line" buffer zone. The de facto partition of Cyprus has
thus undermined the chances of achieving a bicommunal, federal political settlement because the status quo is seen as being preferable to all of
the alternatives. There is an obvious irony to this situation. As Brian
Mandell observes:

> While the current UN Secretary-General's good offices have been most important in reinvigorating the inter-communal dialogue, the preponderant UN role has had the unfortunate effect of removing the incentive for other third parties to be engaged actively in the peacemaking process.[51]

In this regard, the United Nations *qua* third party has become part of the problem, not the solution, in Cyprus.

As we see in the chapters that follow, more recent third-party efforts at intervention in peace building and the implementation of settlements have tried to avoid (explicitly or implicitly) some of the pitfalls of the Cyprus experience. UN peacekeeping mandates have generally tended to be better defined, with a clearer timetable for the deployment and withdrawal of peacekeeping forces. Negotiations aimed at a political settlement have been undertaken prior to, not after, the deployment of peacekeeping forces. Nevertheless, some of the same problems that have thwarted a political settlement in Cyprus are also evident in the cases that follow. Regional actors, for example, can threaten the peace process if they are not explicitly involved in negotiations leading up to a settlement. This was one of the problems in achieving a lasting and durable peace in Cambodia. Conversely, the Salvadoran experience demonstrates how a supportive regional environment can advance the peace process. Ripeness is elusive in the absence of third-party involvement, not just in the negotiation of peace settlements, but also in their implementation, as the failure of successive third-party efforts to end the civil war in Angola demonstrates. At the same time, there have been successes in implementation. Such successes are in large part due to the active and constructive involvement of third parties in all phases of the peacemaking and peace-building process. One such success in recent years is Namibia. In the next chapter we explore why the Namibian civil war ended and why third parties were able to bring peace to Southern Africa.

NAMIBIA

The 1989 resolution of the conflict in Namibia and the subsequent achievement of full independence on March 21, 1990, closed an important chapter in the history of Southern Africa. For the South West Africa People's Organization (SWAPO), formed in 1958, and its leader, Sam Nujoma, who was sworn in as Namibia's first president, independence marked the triumphant conclusion of a struggle that had begun in 1966. For many years Namibia was one of the forgotten conflicts in international relations. The territory had been controlled by South Africa since Germany lost the colony in World War I. In 1968, however, the United Nations changed the name of the territory from South West Africa to Namibia, and in 1973 the UN General Assembly recognized SWAPO as the "sole authentic representative of the Namibian people" after the International Court of Justice ruled in 1971 that South Africa's presence in Namibia was illegal. However, it was not until December 22, 1988, when representatives of Angola, Cuba, and South Africa formally signed an agreement calling for implementation of UN Security Council Resolution 435 (1978), that concrete plans for peace in the region—of which Namibian independence was the central element—were set in motion.

This chapter argues that the reason the Namibian peace settlement succeeded was that it represented the culmination of a lengthy and protracted set of negotiations assisted by third-party mediation, first by the

Western Contact Group and then by the United States. Where the Contact Group lacked leverage, the United States created leverage and developed a negotiating strategy that was more coherent, sustained, and tied to the warring parties' key political interests and objectives. Although the Namibian conflict was in one sense ripe for resolution, this ripeness had to be slowly and meticulously cultivated by outside third parties that recognized that the hurting stalemate on the battleground was amenable to a negotiated settlement. As events were to prove shortly after the settlement was concluded, however, the situation was still highly unstable. When fighting broke out again, third parties were required to stabilize the situation and create an atmosphere conducive to further negotiations and a resumption of the peace process. Third parties were also needed to supervise and control elections, monitor the situation on the ground, and help with the process of promoting national reconciliation and nation building. In several key respects the Namibian experience also serves as a model of how the United States and United Nations can work together and turn a peacekeeping operation into a nation-building one by successfully fusing these two sets of activities. But, as the following case study illustrates, this success was largely the product of staying power by third parties in a difficult situation and the high levels of ongoing support and assistance they provided to Namibia during all phases of the peace process.

The ability of the United Nations to overcome the suspicion and hostility it faced at the beginning of the implementation period was also a key to its success. At the same time, when the United Nations found itself unable to the wield the necessary leverage to keep the parties on track, it was able to turn to other third parties, notably the United States, with the muscle to coax the parties back to the negotiating table.[1]

This chapter first describes the history of the conflict and the negotiations that led up to the peace settlement. Then we examine the outcome of the settlement and its subsequent implementation. Finally, we offer an overall assessment of the Namibian peace process.

History of the Conflict

The conflict in Southern Africa has a long history. Linkage between the conflict in Angola and the conflict in Namibia was formally established by the South African government under the terms it set for the Namibian peace process in 1981, linking Namibian independence to the withdrawal of Cuban forces from Angola. Subsequent U.S. policy tried to gain leverage over South Africa by using linkage to end South African colonialism and achieve a withdrawal of Cuban forces from Angola.[2] However, "informal" linkage between these two conflicts was established much earlier by South Africa's destabilization activities against Angola and by the overlapping dynamics of civil and regional conflicts in the area.[3] The conflict in Angola and the failure of the settlement process there are analyzed in chapter 4.

SWAPO's guerrilla war for the independence of Namibia began in 1966. It enjoyed strong support from the Ovambo people, who constitute approximately 50 percent of Namibia's 1.5 million population. While tribal factions existed, the population was largely unified by the territory's history of apartheid and colonial subjugation. This provided a rallying point for overcoming some of the conflictual elements of traditional tribalism and factionalism that are major features of the conflict in Angola (and even within South Africa's liberation movement). Although SWAPO was dominated by the Ovambo tribal majority, it received support from many of the other tribal factions.[4]

SWAPO established bases in southern Angola and enjoyed the political support of the frontline states and the Organization of African Unity (OAU). In 1978 the Security Council passed Resolution 435, which called for a cease-fire, a UN peacekeeping force, and UN-sponsored elections. Resolution 435 ultimately became the basis for the peaceful independence of Namibia.

A bewildering array of state and nonstate actors were involved at one time or another in this conflict and in the subsequent peace negotiations. In addition to the United States, South Africa, Portugal (as the former colonial power in Angola and Mozambique), the United Kingdom (another colonial power with close ties to South Africa), and the Soviet Union, the other key state actors included Cuba, several frontline states[5]—Angola, Zambia, Mozambique, and Zimbabwe—and, collectively, the member states of the OAU. Leading nonstate actors included various antigovernment guerrilla groups, including the African National Congress (ANC), SWAPO, the National Union for the Total Independence of Angola (UNITA), the Popular Movement for the Liberation of Angola (MPLA), and the Mozambique National Resistance. UN involvement took the form of successive resolutions of the Security Council and direct mediation efforts by the secretary-general and the Western Contact Group, the members of which were the United States, the Federal Republic of Germany, France, Canada, and the United Kingdom.

Third-Party Efforts to Negotiate a Political Settlement

Almost eleven years passed from the time the United States first attempted in earnest to negotiate a resolution to the conflict in Namibia until an agreement was concluded in December 1988. Under the Carter administration, the United States essentially pursued a multilateral approach to mediation that was focused on the Western Contact Group. Under the Reagan administration, the policy shifted to a bilateral negotiating strategy between the United States and South Africa as part of the administration's new doctrine of "constructive engagement." The premise of this doctrine was that the United States would gain leverage on South Africa by recognizing its security interests and by securing the withdrawal of Cuban troops from Angola. A brief chronology of these negotiations follows.[6]

By 1976 the Namibian situation was proving to be increasingly costly to the South African government at a time when it was trying to improve its relations with Africa and the West. The Turnhalle Constitutional Conference was an attempt to dampen growing external pressure for sanctions against South Africa by setting in motion political reforms for an "internal" solution that might eventually pave the road to Namibian independence, but on terms that would be in South Africa's interests and subject to South African control. The goals of the conference were to draft a constitution for Namibia and establish an "interim" government while excluding "nonethnic" parties, such as SWAPO, from any involvement in these deliberations. This did not sit well with South Africa's neighbors, which began to call for a mandatory arms embargo and a ban on new loans to South Africa.

On April 5, 1977, in an effort to head off an internal settlement, the Western powers launched their own diplomatic initiative in the form of the Western Contact Group (WCG). The WCG was initiated by President Jimmy Carter, who was concerned about mounting civil violence in South Africa following violent clashes in the township of Soweto. The WCG started negotiations with South Africa and its neighbors with a commitment to the creation of a Namibian settlement, free elections for an independent government, and the appointment of a special representative to ensure that elections would take place.

The WCG's objective was the creation of a representative government in Namibia without reference to ethnic or racial quotas. The WCG made some progress in getting South Africa to agree to Namibian independence. Outstanding issues in these negotiations included the timing of withdrawal of South African troops from Namibia, a timetable for elections, and the question of ownership of the port of Walvis Bay, which South Africa claimed as part of its territory. SWAPO was unhappy about the direction of these discussions but came under pressure from the OAU to encourage the efforts of the WCG. By September 1977 negotiations had advanced to the most difficult issues.

The WCG's formula called for South Africa to withdraw its forces to one or two army bases prior to UN-supervised elections in Namibia, with the understanding that South African security forces would then be replaced by UN peacekeeping and observer forces. South Africa reluctantly agreed, on condition that both sides of the Angola-Namibia border be monitored to prevent guerrilla infiltrations.

The issue of when to hold elections proved to be more thorny. South Africa favored early elections in 1978 to give the advantage to pro-Turnhalle parties; the WCG favored later elections to allow other groups time to organize. At the same time, South Africa indicated that it would agree to a long-term treaty permitting future Namibian government use of the port at Walvis Bay.

In December 1977 a fourth round of inconclusive talks stalled on the matter of UN involvement in peacekeeping and monitoring of elections in Namibia. Threatened with the termination of oil exports from Iran (its principal supplier of oil), South Africa subsequently agreed to reduce its military forces in Namibia under UN supervision and to allow UN military forces to participate in the monitoring of elections for a Constituent Assembly, which would assume responsibility for drafting a constitution.

Early in 1978 the WCG elaborated a framework for all subsequent negotiations, including the following provisions:

- the appointment of a UN special representative and the formation of a UN planning group to administer Namibia;
- a cease-fire followed by a three-month period during which both sides would redeploy their forces to specified locations;
- elections for a Constituent Assembly under UN auspices; and
- the disbanding of local police forces in Namibia and the release of all political prisoners.

While negotiations were still under way in New York, South Africa increased its military presence in Namibia and launched a series of attacks against SWAPO bases inside Angola. Following these raids, SWAPO broke off talks for several months. In August 1978 UN Secretary-General

Kurt Waldheim issued his report on Namibia, which was based on the report of UN Commissioner for Namibia Martti Ahtisaari. The report, which was accepted by the Security Council as Resolution 435 on September 29, 1978, became the internationally accepted framework for resolution of the conflict. South Africa voiced its objections to the report, complaining that the size of the United Nations Transition Assistance Group, which was to be composed of 7,500 military personnel and 1,500 civilians, exceeded the WCG's proposal. South Africa also objected to the timing of elections because the plan would not allow for independence to be achieved before the target date of December 31, 1978.

South Africa formally rejected the plan on September 20, 1978. On September 29 John Vorster announced his resignation as prime minister and was replaced by a noted hard-liner, the defense minister P. W. Botha. Not only did South Africa's new leadership reject all subsequent UN proposals for a cease-fire, but in March 1979 South Africa began attacking SWAPO bases in southern Angola. Negotiations were suspended but resumed in June 1979 at about the same time as South Africa was taking steps to increase its direct control of Namibia's internal affairs by appointing an administrator-general of Namibia.

On November 6, 1979, in a bid to rescue the stalled peace talks, Secretary-General Kurt Waldheim invited the South African government, WCG members, frontline states, and SWAPO to attend a conference in Geneva to discuss demilitarization proposals. The purpose of these negotiations was to clarify details on a new WCG proposal for a demilitarized zone along the Angola-Namibia border—a proposal that had been provisionally accepted by South Africa, SWAPO, and the frontline states. However, South Africa continued to voice its objections to a number of technical points in the UN proposal, while continuing to insist that the United Nations clearly demonstrate its impartiality before any settlement could be reached.

During this period it became increasingly difficult to focus the political attention of key Contact Group members on the talks. While Britain was busy with independence negotiations for Zimbabwe (Rhodesia), the United States was gearing up for the 1980 presidential elections. In the meantime, South Africa continued its efforts to establish an effective coalition of anti-SWAPO parties to install an internal administration with limited authority under the administrator-general.

By the time "preimplementation" discussions began under UN auspices in Geneva on January 7–14, 1981, South Africa had little incentive to make the necessary concessions that would lead to a settlement. Ronald Reagan was about to be sworn in as the new American president, and South Africa's hope that he would take a more favorable stance toward its interests was soon to be realized. The British government, under Margaret Thatcher, also made clear its opposition to any attempt to impose sanctions against South Africa. The Geneva meeting broke down over the issue of representation and demands put forward by the Democratic Turnhalle Alliance leader, Dirk Mudge, to rescind UN recognition of SWAPO as the "sole and authentic representative of the people of Namibia."[7]

The Reagan administration shifted course to a more interventionist regional and bilateral strategy, labeled constructive engagement. The rationale for this approach was not to impose "blueprints or timetables for change on the South Africans. . . . Rather . . . to help foster a 'regional climate conducive to compromise and accommodation' in both Southern and South Africa."[8] Underlying this approach was the recognition that an improved climate for regional security could happen only if South Africa and Cuban troops in Angola were both recognized as part of the security problem in the region.[9]

During the summer of 1981 apprehensions grew in the Reagan administration about the buildup of Cuban forces in Angola. Apparently responding to a leaked May 1981 State Department memorandum by Assistant Secretary of State for African Affairs Chester Crocker, arguing that Namibian independence should be tied "to a withdrawal of Cuban forces from Angola and a commitment by the Marxist leaders in Angola to share power with Western-backed guerrillas,"[10] Pretoria indicated that it would not enter into implementation of an agreement on Namibian independence unless Cuban forces were withdrawn from Angola. With the increasingly direct role played by the United States in Southern Africa's security problems, the WCG began to fade from the political scene.

In February 1984 the Angolan government negotiated the Lusaka Accord, which defined a "no-go zone for SWAPO and Cuban forces in a large area of Cunene Province" along with "detailed arrangements" for a phased withdrawal of the South African Defense Force (SADF) from Angola.[11] The accord created a joint monitoring commission made up of Angolan and South African forces to monitor the border areas. South Africa and Angola also agreed to the establishment of a U.S. liaison office to physically monitor events in Namibia. The patrolled area covered more than 400 miles of the border, encompassing SWAPO's main infiltration routes into Namibia. Almost as soon as the cease-fire went into effect, South Africa charged SWAPO with violations, using these as a further excuse to slow down South Africa's own withdrawal of forces from southern Angola.

The South Africa–Angola security accord was followed by the Nkomati Accords between Mozambique and South Africa. Both formed part of a coordinated South African strategy to force bilateral dealings with the frontline states and weaken their solidarity. Subsequent talks between Pretoria, SWAPO, and other groups in Namibia proved fruitless because of Pretoria's insistence that a cease-fire precede implementation of UN Security Council Resolution 435. South Africa's insistence that Cuba withdraw its forces from Angola before implementation of Resolution 435 also continued to be a sticking point, as did South Africa's installation of the Interim Central Government in Namibia following the collapse of the Democratic Turnhalle Alliance. Although Angola rejected linkage, saying that the issue of Cuban forces was exclusively a matter of concern between Cuba and Angola, Angola did say that it would consider Cuban withdrawal after South Africa agreed to implement Resolution 435.

In July 1985 the Reagan administration succeeded in persuading Congress to repeal the Clark Amendment prohibiting U.S. assistance to UNITA rebel forces in Angola. With the repeal, the United States gave $15 million in "humanitarian assistance" to UNITA. In April 1986 it was disclosed that, in addition to humanitarian assistance, the United States had begun in January that year to supply UNITA with modest amounts of lethal and nonlethal assistance. In the eyes of SWAPO, the United Nations, the OAU, and the frontline states, the United States was no longer a disinterested third party to the conflict. The Botha government's position was also hardening in response to its own domestic difficulties. The ruling National Party had split, with right-wing members leaving to form their own Conservative Party.

Discouraged by South Africa's lack of progress in abolishing apartheid, however, the U.S. Congress passed the Comprehensive Anti-Apartheid Act on October 2, 1986, over President Reagan's veto. This action was followed by the decision of Commonwealth members to implement the 1985 Nassau sanctions package after the failure of the Eminent Persons Group mission to South Africa.

In November 1987 the situation on the military front began to change. In September South African forces went into Angola in support of UNITA rebel forces, which were in some danger of defeat to a massive Angolan offensive. With Jonas Savimbi's UNITA troops, South African forces were engaged in the siege of Cuito Cuanavale, an Angolan town some 300 kilometers north of the Namibian border. The modest South African force (no larger than a brigade) fought against Cuban forces and the FAPLA (People's Armed Forces for the Liberation of Angola, the military wing of the MPLA) for almost four months and remained deployed in the general area until August 1988. Although there was no decisive battle at Cuito Cuanavale, Cuban president Fidel Castro successfully exploited the situation for propaganda purposes. Thus, "the legend of Cuito Cuanavale is that the SADF was pushed around, defeated, surrounded by hostile forces, and barely able to extricate itself. The reality is that two forces of moderate size tested and checked each other for nine months."[12]

On May 3–4, 1988, regional peace talks resumed between Angola, South Africa, Cuba, and the United States in London. There were further rounds of talks in Cairo, New York, Geneva, and Brazzaville. President Mobutu Sese Seko of Zaire organized the Angolan reconciliation talks, which enjoyed the widespread support of the African nations. Six rounds of negotiations in Brazzaville led to the Brazzaville Protocol of December 1988, which immediately preceded the New York agreements on Namibia and Angola (see chapter 4).[13]

On December 22, 1988, high-level representatives of Angola, Cuba, and South Africa formally signed two agreements (the Tripartite and the Bilateral Agreements) in New York, establishing the basis for peaceful transition in Namibia, cessation of hostilities between South Africa and Angola, and a timetable for withdrawal of Cuban troops from Angola. The Tripartite Agreement called for the implementation of UN Security Council Resolution 435, which required South Africa to reduce its forces from approximately 25,000 troops to 1,500 troops in Namibia within twelve weeks of the agreement's implementation and to confine these troops to two bases.[14] The Bilateral Agreement, signed by Cuba and Angola, set out a withdrawal timetable for the 50,000 Cuban troops, to begin with a 3,000-troop reduction on April 1, 1989. All Cuban troops would be redeployed north of the 15th parallel (200 miles north of the Angola-Namibia border) by August 1989. Twenty-five thousand would be withdrawn from Angola, and the remainder moved north of the 13th parallel (350 miles north of the border) by November 1989. The Cuban departure from Angola would be completed by July 1, 1991. Further provisions of UN Security Council Resolution 435 and the agreements signed in December 1988 included full independence for Namibia by April 1990, preceded by the election of a Constituent Assembly on November 1, 1989, to draft a constitution and organize a new government.

In December 1988 the Security Council unanimously voted to send a mission to Angola to verify the redeployment northwards and the total withdrawal of Cuban forces from that country. This decision was the result of the December 1988 regional accord. The mandate of the United Nations Angola Verification Mission (UNAVEM) ran from January 1989 to January 1991. The verification team included seventy military observers and twenty civilians from Algeria, Argentina, Brazil, Congo, Czechoslovakia, India, Jordan, Norway, Spain, and Yugoslavia. In February 1989 the United Nations Transition Assistance Group (UNTAG) was created by the UN Security Council to monitor the Namibian peace process.

The peace settlement was thus linked to a series of reports, agreements, and discussions concluded in the period 1976–89, which defined both the principles behind the settlement and its manner of implementation. These discussions, which continued during the implementation phase of the settlement process, covered the repeal of various legislation in accordance with Security Council Resolution 435 and the conclusion of negotiations on the following: UNTAG's composition and roles, the status of various police forces in the territory, the electoral legislation and guidelines, and final reforms in the legislation for the Constituent Assembly and the constitution. During the period between the final agreements of December 1988 and the scheduled commencement date of April 1, 1989, negotiations continued on the form and composition of UNTAG pursuant to the secretary-general's report (S/20412) and the demands by the permanent members for a reduction in the scale and cost of the UNTAG mission.

The Role of Ripeness

A structural account of the peacemaking and peace-building process would argue that the conflict met the conditions of ripeness in 1988. The conditions for ripeness include the presence of a hurting stalemate to a conflict and changing perceptions among the parties that the costs of continuing the conflict exceed the benefits to be gained from a negotiated settlement. But the fact that there was ongoing third-party mediation throughout so much of the conflict suggests strongly that this was more a case of cultivated ripeness than one of ripeness emerging by itself from the dynamics of interparty conflict. Of course, defining the moment of ripeness in this case is somewhat problematic. Arguably, the conflict was beginning to approximate the conditions of ripeness as early as 1979–80. The political and economic costs to South Africa were growing: Western countries had earlier raised the stakes with the threat of an oil cutoff, and South Africa's international image was tarnished. However, major unresolved issues lurked just beneath the negotiating table, such as the problems of securing the withdrawal of Cuban forces in Angola and addressing South Africa's broader security interests in the region.

In 1987–88, however, the situation began to change. First, the military equation began to display the elements of what might be termed a *strategic hurting stalemate* in that neither side could hope unilaterally to achieve total victory on the battlefield. This was true of both the Namibian conflict and the linked conflict in Angola. SWAPO was subject to the reprisals of the elite counterinsurgency unit Koevoet (Afrikaans for "crowbar") and elements of both the South West Africa Territorial Force (SWATF) indigenous forces and SADF regulars. South Africa, however, was unable to bring SWAPO to a decisive conventional battle, nor could it hope to win a bush war without a major escalation and commitment of resources. Attempts to strike at SWAPO base camps inside Angola served to widen South Africa's conflict with that country and its Cuban and Soviet backers. Yet, while South Africa's support for UNITA was fairly effective in diverting Angolan and Cuban resources to protect SWAPO operations, the SADF's conventional strikes decreased in their effectiveness as Cuba deployed more and more combat forces in the area. Cuban and Angolan forces were largely unable to do more than stem the tide, however, and their own offensive operations against the SADF and UNITA had only limited success. The resultant stalemate, therefore, was characterized by limited tactical and operational successes, but for the most part neither side had the capability to achieve a strategic victory. This military hurting stalemate had reciprocal effects in the political arena, where support for the continuance of the costly bush war was declining on all sides.

Second, there were growing economic and military costs from the conflict, particularly psychological ones. The South African business community and white opinion were increasingly opposed to the war, and the government itself began to see Angola as a quagmire. This perception, in fact, may have helped pave the way for the rise of the moderate faction of the National Party under Prime Minister F. W. de Klerk.

Third, foreign pressure against South Africa was mounting, as the international community took measures to isolate the country. These included the Nassau package of sanctions adopted by the Commonwealth in October 1985, the decision of the U.S. Congress to override a presidential veto and enact its Comprehensive Anti-Apartheid Act, the modest degree of antiapartheid solidarity subsequently demonstrated by the European Community, and the threat of enactment of the U.S. Total Disinvestment Bill—measures taken in response to growing domestic turmoil within South Africa.[15]

The combination of sanctions, the changing balance of forces in the military arena against South Africa, and the South African white community's growing disillusionment with the war thus helped tip the scales toward a settlement in 1988. Conditions in 1988 approximated those of a hurting stalemate much more closely than they had in 1979–80.

Superpower and Regional Interests

Both superpowers played dual roles in the conflict in Southern Africa: supplying arms to forces they supported and conducting diplomatic activities in the region. The Soviet Union's military involvement in the late 1970s and early 1980s, however, was substantially greater than that of the United States. The Soviet Union contributed about $1 billion annually in arms to Angola during the 1980s, and Cuban forces were providing substantial assistance to the MPLA forces against Jonas Savimbi's UNITA guerrilla movement. Cuban and Soviet assistance to the MPLA was symbolically matched by South African and U.S. assistance to UNITA, resulting in a virtual stalemate in the civil war by 1987.

Whether the Angola-Namibia peace accords were facilitated by the rise of Mikhail Gorbachev in the Soviet Union, the new climate of cooperation between the superpowers, and the changing military-strategic balance between them is questionable.[16] The evidence suggests that Moscow was increasing, not decreasing, its support for FAPLA and for Cuba in the period from 1985 to 1988; at the same time the United States was resuming aid to UNITA and South African troops were actively intervening on UNITA's behalf.[17] Although some scholars argue that Moscow went so far as to pressure Luanda to be forthcoming in the terms of a Cuban withdrawal and to negotiate a compromise with UNITA, American negotiators witnessed no evidence of such behavior.[18] According to Chester Crocker,

Moscow made no changes in the settlement framework. It was not Soviet pressure which got parties to the table. We saw no Soviet evidence of arm-twisting; the Soviet practice of distancing themselves from Castro and racheting down their aid to Cuba did not begin until long after our settlement had been negotiated. . . . At another level, however, their contribution to the 1988 settlement was, first, to stop opposing it, and then to associate themselves with it. This strengthened our hand with each of the parties and raised the price for bailing out.[19]

The evolving relationship between the superpowers in the late 1980s may therefore have had less to do with the settlement and the ultimate success of the peace accords in Namibia than the emerging (and cultivated) ripeness of the situation on the ground. Moreover, the influence of the United States, which played a much more direct role in the negotiations than did Moscow, had less to do with American power projection capabilities, or its economic or military leverage in the region (which was limited), than with U.S. diplomatic skill and influence as a mediator. As Crocker notes, "The parties cared less about the direct, physical leverage the U.S. government could bring to bear than about the intangible, symbolic influence we might wield: our ability to discredit, ostracize, legitimize, and encourage."[20]

The argument is even less compelling that the success of the Namibian peace settlements was due to changing subsystemic or regional balance-of-power influences (if we define the regional subsystem narrowly as the countries in the region). First, the regional balance of power was still heavily weighted in South Africa's favor, notwithstanding the growing stalemate in the military campaign against Cuban and MPLA forces. This is not to say, however, that regional interests (excluding South Africa) played a mixed role in the peace process, with various groups either helping or hindering it at different times. During the preimplementation phase from 1978 to 1988, the frontline states were largely seen as a supportive element in pushing for South African negotiations through UN, WCG, and superpower mediation. But frontline state pressure, with a stress on anti-apartheid action, also served to consolidate South Africa's siege mentality and thus make it reluctant to proceed with Namibian independence for fear that a new "enemy" state would be created along a contiguous northern border. South Africa's national security situation was already complicated by the bush war in Namibia with SWAPO, the linked conflicts being waged in Angola and Mozambique against pro-Soviet, antiapartheid governments, and the internal dynamic of apartheid and the consequent struggle with the ANC (which was supported by the frontline states). Only a change in South African perceptions, as well as an altered calculus by the frontline states over the desirability of continued conflict, could affect the situation. This occurred in 1988.

At the broader level, if one includes the role of Cuba as an extra-regional power but key subsystem player, there was indeed a change in attitudes. Castro was keen to withdraw his forces from Angola if a face-saving way could be found to do so. Jorge Dominguez notes that the Cubans had been in Angola for almost fifteen years. Their force was large enough to defend the MPLA region in Luanda but not large enough to prevent South African incursions into Luanda. Castro built up his forces in Angola in 1987–88 in order to change the balance of power to pave the way for negotiations. In Castro's view, "the South Africans had intervened and tried to solve the Angolan situation militarily, and perhaps they could have achieved it if it had not been for the effort our country made." But as Dominguez writes,

> In the same speech in which he extolled the validity of Cuba's military contribution to the Southern Africa settlement, President Castro praised not only the efficiency of Cuban diplomacy, but also the "positive aspect" of the U.S. role as mediator. In December 1988, at the time of the settlement, Castro certainly did not feel that his government had backed down in the face of a U.S. government success or Soviet pressure. Instead, he said that "in this case our interests coincide, our wishes coincide with the interests and wishes of the United States."[21]

The agreement and subsequent implementation of the accords thus served multiple regional and national interests, with substantial involvement of the region in the implementation process. The continued success of the implementation up to independence was crucially linked to progress in the Angolan internal conflict. From 1989 to 1990 both South Africa and the frontline states were actively involved in trying to broker cease-fires between Angolan factions. It was feared that resumption of generalized hostilities would put an end to Namibian independence, and insulating the conflicts from one another was much emphasized during the implementation phases. For example, the April 1989 incursion by SWAPO did not unduly upset the Angolan peace process, which was then leading to the June 1989 Gbadolite Accords. Likewise, the collapse of the Gbadolite Accords was not allowed to hinder the continued progress of the Namibian settlement, and the fact that a true Angolan cease-fire had not yet been reached at the time of Namibian independence was not allowed to disrupt the Namibian proceedings. Even after independence, the deteriorating situation in Angola was not allowed to spill over into Namibia, which was then approaching its first set of independent elections. Separation of the two situations was achieved with the active support of the frontline states and South Africa.

The Settlement Package: Strengths, Weaknesses, and Ambiguities

What role did the terms of settlement play in cementing the peace process and advancing the process of national reconciliation? The settlement package was both a source of strength and a source of weakness to the overall peacemaking and peace-building process. On the one hand, ambiguity in the Angola-Namibia peace agreements was necessary to reach a consensus. On the other hand, some of the ambiguities came back to haunt the process later on, during the implementation phase of the settlement. The length of the negotiations leading up to the Namibian settlement also created problems as new, unanticipated issues emerged that had not been dealt with in the original architecture of the negotiation. Many of these problems had to be dealt with by the United Nations during the implementation of the peace accords; the fact that it did so successfully contributed to building confidence and trust in the settlement process.

The settlement proposal of April 10, 1978, was submitted by the representatives of Canada, France, the Federal Republic of Germany, the United Kingdom, and the United States (namely, the Western Contact Group) in response to UN Security Council Resolution 385 of January 30, 1976, and formed the initial basis of the eventual peace settlement.[22] The proposal called for the holding of elections for a Constituent Assembly that would, in turn, draft a constitution for an independent and sovereign Namibia, with the independence process to be overseen by the UN special representative (UNSR) assisted by UNTAG. General procedures for the observation of a comprehensive cease-fire under UNTAG supervision were to include (1) cease-fire by all parties, with both South African and SWAPO troops confined to base; (2) subsequent phased withdrawal of all but 1,500 South African troops within twelve weeks and prior to the start of the election campaign, with remaining troops to be withdrawn after elections were certified; (3) citizen forces, commandos, and ethnic forces to be demobilized and command structures dismantled; (4) provision for SWAPO forces to return via designated entry points to participate in elections; and (5) an UNTAG military section to ensure provisions were observed by all parties.

The secretary-general reported on implementation measures following the initial survey mission to Namibia.[23] The implementation plan recommended establishing an UNTAG military component of 7,500 personnel (5,000 personnel in seven battalions, plus 200 observers and a
2,300-person logistics component), the primary task of which would be
support of the civil component. The military component's duties would
include monitoring the cease-fire; confining South African and SWAPO
forces to their bases; assisting in the withdrawal of South African forces;
confining the remaining South African forces until elections were completed; monitoring the borders; preventing infiltration of the borders; and
monitoring the disbandment of citizen forces, commandos, and relevant
command structures.

The UNTAG civilian component was to be divided between civil
police and other nonpolice civilian personnel. The police contingent was
estimated at 360 personnel, with primary duties to be preventing intimidation and interference with the electoral process and helping to ensure
the good conduct of the existing local police forces. The nonpolice civilian component would supervise and control all aspects of the electoral
process, including monitoring of balloting and counting of votes, investigating allegations of fraud or challenges to the results, and generally
working to ensure the fairness of the process; advising the UNSR on the
repeal of discriminatory laws and regulations inhibiting the free and fair
conduct of the elections; and ensuring freedom from intimidation and
investigating allegations of restrictions on free speech, movement, and
peaceful political assembly that would impede a free and fair process.
This civilian component would initially comprise 300 personnel, with a
further 1,200 to be dispatched upon the commencement of the electoral
process. Personnel would oversee an estimated 400 polling stations in
twenty-four regions.

Following this initial plan of action, the central features of which
remained at the core of the UNTAG plan, the secretary-general gave further definition to the UNSR's duties in his "Explanatory Statement" of
September 29, 1978,[24] which was intended to expand on some elements
of his report.[25] Even at this early stage of the planning process, he was
forced to justify the projected costs of the operation in the face of concerns
expressed by some Security Council members. The secretary-general
pointed out that the size of the military component of UNTAG had been
determined following talks with the South Africans on the operational
requirements for a credible force, but the buildup of UNTAG forces

would be gradual and the figure of 7,500 personnel would be viewed as an authorized upper limit, not as an absolute requirement. The secretary-general also reported that conditions had not yet been reached for the process to commence, despite assurances of cooperation by the relevant South African and SWAPO parties. SWAPO had agreed to observe and sign cease-fire proposals in a letter dated September 8, 1978.[26]

Follow-up agreements in 1982 elaborated the principles that would guide the elections, the formation of the Constituent Assembly, and the subsequent authoring of a constitution. A series of "impartiality agreements"—concluded in private but later released—were also essential features of the eventual settlement process. It was agreed that the South West Africa Police Force (SWAPOL) would continue as the primary enforcer of law and order, under the scrutiny of the administrator-general (AG) and the UNSR, in conjunction with the civilian police monitors of UNTAG, to ensure correct action. SWATF would be monitored and its command dismantled by UNTAG during "the demobilization of all citizen forces, commandos and ethnic forces, and the dismantling of their command structure."[27]

These extensive agreements were the basis of the negotiations that finally resulted in the 1988 accords; they formed the central core of the settlement plan as it was eventually conceived. The centrality of these agreements was reiterated by the secretary-general in his report of January 23, 1989.[28] In further detailing the particulars of the settlement plan in part II of the report, the secretary-general referenced two additional related agreements involved in the settlement plan negotiations. These were the 1982 agreement[29] that UNTAG would monitor SWAPO bases in Angola and Zambia (this agreement was distinct from the UNAVEM mission detailed in S/20338 and Security Council Resolution 626),[30] and the November 1985 agreement[31] on the system of proportional representation for the elections slated under Security Council Resolution 435.

On the matter of police monitors, estimates were continually revised to account for the fluctuating strengths and composition of local forces. The original 1978 requirement of 360 police observers was predicated on a territorial police force of about 3,000. As noted by Security Council Resolution 629, however, the strength of those forces had risen considerably in the intervening years to an estimated strength of 8,300 in October 1988. Although the controversial 3,000-man counterinsurgency unit, Koevoet, was to be disbanded under UNTAG supervision, the UNSR and secretary-general felt that the police observer contingent must be increased to at least 500 in the interim. These police forces were to play a crucial role in the settlement process, not only by monitoring the conduct and behavior of SWAPO forces, but also by helping to promote dialogue and build confidence in the settlement process.

The military tasks of UNTAG as described in the original report of 1978 were modified by the addition of three new missions: (1) monitoring of SADF personnel, who would continue to perform civilian functions in the transition period; (2) monitoring the restriction of SWAPO troops to bases in Angola and Zambia; and (3) ensuring that military installations along the northern border (with Angola) were deactivated and placed under UN control, and providing security for these installations.[32] Altogether, these tasks and the military mission as a whole were estimated to account for 75 percent of UNTAG's total mission costs. Not surprisingly, especially because they stood to contribute about 57 percent of the total peacekeeping costs, the permanent members of the Security Council pressed for substantial reductions in the military component—arguing that positive improvements in the relations of the region warranted such reductions—while changing none of the mission requirements. But the members of the frontline states argued that the situation had in fact become more complex—especially in the matter of consolidated and expanded police forces—and that an *increase* in the numbers of the military mission was in fact desired. In the end the authorized upper limit remained at 7,500 personnel, but the initial deployment was cut to three 850-man battalions, 300 observers, a 100-man headquarters, and 1,700 logistics personnel, with supplementary forces on standby, for a total actual deployment of 4,650 personnel, which cut projected UNTAG costs from about $700 million to approximately $416 million. This did not, however, include the costs of the separate UN High Commission on Refugees (UNHCR) mission to repatriate refugees, which would be funded from other sources. Lieutenant Prem Chand of India was designated the force commander.

Finalization of these arrangements would depend on the appropriate personnel being found from national contributions, as well as funding being agreed to through the normal procedures. There was also the issue of a formal cease-fire date, which would give expression to the de facto cease-fire in effect since August 10, 1988. The secretary-general requested a more formal timetable for the cease-fire from SWAPO and South Africa; he urged restraint in the interim on both sides to avoid jeopardizing either the de facto cease-fire or the April 1 implementation schedule. The success of these revised plans, in the secretary-general's view, was clearly reliant on the continuance of the status quo among the parties.

A key question is whether the conditions or assumptions under which a negotiated settlement was reached reflected the situation on the ground and whether during the postconflict, peace-building phase of the agreement there was any change in these assumptions or on the ground.

It is fair to say that the negotiated settlement did fairly accurately reflect the situation on the ground at the time, with negotiations constantly being updated to reflect changing circumstances. Assumptions about negotiations did not seem to change in any substantive manner in the postconflict phase, except to the extent that it was necessary to refocus attention on SWAPO as a formal party to the process following the April incursion. The peace process was otherwise largely unimpeded. Difficulties that were experienced were normally temporary and quickly overcome, generally with the assistance of UNTAG.

Although the agreements had been concluded over a period of more than ten years and sought to reconcile a diverse range of interests, a number of issues remained unresolved and were left to subsequent negotiations, while other issues emerged that could not have been anticipated. These issues, which varied in significance and impact, included the following:[33]

- *Walvis Bay.* This territory was not specifically mentioned in Security Council Resolution 435's reference to "the whole of Namibia," as to have expressly included or excluded it would have meant rejection by either South Africa or SWAPO. Although Security Council Resolution 432 of July 1978 had specifically called for the reintegration of Walvis Bay into the Namibian territory, it remained a controversial issue in the negotiations until both parties agreed later in 1978 to postpone agreement. In the interim, South Africa was not to use the port in any manner prejudicial to either Namibian independence or the economy.[34] The status of neither Walvis Bay nor the nearby offshore islands had been decided at the time of implementation.

- *Constituent Assembly.* Despite agreement on general principles, the settlement plan lacked specifics on ratification and procedures for choosing the first government.

- *Constitutional principles.* These were agreed upon by SWAPO and South Africa, but there was no a priori legal requirement for the new Constituent Assembly to abide by them. During implementation, this caused a division between SWAPO and UNTAG, on the one hand, both of which felt that the assembly should be free to choose applicable principles, and South Africa and several Namibian political parties, on the other hand, which felt the agreed-upon principles should form the core of the constitution. Debate focused on whether a new assembly could, in effect, have the core of its constitution dictated by previous agreement.[35] South Africa stressed previous Security Council decisions reaffirming the 1982 principles as an integral element of the settlement, as stated in S/20412, and urged they be upheld.[36]

- *Discriminatory legislation.* A narrow interpretation was given to the repeal of discriminatory legislation and regulations, revoking only those laws that would directly inhibit participation in the electoral process. Other legislation was not so easily addressed because the issues involved had not been directly specified.

- *Parties to the settlement.* The 1978 cease-fire proposal applied only to SWAPO and South Africa. UNITA was not specifically included and thus could act as a potential spoiler. Further, some of the local forces, such as Koevoet, had been formed after the 1978 provisions on disbandment of forces and were thus not specifically mentioned. These units continued to function under the AG as part of the police force, carrying out actions against SWAPO and its supporters. Koevoet would remain a controversial element in implementation right up to the elections.

- *Dispute resolution procedures.* No formal mechanism existed for resolving disputes between the AG and the UNSR. Martti Ahtisaari, as UNSR, was not given a formal mechanism to exercise power in pursuit of UNTAG's mandate, and thus he had to rely on informal means. The limited leverage the UNSR enjoyed insofar as he could refer problems to the joint commission, the secretary-general, and even the Security Council was enhanced by the fact that he too had to be satisfied with each step of the process before it could move forward.

- *Continuing disputes over the size of UNTAG.* Debates in the Security Council and General Assembly about the size and composition of UNTAG led to delays. At one point the debate became so acrimonious that the General Assembly threatened to withhold funding. The purchase of vehicles (especially mine-resistant vehicles) and supplies from local sources (namely, South Africa) also prompted debate. Agreement on this latter issue was not reached until March 1. The net result was a delay in the deployment of UNTAG forces and suitable equipment. Only 1,000 troops were in the territory on April 3, and none of the infantry battalions had been deployed. Initial units were unequipped to assume patrol duties in Namibian terrain.

Several contentious issues emerged concerning the interpretation of various aspects of the agreement and the manner of their implementation. These focused on the development of a legal framework for elections in accordance with Security Council Resolution 435, including electoral procedures, constitutional development, and repeal of discriminatory laws. A second issue was the disbandment of local forces such as Koevoet and their role in SWAPOL. A third concerned the problem of detainees. These issues are examined, in turn, below.

On the legal framework issue, as Robert Jaster notes, the South African AG, Louis Pienaar, was in a difficult spot between his own government and the UNSR.[37] Pienaar was appointed in 1985 as a representative to the Transitional Government of National Unity (TGNU) that had since become defunct and, in any case, had never been recognized as valid by the United Nations. Under the old system, he had enjoyed wide administrative and review powers, but under the transition process he was placed between a reform-oriented majority, a vocal white South African lobby, his own government's wishes, and the review power that the UNSR held over him. This, Jaster observes, often left the AG in a difficult position when trying to deal with various aspects of the legal and administrative reforms; he seems to have been trying to satisfy too many political masters and wary constituents. The result, at times, was some odd first drafts of reform laws and an occasionally antagonistic relationship between the AG and UNSR.

Three major groups of laws needed to be enacted in accordance with the settlement plan: laws creating a suitable environment for Namibian political participation; electoral administration laws to ensure free and fair elections; and laws on the Constituent Assembly. Throughout this process, the AG was responsible for primary drafting of the laws in consultation with and under the review of the UNSR. In some cases, laws had to be made public for comment or referred to appropriate governments and the United Nations. Laws became valid only after final approval of the UNSR.[38]

Dispute over electoral laws was prolonged. The AG's initial draft of July 21 was almost universally rejected by most parties on the grounds that it was too centralized, required all vote counting to be done in Windhoek, compromised the secrecy of the ballot, denied parties access to polling stations (to prevent intimidation of voters), and allowed South African electoral officials to guide illiterate voters during the voting process.[39] International pressure—including a U.S. congressional review and a UN resolution sponsored by the Commonwealth nations (Security Council Resolution 640, August 29)—forced revision of this draft law by the AG. UN legal specialists were sent to assist with the revision and negotiation, and agreement was reached on October 6. The new law eliminated the use of numbered envelopes, instituted a decentralized vote count, permitted UNTAG supervisors to be present when voting procedures were explained, and allowed parties access to polling stations.[40]

The initial draft of laws on the Constituent Assembly submitted by the AG on July 21 was wholly unacceptable to almost all parties concerned. The proposal gave the AG power to control procedures of the assembly and constitution, gave South African territorial courts review powers over the assembly, endorsed the 1982 Constitutional Principles agreement, and required assembly members to swear their oath of allegiance before a South African judge. In addition, the AG was designated president pro tem, and the assembly would be capable only of "recommending" actions to the AG, who could choose to use a veto or not to act. Controversy over the draft resulted in its being temporarily shelved in order to avoid linkage with the electoral law then under negotiation, with Security Council Resolution 640 addressing the issue in the interim by charging the secretary-general with ensuring that the law "respects the sovereign will of the people of Namibia." The AG soon dropped his proposals to have full review powers in the assembly, but negotiation was prolonged on the issue of the 1982 Constitutional Principles. SWAPO and UNTAG argued that the assembly should not be bound by the agreement, while other political parties and the AG argued that the principles were a central element of the settlement plan as agreed to by SWAPO. UNTAG was seen by many as being too partial to the SWAPO position, and the argument was made that if SWAPO could reject the 1982 principles, then other parts of the settlement plan being "imposed" could also be rejected on similar grounds. The UNSR argued that the assembly should be free to decide on the content of the constitution, deriving its authority from the elections instead of South African or international law.[41]

In the end, the law passed on November 6 gave the Constituent Assembly the task of drafting a constitution to be adopted by a two-thirds majority, determining the date for independence and then formally declaring that independence, and forming a government according to eventual constitutional rules. Importantly, as the secretary-general pointed out, the law made explicit provision that no external court of law would have the power to interfere with or review the decisions of the assembly (at least during the interim, until such provisions were granted by the assembly in the constitution).[42]

A second extremely controversial issue concerned the disbandment of local forces—in particular, the local ethnic forces that had been recruited into the South African military and police apparatus. These included units such as SWATF and, at a later date, the even more controversial Koevoet unit.

SWATF was explicitly singled out for disbandment by the 1982 "informal checklist"; this was largely completed by May 27 (except for two battalions of bushmen).[43] Koevoet, however, remained a continual source of disagreement between the AG and the UNSR, as well as between SWAPO and the AG. According to the secretary-general's report of January 23, 1989, the force was considered a paramilitary unit to be dismantled.[44] The South Africans announced its disbandment in December 1988, but it soon became evident that Koevoet had been incorporated almost wholly intact into SWAPOL. The unit, known for its effectiveness against SWAPO and also for its brutal, unconventional tactics, was a constant concern for both SWAPO and the UNSR, mainly because it continued to utilize its trademark "Casspir" mine-proofed armored vehicles equipped with heavy weapons and because it seemed to take every opportunity to antagonize SWAPO rallies. The continued existence of the unit contravened the spirit of the settlement plan, as well as some specific provisions regarding the weapons SWAPOL could carry and the people considered suitable for employment in its ranks. On September 28, South Africa finally agreed that the Koevoet personnel would be demobilized immediately; by late October the problem was finally resolved.

A third issue that developed into a significant controversy was the repatriation of detainees. This was a specific provision of the settlement plan to be dealt with early in the process, and the UNSR was mandated to ensure that all detainees had been released. In the first two months of the process, several human rights groups—including the International Society for Human Rights and Amnesty International—along with the SWAPO-Democrats party (a reactionary anti-SWAPO group), claimed that SWAPO was holding some 260 personnel in Angola. SWAPO initially denied the reports, but in late May announced it had released prisoners in Angola. After interviews by UNTAG personnel, 232 detainees were flown back to Namibia by the UNHCR through July and August. On July 20 the South Africans also released a number of remaining political detainees. Throughout the repatriation of SWAPO detainees, there were reports that many had been tortured and that a large number might remain unaccounted for. The issue was taken up by two detainee organizations hostile to SWAPO, the Parents' Committee and the Political Consultative Council, which released additional lists of names and, along with church and civil organizations, demanded UN investigations into the alleged SWAPO abuses.

SWAPO largely ignored the allegations, although it admitted to having detained people in the past. As a result of UN and international pressure, SWAPO eventually invited the UNHCR and human rights groups to tour its camps. UNTAG compiled a separate list of 1,100 names and received permission from Angola and Zambia to conduct on-site inspections. All camps were investigated to UNTAG's satisfaction; its report of October 16 stated that it had uncovered no evidence of additional detainees.[45] After the investigation, however, its consolidated list still contained 263 names that were unaccounted for. The South African foreign minister criticized the report as being totally inadequate in a letter to the secretary-general on October 13, and alluded to the United Nations' partiality for SWAPO.[46] The secretary-general maintained that the investigation had been as thorough as possible, but that UNTAG would continue to investigate.[47] Many groups claimed the whole investigation to have been a whitewash and exploited the controversy to their political advantage in the election campaign that followed.[48]

Most of the above issues were not overly serious, though several led to sharp disagreements. Continuing consultation and negotiations among the parties to the accords, assisted by third-party mediation, prevented these difficulties from scuttling the peace process. As we will see, this factor, along with the contribution of the United Nations to the establishment of a secure political environment conducive to free and fair elections, helped to keep the settlement process on track.

Third Parties and the Implementation of the Peace Settlement

Implementation of the Namibian peace accords formally began at midnight on March 31, 1989, in anticipation of the April 1 official cease-fire date and scheduled commencement of the Namibian peace process. However, some time before dawn on April 1, more than 2,000 heavily armed SWAPO guerrillas entered Namibia from neighboring Angola. This was in direct violation of the Geneva Protocol of November 1988, which called for "reciprocal military restraint by the Cubans and SWAPO."[49]

The evidence clearly suggests that SWAPO numbers and equipment— at least among the actual incursion forces—were insufficient for anything more than a limited guerrilla offensive. The offensive was undoubtedly a threat, however, and South African intelligence sources made much of other buildups and redeployments occurring inside Angola.[50] SWAPO forces were outnumbered by the South Africans, even if the latter were confined to base and in the process of demobilizing. South Africa had been aware since mid-March that SWAPO was massing its troops, but its warnings to UNTAG had gone unheeded. Had the UNSR not finally given his permission for South African troops to leave their bases in response, South Africa would not have stood idly by while SWAPO rampaged across the territory. Once South African troops were released to bolster the police forces already engaging the rebels, the battle was predictably short and one-sided, with SADF forces killing more SWAPO troops than in any other single battle. The final toll was estimated at over 300 SWAPO dead at a cost of about 30 SADF personnel.

Given these details and keeping in mind the context of a hurting stalemate, we can find few persuasive explanations for SWAPO actions. Explanations of SWAPO's motives are necessarily speculative. One explanation deals with a long-standing SWAPO claim that its units should have been allowed to occupy bases or de facto areas inside Namibia at the time of independence. The denial of these requests by South Africa in 1978 and 1979, which broke off discussions over the matter, forced SWAPO to drop them. This did not mean the issue was closed, however. Following the incursion SWAPO claimed that its units had been peacefully gathering at "bases" inside Namibia in preparation for disbandment by UNTAG forces, as called for in the settlement proposal.[51]

Most sources concur that SWAPO may have felt that having troops inside Namibia at the time of implementation would be an important public relations coup, especially to reaffirm support among the Ovambo population—SWAPO's primary support group—and also perhaps to impress the remainder of the populace. Jaster notes that this might have had a more positive effect had SWAPO eluded South African forces and been able to receive protection from UNTAG.[52] As it was, however, the incursion served to alienate SWAPO from some of its potential support, further increased distrust among the white populace and South Africans, and brought a backlash of criticism from many of SWAPO's diehard supporters. SWAPO's initial denial of the incursion was rejected by the international community; SWAPO received rebukes from several frontline states, including Angola, which had given guarantees that SWAPO forces would stay above the 16th parallel until the formal time for their repatriation arrived. This had been part of the Geneva Accord of August 1988, and SWAPO had subsequently given assurances in correspondence with the secretary-general that it would abide by the settlement proposals. However, SWAPO was not a formal signatory to those agreements and had thus never given its written assent to them, even though, according to the interpretation of most Western sources, SWAPO had done so at least indirectly through third parties.[53]

As a result of these incursions, South Africa was able to claim that it was the injured party, although it was widely criticized for the brutal way it had hunted down the insurgents during the mopping-up operations. UNTAG and the UNSR also received a fair amount of criticism for their ineffective response, but Jaster places some blame on the Security Council, whose delays had in turn seriously delayed the force's deployment.[54]

The issue of SWAPO's incursion was immediately taken up by the joint commission, which met in emergency session April 8–9 outside Windhoek. The commission issued the Mount Etjo Declaration on April 9, coinciding with a de facto suspension of UN Security Council Resolution 435. The commission was created to oversee the implementation of the accords. According to the American mediator who proposed it, the commission was to serve as a political forum in which the parties could voice their concerns and resolve problems that arose: "It would not duplicate the role of UNTAG or the UN Secretary-General, but would serve as a mechanism for ongoing contact and communication among the signatory parties."[55] The commission served broader political objectives as well. The Soviets' membership was a strong incentive for them to support the regional peace process. From the South African viewpoint, the commission established a mechanism to review commitments and ensure that the peace process remained on track. It also kept the United States involved in the peace process once the agreement had been signed.[56] Such foresight reaped immediate dividends after the SWAPO incursion. The commission was then ready to swing into action and put

the peace process back on track. U.S., Soviet, Angolan, and Cuban officials met in emergency session accompanied by UN officials and developed a new set of understandings. (By coincidence Margaret Thatcher
was also in Namibia. "She helped keep the South Africans from tearing
up the Brazzaville and New York accords. She also provided strong leadership to Martti Ahtisaari, . . . who had authorized the South Africans to
use force to halt the SWAPO incursion."[57])

The Mount Etjo Declaration clarified the situation to a degree, ordering
all SWAPO troops still in the territory to present themselves at a number
of border assembly points or assembly areas inside the territory.[58]
UNTAG monitors at these locations would then escort the SWAPO members back to Angola, where they would be required to return above the
16th parallel. If SWAPO members chose to stay in Namibia, they would
have to surrender themselves and their weapons to UNTAG. The withdrawal was to be completed by April 15 to the satisfaction of the AG and
the UNSR. However, SWAPO combatants avoided the assembly points
because SADF forces were still deployed at many of these locations. Further negotiations led to an agreement to confine SADF forces at their
bases while SWAPO forces returned to Angola, followed by the release of
SADF forces to verify their return. In response to these events, the United
Nations accelerated the deployment of its forces and was subsequently
able to fulfill the military component of its mandate without experiencing
major difficulties. With simultaneous withdrawals of Cuban and South
African troops, both carefully monitored by the United Nations and external observers, neither group had much opportunity to take substantial
advantage of the situation even if there had been the political will to do
so. Thus, military stability on the ground was achieved with the assistance of various third parties: the United States, the United Kingdom, and
the United Nations. The latter monitored and supervised the withdrawal
and demobilization of forces.

The commission continued to meet every month thereafter to iron out
lingering problems and difficulties between the parties. SWAPO soon
agreed to withdraw its forces to Angola under UNTAG supervision by
April 15. Withdrawal could not be confirmed by that date, and South
African troops were only gradually returned to base after the joint commission granted South Africa more time to verify the withdrawals. This
further attests to the importance of third parties in cultivating the moment
of ripeness and fostering the right conditions for a peace settlement to
take root.

In May 1989 talks resumed between Angola, Cuba, and South Africa aimed at putting the Namibian independence process back on track. By July the conditions specified in the original timetable were being met, including the withdrawal of South African forces and the return of Namibian exiles for elections scheduled for November 1, 1989. However, the political atmosphere continued to be plagued by fear and intimidation on all sides, particularly by Koevoet forces. The United Nations threatened that continued action by the unit might jeopardize the upcoming elections and called for a demobilization of the Koevoet forces.

SWAPO clearly had the most to gain from the achievement and implementation of a settlement; SWAPO was also favored in the upcoming elections. South Africa was concerned about the emergence of a reactionary SWAPO government based on socialist principles, while SWAPO was concerned about a continuation of apartheid. Efforts to mollify these mutual suspicions and concerns resulted in negotiation of guiding principles to ensure that the new government would be suitably democratic and based on fundamental human rights. In practice, these principles were almost fully adopted by the Constituent Assembly in drafting the Constitution, and the Namibian government and Constitution are now among the most progressive and democratic in all of Africa.

To supervise and control the elections the United Nations trained and fielded more than 3,000 personnel drawn from the UN professional staff and more than 100 member countries. This number included 1,758 electoral supervisors who supervised each of the 358 polling stations and the subsequent tabulation of the vote, 358 UNTAG military personnel who guarded the ballot boxes, and 1,023 CIVPOL (Civilian Police) personnel who supervised security at the polling and counting stations.[59] As one observer writes:

> With hindsight, it is clear that the UN civilian police played a more critical role in the settlement process than had been anticipated. . . . While CIVPOL was restricted by its mandate to a "supervisory" role, it managed to have a salutary impact on the practices and behavior of the SWAPOL forces. It also played an important role in building confidence in the settlement process through its efforts to promote dialogue among the frequently divided communities in which its members lived and worked.[60]

UN civilian personnel, located in the forty-two field offices UNTAG established throughout the country, also performed a key role in reconciliation. These field offices, which were set up by the secretary-general in his report of August 29, 1978 (S/12827), were in both concept and establishment the initiative of UN officials such as Martti Ahtisaari, Cedric Thornberry, and Hisham Omayad, who had extensive knowledge and experience of the region. The function of these offices was to undertake activities beyond the technical aspects of electoral supervision, including establishing and maintaining regular contacts and liaison with all local officials and with local leaders of all political parties and organizations; ensuring that local officials and the population were fully and accurately informed about the organization and functions of the United Nations and UNTAG; observing political activities in the area; resolving complaints and appeals; and settling local disputes through discussion and consultation with the local authorities. Clearly more than supervision, these duties were in the realm of consultation and conciliation—or simply good, old-fashioned diplomacy. The personnel who headed these field offices were carefully selected for their posts and given special training in the consultation and problem-solving techniques needed to perform their jobs effectively.[61]

Results of the November 7–11, 1989, election gave SWAPO 57.3 percent of the vote (41 seats), the Democratic Turnhalle Alliance (DTA) 28.6 percent (21 seats), and the United Democratic Front of Namibia (UDF) 5.6 percent (4 seats); four other parties split the remaining seats (gaining between 1 and 3 seats each). Ten parties ran candidates in the elections. For a total of 72 seats, 680,688 votes were cast (more than 97 percent of registered voters); only 1.4 percent of the ballots were invalidated as spoiled or illegitimate. As expected, SWAPO took the majority vote in the dominant Ovambo region, but its victories in other areas were less clear and it lost many tribal districts altogether. The vote satisfied SWAPO and its supporters, by and large, allowing SWAPO to take the lead in the government and new state. At the same time, the absence of a clear two-thirds majority meant that SWAPO was unable to impose a one-party state if it had wanted to and would instead face a fairly strong democratic opposition. Given the virtual impossibility of a SWAPO defeat, the slim majority and strong opposition were the best that South Africa could hope for under the circumstances.

Namibia's political parties were able to work together in parliament. The slight SWAPO majority was countered by a vocal and coordinated opposition. Further, the mix in parliament meant that SWAPO had to adopt free-market economic principles. Additionally, SWAPO and the other parties demonstrated their commitment to working together through the formation of an executive branch drawn from a wide cross section of racial, ethnic, and political groups. Whites were encouraged to remain in the country and continue to play an important role in the government and civil service, including the police and military. Elections were initially marred by interparty violence, mainly mutual intimidation conducted by SWAPO and South African–supported parties such as the DTA and SWAPO-Democrats. This behavior eventually stopped and the parties have worked together fairly well since then.

After independence the SWAPO party congress held in December 1991 further moderated the party's policies, endorsing policy changes that stressed education and teaching reforms, legal changes to combat increasing crime, a gradual increase in the size of the military and the creation of a navy, fiscal discipline, foreign investment and marketing of products abroad, and more savings and farming. The party also announced that it was changing from a liberation movement to a mass political party, and all references to the People's Liberation Army of Namibia were removed.[62] The DTA also announced some policy shifts to bring it into line with the current political climate and renamed itself "DTA of Namibia."

In September 1992 preparations began for the first series of postindependence elections. The elections would be held between November 30 and December 5 in ninety-five constituencies in thirteen regions, with six to ten constituencies per region. Simultaneous elections would be held for the National Council or second chamber in parliament, with regional councils electing two members each.[63] Elections went ahead as scheduled with 500,000 voters, 77 percent of the eligible population, registered. SWAPO won nine out of thirteen regions; the DTA won three; and the thirteenth region was split between SWAPO, the UDF, and the DTA. SWAPO secured a majority in thirty-nine of forty-eight local authorities, with the DTA gaining a majority in seven and the UDF a majority in two. There were no reports of fraud or irregularities.[64]

The SWAPO-led government also entered into negotiations with several neighboring states on border issues, and concluded negotiations with South Africa on the status of Walvis Bay and the Penguin chain of offshore islands.

Assessment and Conclusions

Why was the Namibian peacemaking and peacekeeping operation the success that it was? In contrast with the case of Cyprus, how was a political settlement negotiated in Namibia that brought warring parties at both the subnational *and* the regional levels to the table, and how did the subsequent peacekeeping operation help to consolidate the peace?

First, third-party–mediated negotiations were conducted on two tracks. South Africa's interest in seeing Cuban troops withdrawn from Angola in the interests of regional stability were successfully linked to a policy of ending apartheid rule in Namibia and legitimizing SWAPO and Namibian desires for independence.

Second, once a settlement was achieved it became crucial to ensure that the military situation remained relatively stable during the implementation process, both within Namibia and in neighboring Angola (see chapter 4). This was no easy task for U.S. negotiators or for UN peacekeepers. Distrust and hostility were pronounced, and isolated incidents of violence occurred during this process—the most notable, of course, being the SWAPO incursion of April 1. UNTAG was constituted to conduct multiple peacekeeping tasks in support of the implementation process. Aside from major criticism of its inability to respond to the April 1 incursion, the force was recognized as largely successful in conducting its primary missions. The fact that UNTAG was not properly deployed prior to the April 1 deadline—and thus was not in a position to prevent or adequately react to the incursion—has been blamed chiefly on wrangling in the United Nations and on the desire of the great powers to downsize the force, and not on any inherent fault with the force itself.[65] However, even if the force had been properly deployed, it is uncertain whether it could have had an adequate deterrent effect, or given its inexperience in the unique bush warfare of the region, whether it would have been able to combat the offensive without significant South African help. Moreover, had the United Nations found itself involved at the very outset of its operations in a major counteroffensive against SWAPO, its very neutrality would have been called into question and its subsequent mission might have been seriously jeopardized. Thus, its inability to deal with SWAPO on a military basis was largely fortuitous.

The United Nations obviously played a key role in all stages of the implementation process, primarily through UNTAG, but also through the independent UNSR, associated UN agencies such as UNHCR, and the continued involvement of the Security Council and General Assembly in the entire process. Additionally, the OAU and the frontline states were closely involved in the process by helping to ensure that SWAPO abided by agreements and by forming an essential line of communication during several stages of the negotiations. The United States and the Soviet Union, along with Western Contact Group members, were also part of both the negotiation and the settlement phases of the peace process.

In the settlement and implementation phase, the United Nations played a major controlling role in overseeing the AG's implementation of the agreement. The United Nations was often involved in direct bilateral negotiations with the AG on changes to legislation; it also acted as an intermediary for the parties and assisted the bilateral negotiations between SWAPO and the South Africans—especially on points of contention that arose during the election process. Through the UNSR, the United Nations was ultimately responsible for approving the entire process at each stage, giving the organization considerable powers and a dominant role.

Other aspects of the peacekeeping mission included civilian police and elections monitoring. The United Nations was criticized for inadequately forceful responses early in the process toward the continued existence of Koevoet, and for its response to some allegations of electoral intimidation and interparty violence.[66] Other than this, the police mission was successful and was eventually expanded.

As the prime agency overseeing elections, UNTAG was effective in upholding adequate international standards and facilitating the process.[67] UNTAG officials also provided important advice and assistance in interpreting and applying electoral laws and regulations to local officials who had little experience with elections. The electoral campaign was conducted under a "Code of Conduct" that was signed by all Namibian parties. Party representatives also met on a bimonthly basis at the national and regional level under the chairmanship of UNTAG officials. Disputes between the parties were mediated by UNTAG officials. In the period following the elections, UNTAG field offices brought together representatives of all political parties, and church, ethnic, and community leaders in "reconciliation meetings" aimed at promoting tolerance and reconciliation.

UNTAG was also considered fairly effective in coordinating some of the refugee relief and humanitarian assistance operations in conjunction with the International Committee of the Red Cross and UNHCR. These were some of the least controversial aspects of the mission, but they were important in ensuring that expatriates were returned, cared for, and identified for voter registration. This part of the mission was funded from separate budgets, although conducted under UNTAG's aegis.

In addition to the United Nations, several national, regional, and international agencies contributed to the implementation process, including the OAU, EC country missions, human rights groups, antiapartheid groups, and church groups. Several nations—including the United States, other joint commission members, and Commonwealth members[68]—likewise made very valuable contributions.

A major role was played by the United Nations in areas of mediation, conciliation, and fact finding, with Special Representative Ahtisaari bearing primary responsibility. Many of his decisions were reviewed in New York prior to implementation. The negotiation role of the UNSR was central, given his generally wide powers, but constant liaison with New York and international attention may have constrained his freedom to act independently at times.[69] On the other hand, his right of veto over the entire process and his ability to appeal to New York when negotiations bogged down, or when parties displayed intransigence, gave him additional authority and power.

Because a conciliatory framework had been laid down during the implementation process, rival factions were able to work out their differences on the Constitution and matters of daily governmental business. Since independence there has been no significant breakdown in internal relations, and subsequent independent elections held in accordance with the Constitution in November and December 1992 were conducted without apparent incident. The entire UNTAG mission is thus considered, in general, to have been a model of efficiency and success.

In sum, the 1988 peace accords that gave Namibia its independence and led to the phased withdrawal of Cuban troops in Angola were the culmination of a lengthy set of negotiations that the Carter administration began as a broad-based multilateral undertaking and that the Reagan administration narrowed into a triangular one. Third-party–assisted negotiations, first by the WCG and then by the Reagan administration, were key to the eventual resolution of the conflict. The ripening of the conflict thus could not have occurred without the assistance of third parties. Through the passage of resolutions, mediation, and sharpening definitions of the negotiating agenda, the parties were coaxed to the negotiating table.

Once a settlement was reached, however, third parties were required to ensure that the settlement process remained on track and was not derailed by the great mistrust and hostility that characterized relations between the parties. The potential for backsliding into armed violence and confrontation was real and ever present. When a renewed outbreak of fighting did occur, UNTAG had to act swiftly to ensure that violence did not escalate. But UNTAG's role went well beyond peacekeeper, monitor, and supervisor of elections to that of conciliator, mediator, arbitrator, and negotiator at both local and national levels during implementation of the peace settlements. In this role it was supported by the secretary-general and the five permanent members of the Security Council, the United States in particular.

Although the conflicts in Namibia and Angola were fueled by the Cold War and the prospects for settlement hinged on the withdrawal of Cuban troops from Angola, it would be a mistake to attribute the resolution of the Namibian conflict solely to superpower détente. The rise of Gorbachev to power coupled with improved U.S.-Soviet relations in the 1980s removed some obstacles, but more important was the shifting correlation of forces at the regional and extraregional levels. First, the South African government and public were increasingly frustrated by a war that was stalemated on the battlefield. Second, Cuba's Castro deserves credit for seeing the handwriting on the wall. The war was taking its toll on the Cuban economy. The Cubans' buildup of forces in Angola in December 1987 was intended to strengthen their bargaining position at the negotiating table so that they could withdraw their forces without losing face.

Taken together these factors suggest that the prospects for achieving a durable peace settlement depend ultimately on the interests and perceptions of the parties to the conflict; the methods, skills, and timing of the intervention by mediators; "cultivated ripeness"; and a reconciliation process that is sustained during implementation by third parties that can perform a variety of functions that help ensure the parties' continued commitment to the peace process. To perform these functions effectively, however, third parties must have staying power, resources, and a commitment to the peace process itself. These conditions were met in Namibia. But, as we see in the next chapter, in Angola they were not.

ANGOLA

The origins of the conflict in Angola date back to the April 1974 military coup in Portugal that overthrew the government of Marcello Caetano. The new government pledged that it would grant independence to Portugal's African colonies, and within a few months negotiations for Angola's independence began. However, no single group or leader emerged in Angola to which Portugal could turn over the reins of authority. Rather, three major groups vied for power: the National Front for the Liberation of Angola (FNLA, which had ties to Zaire), the Popular Movement for the Liberation of Angola (MPLA, which had support from Cuba and the Soviet Union), and the National Union for the Total Independence of Angola (UNITA, which received some support from China).

The Alvor Accord on Angolan independence was signed in Alvor, Portugal, on January 15, 1975. The accord was to involve a tripartite transitional coalition government headed by a Portuguese high commissioner and assisted by a presidential council with a rotating chairmanship. Under the terms of the accord, Angola would become independent on November 11, 1975. But, almost as soon as it was created, the transitional government was undermined by factional warfare that Portugal, in its haste to get out of Angola, did little to stop. As each faction turned to its outside allies for assistance, the situation in Angola deteriorated further. South Africa sent forces, including former Portuguese colonial units, to

Angola to support the FNLA and UNITA. Both Cuba and the Soviet Union provided help; the Soviets were directly involved in combat operations and supplied military advisers and personnel.[1]

By the 1980s the Cuban presence had grown considerably, and the civil war in Angola became linked to the war for independence in Namibia. The South West Africa People's Organization (SWAPO), which had bases in Angola and launched its raids from Angolan territory, enjoyed the backing and military support of the MPLA. South Africa, in turn, was involved in a war against not only SWAPO but also the MPLA and the Cuban troops, which were seen as posing a major threat to South Africa's interests in the region. Moreover, South Africa backed UNITA in Angola's civil war, as did the United States, because of the perceived threat of communism in the region.

The early 1980s were also characterized by the increasing desire of many Western and African states to bring peaceful democratic change to Southern Africa. In particular, this period was marked by persistent American efforts to end apartheid in South Africa. The Reagan administration decided that the key to bringing about peaceful democratic change in South Africa was first to secure Namibian independence, which, in turn, could only occur if Cuban forces were withdrawn from Angola. This, furthermore, required a move toward ending the civil strife in Angola. Hence was born the multipronged policy of "constructive engagement."

This chapter explores why the first phase of the peace process in Angola, which centered on the implementation of the Angola-Namibia peace accords, succeeded, and why the second phase, which centered on the implementation of two subsequent accords, the Gbadolite and Bicesse Accords, failed. The argument of this chapter is that continuation of the civil war in Angola was due, in part, to a lack of ripeness in the conflict itself. Although the civil war exacted a enormous price on the people of Angola in loss of human life and forgone economic opportunities,[2] the MPLA and UNITA leaderships continued to believe that they could achieve their aims through a military rather than a political solution. However, there was a moment when the conflict did appear to be ripe for resolution. That came in May 1991 with the signing of the Bicesse Accords. But the inability of third parties, notably the United Nations, to provide the resources needed to implement the 1991 peace accords doomed them to failure in the face of widespread cheating and noncompliance.

The failure of the Bicesse Accords is a striking illustration of the proposition that if third parties fail to invest adequate resources into the implementation of a peace settlement, particularly in the monitoring of cease-fires and demobilization of forces, the peace process is much more likely to end in failure. There is strong evidence in this case that the failure of the United Nations to do precisely that was a key factor in the collapse of the Bicesse Accords. To be sure, the agreement itself had some major weaknesses. Notable among these were the lack of adequate power-sharing provisions and the winner-take-all elections once a cease-fire and partial demobilization were completed. But it is conceivable these problems might have been surmounted, or at the very least addressed in follow-on negotiations, had the peace process moved forward and a modicum of trust developed between the parties. In this case, a weak third-party presence helped doom the peace process.

Without doubt the United Nations learned from this failure; after a new round of negotiations, which were concluded in 1995, the decision was made to deploy a much larger peacekeeping force to monitor implementation of the new accords. The price of the earlier failure, however, was a civil war that continued for three more years at great cost in human life and suffering. As Chester Crocker, the former U.S. assistant secretary of state for African affairs under Ronald Reagan, notes:

> Faced with mounting worldwide peace-keeping costs and peace accords that limited the UN's implementing role, the Security Council decided to bring peace to Angola on the cheap. UNAVEM II's mandate was confined to observing, monitoring, and facilitating the performance of the Angolan parties.[3]

But the penny-wise approach of the United Nations to peacekeeping and electoral supervision exacted a huge price: within weeks of the Angolan elections, the MPLA and UNITA were at war with each other again. Although the parties themselves bear primary responsibility for this suffering, the international community bears some responsibility too for its unwillingness to commit the requisite resources and to exert sufficient pressure to end a brutal war that had gone on for far too long.

Third-Party Efforts: The Angola-Namibia Peace Accords

Although the road was a long and tortuous one, the United States played a key role in the negotiation of a peace settlement that paved the way for

Namibian independence and led to the withdrawal of foreign troops from Angola and Namibia. As the following review of the negotiations leading to the Angola-Namibia peace accords indicates, the peace process was cultivated and ripened with American assistance. Had the United States not undertaken the kind of diplomatic "constructive engagement" it did, it is unlikely that the parties would have negotiated and concluded a peace treaty that ended interstate warfare in the region.

Efforts to seek a negotiated withdrawal of Cuban troops from Angola began haltingly in 1983. If South Africa were to withdraw its forces from Angola's border, the United States would have to deliver a Cuban withdrawal from Angola. The United States drafted a timetable for Cuban troop withdrawals, which was presented to the MPLA. But U.S. mediation efforts were hampered by the changing military balance between UNITA and the MPLA and continued forays by the South African Defense Force (SADF) into Angola. Nonetheless, in December South African foreign minister R. F. (Pik) Botha advised UN Secretary-General Javier Perez de Cuellar that South Africa would be prepared to begin trial troop withdrawals at the end of January 1984 in an effort to foster a Namibian settlement, conditional upon Angola's not exploiting the situation. Angolan president dos Santos, in a letter to the secretary-general on December 30, accepted the possibility of a truce between the two nations.

On February 16, 1984, after a several rounds of intensive negotiations, the Lusaka Accord was concluded between Angola and South Africa, with the help of U.S. mediation. Under the terms of the agreement, South Africa would withdraw its forces from Angola while SWAPO and Cuban forces would agree to stay out of a large part of Cunene Province, which bordered on Namibia. The United States also agreed to commit a few U.S. representatives to assist a joint South African–Angolan commission charged with monitoring the accord. But there were repeated delays in deploying the commission and implementing the accord, and a continuing pattern of distrust and fear threatened to derail the plan entirely.[4]

As a result of the impetus provided by the Lusaka Accord, Chester Crocker met with Pik Botha in October, transmitting new Angolan proposals on a linked Angola-Namibia settlement. Crocker viewed the proposals as an important step forward, constituting Angolan acceptance of the linkage principle, which the Angolan government had earlier rejected.[5] The proposals contained specific suggestions on the withdrawal of South African troops, the implementation of UN Security Council Resolution 435, the establishment of a cease-fire with SWAPO, the withdrawal of Cuban troops once the implementation of Resolution 435 had begun, and the guarantee of Namibian independence and Angolan territorial integrity. On November 17 Angola submitted its plan to the United States, which forwarded a copy to the United Nations.

In March 1985 the United States presented Angola and South Africa with compromise proposals based on their previous positions. But hopes for any sort of movement in negotiations were dashed when South Africa moved on April 18 to unilaterally establish an interim administration in Namibia. The United States refused to recognize any transfer of power to the new entity, realizing that this was a slap in the face to its diplomatic efforts. In May, after a South African commando team was intercepted while trying to sabotage an oil installation partially owned by the Gulf Oil Corporation, South Africa admitted it had conducted "covert military reconnaissance forays" into northern Angola. This was followed by an SADF raid against "alleged" African National Congress targets in Botswana.[6] When U.S. ambassador Herman Nickel was recalled from South Africa to protest the attack on Botswana and the sabotage attempt on the oil facility, constructive engagement seemed to be all but dead. On June 20 the Security Council adopted Resolution 567 condemning South African military aggression in Angola and demanding unconditional withdrawal of South African forces from Angolan territory. The United States voted for the resolution, sending a clear signal of disapproval to South Africa.

Little progress was made in U.S.-assisted mediation efforts until April 1987, when the United States resumed talks with Angola in Brazzaville, Congo. The talks previously had been broken off by Angola to protest the February 1986 announcement of American covert assistance to UNITA. There was a second round of talks in July between American and Angolan officials in Luanda regarding the timetable for Cuban troop withdrawals and Namibian independence, but Crocker later dismissed these talks as "basically a waste of time."[7] In September American officials again met with Angolan officials in Luanda regarding Resolution 435 and the peace plan, hoping to clarify certain ambiguities in the Cuban troop withdrawal schedule.

While the United States was trying to press Angola to be more explicit about a timetable for Cuban troop withdrawals, South African forces, which were aiding UNITA, were involved in clashes with Cuban troops on the outskirts of Cuito. On December 23 yet another UN Security Council resolution was passed condemning delays in the withdrawal of South African troops from Angola. Although South African foreign minister

Pik Botha rejected UN demands for a complete withdrawal, he acknowledged that a gradual SADF withdrawal from Angola was under way.

In January 1988 a new round of talks began in Luanda between American and Angolan officials, joined for the first time by Cuban officials.
These talks led to Angola and Cuba's jointly agreeing on February 1 to a
total withdrawal of troops from Angola as part of an overall peace package. Then in March South African defense minister General Magnus Malan
proposed a direct deal to the Soviets calling for a withdrawal of South
African forces from Angola in return for a Soviet commitment to the establishment of a neutral government in Angola. He made no mention of
Namibia. The Soviets rejected the offer. However, Malan's initiative
occurred almost simultaneously with a new round of meetings held in
Geneva between Crocker and Foreign Minister Botha. In Geneva the
United States was presented with an MPLA-approved timetable for Cuban
troop withdrawals, which the United States then presented to the South
African government. Although Botha claimed that the proposals lacked
specific details, they served as a promising start.

Formal negotiations involving direct, face-to-face meetings between
Angola, Cuba, and South Africa under U.S.-led mediation began in London
on May 2, 1988. A follow-up meeting occurred on May 13 between South
Africa and Angola in Brazzaville, without representatives from the United
States or Cuba present. As Crocker notes, "The meeting accomplished
nothing."[8] Over the next eight months, there were to be eleven more
meetings—what might be termed a negotiating marathon—before an
agreement was reached. During this period the superpowers jointly
announced their support for Namibian independence and the withdrawal
of Cuban forces from Angola; Resolution 435 was reaffirmed by Angola,
South Africa, and Cuba; South Africa pledged to withdraw its troops from
Angola; a cease-fire was concluded; Namibian elections were scheduled;
the joint commission charged with overseeing the cease-fire, and the
implementation of Resolution 435 was established; and the United Nations
approved the dispatching of a technical team to Namibia to prepare for
the arrival of the United Nations Transition Assistance Group (UNTAG).

On December 13 the Brazzaville Protocol was signed by South Africa,
Angola, and Cuba. The protocol reaffirmed the "Principles for a Peaceful
Settlement in Southwestern Africa" as initialed in New York on July 13
and ratified by the parties on July 20. A joint commission comprising the
three parties, along with the United States and the Soviet Union as
observers (with Namibia to join when it achieved independence), was

established to deal with issues arising from the Tripartite Agreement, which was to be signed December 22 and to include the signing of a Bilateral Agreement on Cuban troop withdrawals. The joint commission was not, however, to supersede either UNTAG or the UN verification authority in Angola.[9]

One week later the UN Security Council passed Resolution 626, which chartered the United Nations Angola Verification Mission (UNAVEM) for a period of thirty-one months, with the mission to enter into force upon the signature of the Tripartite and Bilateral Agreements. The mission, to comprise seventy military and twenty civilian personnel headquartered at Luanda, would provide observer teams to monitor the ports and airports that the Cubans would use for departure, and to ascertain the exact number of Cuban troops present in the country. The Cubans were to give UNAVEM seven days' notice of any troop withdrawals or rotations, and a joint commission with UNAVEM, Cuban, and Angolan representatives would monitor activities in the various zones, with UNAVEM to have free access for verification. Advance parties were scheduled for deployment around January 13, 1989, with the remainder on or about March 20. Brigadier-General Pericles Ferreira Gomez of Brazil was confirmed as UNAVEM's chief military observer on December 23.[10]

On December 22, 1988, the parties met at UN headquarters in New York to sign the Tripartite and Bilateral Agreements on Angola and Namibia.[11] The Tripartite Agreement predominantly concerned the implementation of Resolution 435, but paragraph 4 specified the inclusion of the Angola-Cuba Bilateral Agreement on a "staged and total withdrawal" of Cuban troops and arrangements concluded with the Security Council to verify their withdrawal. Paragraph 5 specified that the parties agreed to refrain from the threat or use of force and not to allow their territory to be used by other parties to wage aggression on one another. Paragraph 6 included a pledge of noninterference in the internal affairs of neighboring states. The agreement was signed by Afonso Van Dunem of Angola, Isidoro Octavio Malmierca of Cuba, and Pik Botha of South Africa.[12]

The Bilateral Agreement between Angola and Cuba was to terminate the "Cuban internationalist military contingent" in Angola. Article 1 of the agreement specified that a baseline Cuban force of 50,000 men would be redeployed in stages above the 15th and 13th parallels, a redeployment to be completed by July 1, 1991.[13] Under Article 2, the two governments retained the right to modify or alter their obligations in Article 1 should flagrant violations of the Tripartite Agreement occur. A UN verification force was further requested by Article 3, with a matching protocol to be agreed upon.[14]

At the time of the 1988 Accords, the relationship between Angola, Cuba, and South Africa was still tense militarily, but it had improved diplomatically through the negotiation process. The timetable and format for Cuban and South African troop withdrawals had been established in detail, easing the general situation over Angola, but UNITA had not been party to the agreement and vowed to continue fighting (and did so). South Africa had also received reassurances from Angola that SWAPO troops would be restricted above the 16th parallel (100 kilometers north of the Angola-Namibia border) during the presettlement process.

These agreements followed what was generally seen to be a military stalemate, especially between Angola, Cuba, and South Africa as characterized by the siege of Cuito Cuanavale and subsequent operations (see chapter 3). The addition of Cuban troops to the Angolan struggle served to counter South Africa's conventional force advantages on the ground and in the air. Neither the MPLA nor UNITA as individual entities seemed capable of launching large, strategic offensive operations without support from their respective allies. However, with the withdrawal of Cuban and South African military support, sporadic battles, largely initiated by UNITA, continued throughout the country following the successful negotiation and implementation of the Angola-Namibia accords.

Similarly, the level of trust appeared to have been moderate between the parties (South Africa, Angola, Cuba); each side needed reciprocal withdrawals to stabilize the situation but was uncertain about whether its withdrawal could be accomplished without harassment or whether withdrawal would leave it open to offensive action. The political climate improved between South Africa and Cuba as a result of U.S.-initiated talks between their military commanders. The problem, however, was that UNITA did not agree to stop attacks on Cuban forces, even though South Africa agreed to withdraw the SADF. And the MPLA offers of general amnesty to UNITA fighters seemed disingenuous because the MPLA did not extend the same offer to Savimbi nor did it offer him a role in a coalition government.

Given the relative military power of Cuba and South Africa in Angola prior to the accords, it was generally agreed that a military stalemate was in effect and that victory was not readily—if at all—available on the battlefield. The linkage of the Namibian and Angolan situations was also recognized as almost unavoidable, given the mounting costs to South

Africa of the SWAPO bush war and conventional-force incursions into Angola in support of UNITA, and to Angola and Cuba of fighting the war with UNITA and South Africa. Linkage was all the more likely given the pressures being exerted by the Reagan administration's policies on the area and by the Soviet and Cuban presence in Southern Africa. Both the general assumptions and the military situation in these cases appeared to remain constant in the latter stages of the negotiations, but earlier negotiations were characterized by frequent resumption of hostilities in the belief that a military victory was feasible. While there was continued sporadic fighting in Angola during the implementation process, Cuban troops largely stayed clear of open hostilities in the agreed zones, leaving any offensives up to the military forces of the MPLA, the People's Armed Forces for the Liberation of Angola (FAPLA). The military situation between FAPLA and UNITA's military forces, the Armed Forces for the Liberation of Angola (FALA), appears to have remained relatively balanced throughout this period; both sides continued to receive material aid from their respective sponsors so that neither would be able to achieve a clear advantage. It was also still constantly assumed that a full breakdown in the Angolan situation would threaten the Namibian process, and all efforts were made to keep the Angolan process on track and in control during the Namibian independence process. While Cuba did suspend its withdrawals for one month due to UNITA offensive action, they were quickly restored. Both the United States and South Africa also pressured UNITA to keep its attacks from halting Cuban withdrawals.

Superpower and Regional Interests

How did regional and great powers contribute to or detract from the peace process both before and after the signing of the Angola-Namibia peace accords? On the one hand, superpower pressure was clearly instrumental in moving the peace process forward. U.S. motives for pushing the Angola-Namibia agreements appeared to stem from not only Cold War systemic (or superpower rivalry) concerns about the Soviet and Cuban presence in Southern Africa, but also a desire to bring about peaceful democratic change in Southern Africa. The Soviets and Cubans appear to have been motivated by a desire to consolidate their extensive and costly commitments in Angola, to finally achieve the implementation of Resolution 435, and to see South African interference reduced in Angola and Namibia. Support from the two superpowers was also required to move negotiations directed at ending the internal civil war in Angola, because neither the African states nor Portugal had the requisite leverage over the parties. This leverage, important as it was, was not strong enough to prevent backsliding into armed confrontation once the May 1991 accords began to fall apart. This was because the civil war in Angola was intractable as a result of the high levels of distrust between UNITA and the MPLA, and a continued preference for military rather than political options.

Support from the major regional power, South Africa, was also essential for the regional peace process to move forward. For South Africa the loss of Namibia could only be balanced by Cuban withdrawal from Angola, which was seen as the greater threat—to Namibia and South Africa itself. The fact that the UN and UNTAG forces, combined with the Cuban troop withdrawals, were able to give South Africa the requisite guarantees that Namibian elections would be fair and impartial and that independence would not lead to an expanded Cuban presence along South Africa's borders was important in persuading South Africa that the peace process was more desirable than continued military operations (these having largely reached a stalemate in any case).

South Africa was also supportive of peace initiatives directed at ending the civil war in Angola. However, it was able to exercise only limited influence on negotiations and a settlement because it was not trusted by the MPLA.

For Angola the continued South African presence in Namibia and frequent South African incursions into Angola in support of UNITA could be reduced by achieving Namibian independence, which would eliminate South African and UNITA operating bases in Namibia and sever direct South African–UNITA supply lines. Thus several military and political strategic advantages could be gained in addition to the general peace and stability in the region that would arise from the proposed changes.

SWAPO and UNITA's exclusion from the Angola-Namibia negotiations of 1988, however, appears to have been a root cause of their later aggression and lack of support for some of the agreement provisions. SWAPO's desire to establish a presence inside Namibia prior to the implementation phase—for either military or political reasons—apparently played a role in the incursions of April 1, which very nearly upset the entire peace process. These incursions resulted in a decisive military defeat for SWAPO forces and negatively influenced the support SWAPO received from the frontline states and some key groups in Namibia.[15] UNITA had withdrawn from the negotiations. The group claimed that its exclusion from negotiations and the lack of an internal settlement for Angola would threaten the viability of the peace process. As we will see, even though this threat proved hollow, the challenge of bringing UNITA into direct negotiations with the MPLA to end the civil war in Angola proved formidable.

Third Parties and the Implementation of the Peace Settlement

As discussed in chapter 3, implementation of the Angola-Namibia peace accords began on April 1, 1988, coinciding with the implementation of the Bilateral Agreement on Cuban troop withdrawals and the arrival of UNTAG forces in Namibia. The implementation stage was interrupted by a SWAPO offensive launched on the eve of April 1, which caught UNTAG, still in its deployment phase, off guard and forced the United Nations to request assistance from South African troops to put down the insurgency. The situation was restored following operations by South African units and negotiations between the parties at Mount Etjo. The implementation phase followed the initial agreements by four months to allow South African, SWAPO, and other troops in the Angola-Nambia area to move to agreed-upon encampments. In Angola, implementation of the accords began prior to April 1, with the first withdrawal of Cuban troops occurring as a goodwill gesture in accordance with the proposed timetable.

There were few, if any, changes in the interpretation of the agreement during its implementation. The Cuban troop withdrawals went relatively smoothly, and all of the major powers remained committed to the peace process. The lack of a true internal process for Angola meant that there was continued fighting to gain an advantage in the stages preceding final Cuban withdrawals, but this did not alter the commitment of the key players to the settlement and implementation of the accords.

Third-Party Efforts: The Gbadolite Accords

Although the Angola-Namibia peace accords addressed several key elements of the civil war in Angola—namely, the problems of Cuban troops in Angola and South African support for UNITA—it soon became clear that the war between UNITA and the MPLA would not stop unless further steps were taken.[16]

The first attempt to negotiate an internal settlement of the conflict in Angola came with the Gbadolite Accords of 1989, a regionally inspired and negotiated peace initiative. There was no real implementation of this accord because the negotiated cease-fire and other steps agreed to in the Gbadolite Declaration broke down almost immediately; fighting resumed sporadically throughout the country almost as soon as the ink was dry. Attempts to restore the peace agreement by African and other mediators were unsuccessful, except for very brief periods, and fighting continued through 1989.

The military situation was ostensibly at a stalemate because of the reduced support to both parties with the phased withdrawals of Cuban and South African forces from Angola. However, the problem was that both UNITA and the MPLA retained sufficient military capabilities to launch independent offensives. As a consequence, in the minds of the parties the military option was not yet exhausted. Furthermore, the great mistrust between MPLA and UNITA leaders at the time the accords were negotiated was exacerbated by the breakdown of the African-sponsored mediation effort and the ongoing disagreement about what actually had been decided.

In fact, the general lack of precision of the Gbadolite Accords was a prescription for failure. Because there was no formal written accord, the substance of the agreements was left to the interpretation of the individual parties. These interpretations were highly conflictual and led to a rapid breakdown in the central cease-fire provisions. Many of the African leaders claimed that Savimbi had accepted a period of exile as demanded by dos Santos; Savimbi very quickly denied this and President Mobutu of Zaire claimed Savimbi had never agreed to exile. Savimbi may have agreed to go into exile provided that this was kept secret; however, when Kenneth Kaunda of Zambia went public with the exile story, Savimbi may have been forced to retract his acceptance. There were also reports that Mobutu, anxious for an agreement, had given the parties his own ambiguous interpretations of what the other had agreed to, leading to further complications in the implementation process.

This was the first major attempt at an internal resolution to the Angolan situation, but it clearly lacked sufficient precision and scope in its provisions to be effective. Furthermore, the wide "zone of ambiguity" in the agreement, which was immediately contested by the parties, proved counterproductive, serving to raise rather than ease tensions.

Third-Party Efforts: The Bicesse Accords

A new round of talks, this time under Portuguese mediation, began in April 1990. Delegations led by MPLA foreign minister Van Dunem and UNITA foreign minister Fernandes first met for secret talks on April 24 in Evora, Portugal. The Portuguese foreign minister emphasized that his country was not assuming a direct mediating role, which was still held by Mobutu of Zaire, but was just offering Portugal's "good offices" for preliminary discussions.[17] However, it would not remain this way for long.

On May 17 talks were held in Zaire between Savimbi and U.S. assistant secretary of state Herman Cohen. Following the talks Fernandes flew to Lisbon with new proposals for a cease-fire. The Portuguese secretary of state for foreign affairs, José Durão Barroso, then flew to Luanda to meet with President dos Santos. Barroso was seen as a key player in the negotiations, having just finished talks with Yuri Yukalov, director general for Africa in the Soviet foreign ministry. A joint Soviet and Portuguese statement stressed positive developments, but Yukalov said the Soviet Union would not stop supplying the MPLA until the United States terminated its assistance to UNITA.[18]

The announcement came the weekend of May 19 that Angola and Namibia had agreed to form a joint border commission after meetings between Angolan defense minister Pedro Maria Tonha Pedale and Namibian home affairs minister Hifikepunye Pohamba. Pohamba and Pedale issued statements that border security had been strained due to UNITA activity and that the pact would allow Namibia to react to UNITA attacks. But the two nations denied that they were forming an alliance against UNITA. Troops were not to be allowed to cross the Angola-Namibia border.[19]

In June a second round of secret direct talks in Portugal ended abruptly when Savimbi recalled the UNITA delegation over supposed misunderstandings in communications. Talks hinged on an agreement to hold elections and establish a multiparty system.[20] On June 20 the Angolan information minister issued statements warning UNITA of the consequences of breaking off talks, and said that the subject of the Portugal meetings had been discussed beforehand. The Angolan government said it was willing to proceed but that UNITA was being irresponsible and was delaying stabilization efforts.[21] The central committee of the MPLA announced in early July that the government would "evolve towards a multi-party system," paving the way for further Portuguese-mediated talks later in July.[22]

It was reported in mid-July that the United States was also resuming direct high-level talks with Angola, ostensibly regarding easing the passage of Red Cross supplies to refugees. During the second round of talks, the MPLA's attempt to obtain a broader understanding of the principles of a final political settlement had taken UNITA by surprise. UNITA had subsequently dropped its demands for a role in a transitional government, saying that it was ready to be an opposition party. The major sticking points were the MPLA's refusal to officially recognize UNITA and disagreements regarding cease-fire enforcement.[23]

The parties decided to meet again in Portugal in August. At the same time, the military campaign shifted to the north, near Beu.[24] Meeting with Portuguese prime minister Anibal Cavaco Silva in São Tomé on August 9, dos Santos said that UNITA military actions were hindering negotiations and warned that if they increased, they would be met with an "appropriate response."[25] On August 11 UNITA radio reported attacks on government forces in Malanje Province, with large quantities of equipment destroyed or captured.[26]

The Portuguese realized that they needed more leverage if the negotiations were to move forward. And as the United States and the Soviet Union had agreed to work jointly on the Angolan peace process following meetings between U.S. secretary of state James Baker and Soviet foreign minister Eduard Shevardnadze in Siberia in August 1990,[27] when peace talks resumed American and Soviet officials attended as "observers." UNITA issued several new demands at the talks, including formal recognition and a fixed date for elections before it would agree to a truce. The Angolan government said that the fighting would have to stop first. Each side continued to call the other's position irresponsible and an impediment to the peace process.[28]

President Mobutu said that Savimbi had agreed to a cease-fire and a dialogue with the government on September 15.[29] This announcement was followed by the statement of Portuguese secretary of state Barroso that the MPLA and UNITA had agreed in principle that the United States, the Soviet Union, and Portugal should monitor an eventual cease-fire. After four days of talks the parties reached a consensus on a need for international monitoring but were unsure if military personnel would be used.[30] Following the fourth round of negotiations in Portugal at the end of September, the United States and the Soviet Union indicated their willingness to police a potential cease-fire and elections.[31]

On November 20 a fifth round of talks ended in Estoril, Portugal, without agreement on a cease-fire, but Barroso reported progress, saying four-fifths of a peace settlement had been agreed to by both sides. The issue of UNITA recognition had been settled, but how this was to be achieved had not been resolved. A sixth round of talks was due to be held before January 1991. The documents were assembled by Portuguese mediators from the proposals of both sides, despite mutual accusations that each lacked the will to implement a cease-fire. The issue of integrating the two armies was not discussed, but both had agreed on steps to implement a cease-fire, including formation of a joint verification commission and confinement of troops to predetermined zones. Observers from the United States and the Soviet Union were also present at these talks.[32]

After a six-day congress the MPLA endorsed plans to end one-party rule with new laws to be enacted by January. UNITA said it would sign the cease-fire if the MPLA congress approved multiparty rule. A second congress would be held between March and June 1991 to make final decisions regarding the MPLA as a party; the MPLA had already decided to abandon Marxism for democratic socialism and to hold direct elections for president and legislature by secret ballot. The new laws would guarantee freedom of expression and a right to strike and would suspend formal links between the armed forces and the MPLA.[33]

After meeting with President George Bush in December, Savimbi announced that peace prospects had improved due to American and Soviet efforts. Savimbi said his goal was a truce in early 1991 and the holding of elections by the end of the year; the factions in Angola reputedly were close to agreement. Shortly after Savimbi's meeting with Bush, five-party discussions were held in Washington between the United States, the Soviet Union, Portugal, the MPLA, and UNITA. Savimbi had previously met with Soviet foreign minister Shevardnadze. The U.S. State Department said that the talks were very significant in light of past Soviet ties with the MPLA and thereby sent an important signal to the Angolan government. Shevardnadze himself commented that a peace plan could lead to a cutoff in arms shipments.[34] On December 29 Baker and Shevardnadze worked out detailed cease-fire proposals and a "zero-zero" option of coordinated arms supply cuts to follow the conclusion of an agreement. Their proposals called for a halt to the fighting, then simultaneous separation of the parties and the stationing of monitors, followed by a formal cease-fire. The goal was to avoid a repetition of the 1989 breakdown in the Gbadolite Accords.[35]

UNITA held its own conference on the negotiating process in Jamba from December 28 through January 2. The conference included political bureau and central committee members, members of the armed forces supreme command, UNITA foreign representatives, and various observers. The conference expressed total support for UNITA-MPLA negotiations to find a political solution to the war; recommended that the MPLA submit, for UNITA review and input, a draft law on parties for debate; supported documents issued at the end of the Washington talks of December 13 as the only valid basis for continued negotiations; recommended that the United States and the Soviet Union become directly involved in the negotiations; recommended that the UN secretary-general be invited to appoint an observer to the negotiations; and reiterated UNITA's position that a UNITA-MPLA cease-fire should be witnessed by U.S., Soviet, Portuguese, UN, and OAU officials in order to bind the parties domestically and internationally.

Within the MPLA a military and cabinet shuffle was also under way, ostensibly as a series of reconciliatory and tactical moves to place supporters in government positions prior to the peace talks with UNITA scheduled for later in January. A former FNLA prime minister, Johnny Pinnock Eduardo was appointed deputy foreign minister, and Defense Minister-General Pedro Maria Tonha was appointed chief of staff. Many saw Tonha's appointment as an MPLA effort to depoliticize the army.[36] But in early February the sixth round of peace talks stalled almost as soon as it began. The Portuguese said that the MPLA had refused to sign documents setting out previous oral positions establishing a framework for a cease-fire and multiparty elections, adding new elements to the negotiations. The MPLA refused to sign the documents unless a specific date for the cease-fire were set; UNITA responded that it would negotiate only if a date for elections were also set. Negotiations were set to resume in March.[37] But by the middle of February, heavy fighting was occurring in northern and central Angola. UNITA forces isolated and attacked the northern port of Ambriz, with both UNITA and MPLA claiming to control the city. The MPLA meanwhile blamed UNITA for trying to subvert the peace process by force, arguing that UNITA remained unprepared for peace.[38] Fighting was also spilling over into neighboring Namibia. Angolan aircraft were responsible for a bombing attack on Bagani in northern Namibia. Angola charged that the area was the site of camps set up by the South Africans to run destabilization operations, and that these continued to be run by South African and UNITA rebels. South Africa announced it was sending a senior official to the area, and the Angola-Namibia border commission announced it would hold an emergency meeting.[39]

President dos Santos met with President Sassou-Nguesso of Congo, President da Costa of São Tomé and Principe, and President Bongo of Gabon in Libreville, Gabon. Dos Santos announced that the Angolan government had proposed April 15 as a cease-fire date, and that UNITA would study the proposal on February 21. The government was also said to have begun revising the constitution and other laws related to the elections. Dos Santos declined to hold direct meetings with Savimbi, claiming that they would complicate matters and detract from the Portuguese-led mediation efforts.[40]

In early March U.S., Soviet, and Portuguese representatives meeting in Lisbon called for UNITA and the MPLA to meet in Portugal before the end of the month. UNITA was called upon to supply a realistic timetable for elections and to support the peace process in its public dialogue. Angolan foreign minister Van Dunem, however, continued to blame UNITA for attempts to sabotage the peace process.[41] Nevertheless, on April 4 talks resumed in Estoril. The MPLA delegation was headed by Lopo Do Nascimento, and the UNITA delegation by Vice President Jeremias Chitunda, with UN representative Colonel Dermont Gamley observing and Portugal continuing as mediator.[42] As the talks continued, the MPLA accused UNITA of launching a new military initiative in an attempt to strengthen its position in the negotiations.[43] But at the end of the month, in an address to an extraordinary congress in Luanda, dos Santos announced that he had agreed to a Portuguese proposal for a cease-fire beginning in May.[44] Savimbi, speaking from London, stated that agreements leading to a cease-fire and elections were to be initialed in Lisbon on April 30, with a formal signing ceremony to occur at the end of May. Savimbi said all the negotiations were completed and awaiting signature, which would be witnessed by U.S. secretary of state Baker, Soviet foreign minister Alexander Bessmertnykh, and the UN secretary-general, Perez de Cuellar. Elections were slated to occur in September or November 1992; Savimbi said a UN peacekeeping force would be sent to Angola twenty days after an agreement was reached.[45]

The Settlement Package: Strengths, Weaknesses, and Ambiguities

On May 2 the Bicesse Accords were initialed by the parties in Estoril, bringing the cease-fire into effect on May 15 at midnight, with verification to be carried out by the United Nations. The peace plan was mediated by Portugal, with observers from the United States and the Soviet Union. It consisted of four main parts: (1) the Cease-Fire Agreement; (2) the Fundamental Principles for the Establishment of Peace in Angola; (3) the Concepts for Resolving Issues Still Pending between the Government of the People's Republic of Angola and UNITA; and (4) the Protocol of Estoril.

Cease-Fire Agreement

The cease-fire was to be total and would allow for free movement throughout the country, with overall supervision by UNITA and the MPLA government acting within the framework of the Joint Political and Military Commission (CCPM). The United Nations was invited to send monitors at the request of the government. The cease-fire would include the cessation of hostile propaganda as well as armed hostilities. The parties also agreed to end their acquisition of lethal materials; the United States and the Soviet Union would support the agreement by halting their arms supplies and encouraging others to do so as well. The cease-fire further entailed the release of prisoners held by the two sides. All offensive movements and redeployments to new areas, as well as all patrols outside of designated areas, were restricted. In addition, the parties were not to plant new mines or impede mine-clearing operations.

Verification of the cease-fire was to be monitored by a Joint Cease-Fire Verification and Monitoring Commission (CMVF) composed of UNITA and MPLA members, plus observers from the United States, the Soviet Union, and Portugal, with UN representatives also invited to observe. The CMVF would report to the CCPM; UN monitors would operate under their own command structure verifying that the CMVF was fulfilling its duties. The CMVF was given a broad mandate of supervision, patrolling, investigation, and reporting. The CMVF would monitor the assembly of troops in designated areas, overseeing their demobilization and reintegration into civilian life or into the unified armed forces, and would ensure that in the interim their arms were suitably safeguarded. Notably, the CMVF was also charged with investigating allegations of possession and use of chemical weapons by the parties.

The cease-fire timetable over a sixteen-month period was as follows:

- May 1, 1991: Cease-fire initialed.
- May 15, 1991: De facto suspension of hostilities.

- May 29–31, 1991: Signature of the accords, with the CCPM and CMVF to take office, monitoring groups to move into position, and the United Nations to begin verification operations.
- June 15–30, 1991: Completion of establishment of monitoring and verification system.
- July 1–August 1, 1991: Movement of forces to assembly areas.
- August 1, 1991: Verification of the demobilization process and creation of unified armed forces.
- September–November, 1992: Elections to be held.

Fundamental Principles for the Establishment of Peace in Angola

UNITA agreed to recognize the state of Angola, its president, dos Santos, and the MPLA government until elections were held. In return UNITA was to acquire freedom of political expression and participation once the cease-fire took effect. The government would consult with all parties on changes to the Constitution. Elections would take place following an internationally supervised registration, and monitors would ensure that the elections were fair and free. Additionally, the agreement called for respect for human rights and basic freedoms, including freedom of association; the creation of a neutral national army by the time of the elections; and a cease-fire throughout the country.

Concepts for Resolving the Issues Still Pending between the Government of the People's Republic of Angola and UNITA

UNITA would acquire the right to conduct its political activities freely upon signature of the cease-fire. The parties were also to decide on a date for the holding of elections. The Angolan government agreed to hold discussions with all political parties. The cease-fire obliged all parties to desist from receiving lethal materials. Overall implementation of the cease-fire would be the responsibility of the Angolan parties operating under the CCPM, with international monitors to verify the cease-fire and work with the parties. The parties also agreed to hold internationally supervised elections; monitors would remain until the elections were certified free and fair.

Protocol of Estoril

The protocol set out six main areas of agreement between the MPLA and UNITA.

- *Elections.* Elections would be held for the president and the legislative assembly by secret ballot and under a majority system, with a second ballot in the event that no party received a majority the first time. The elections would be preceded by an official campaign period, and all adult voters would be eligible, in accordance with the rules to be decided by a multiparty consensus. Representatives from Portugal, the United States, and the Soviet Union would serve as observers, with the understanding that elections would be held by November 30, 1992.
- *Joint Political and Military Commission.* The CCPM would be established and charged with the overall supervision of the peace process. It would be assisted by three subcommissions: the CMVF, the Joint Commission for the Formation of the Angolan Armed Forces (CCFA), and the Political Commission. The CCPM would end its activities once the elected government took office.
- *Principles related to internal security between cease-fire and elections.* All basic freedoms would be granted to the citizens of Angola. The neutrality of the police would be verified by national and UN police observers. UNITA would be responsible for the protection of its members; UNITA representatives acting in this capacity would be given police status.
- *Political rights to be exercised by UNITA.* After UNITA registered as a political party under government legislation, it would be accorded the full rights of a political party with freedom to recruit members, hold rallies, run for elections, and have access to government media.
- *Administrative structures.* The existing central government administration would be extended to areas not yet under its control (that is, those areas under UNITA control).
- *Formation of the Angolan armed forces.* Politically neutral armed forces incorporating military forces of the MPLA (FAPLA) and UNITA (FALA) would be created before the elections, under the supervision of the CCPM and the CCFA, with a total strength of 50,000 personnel (40,000 army, 6,000 air force, 4,000 navy).[46]

Implementation of the Bicesse Accords began almost immediately after the accords were signed but involved a phased process. The agreement was precise as to the areas to be covered by the agreement, and in the general ordering of the peace process. A cease-fire, de facto as of May 15 and formal as of May 31, would precede the phased assembly, disarming, and demobilization of factional military forces; the phased creation of a unified national military; the enactment of electoral reform laws; and the eventual elections, to be held no later than November 1992. This satisfied, in general terms, the major positions of both sides. The MPLA had wanted an effective cease-fire before it was willing to discuss elections and the establishment of an interim government with UNITA, while UNITA had held that it would not accept a cease-fire until a precise timetable for elections had been agreed upon. The ambiguities that remained in the agreement centered on how the process would actually be implemented, monitored, and verified. Internal implementation and verification of the process was to be carried out by the CCPM with the assistance of subcommissions, namely, the CMVF, the CCFA, and the Political Commission. The CCPM was to be a five-party commission, comprising the MPLA and UNITA as well as the observer "troika" of Portugal, the United States, and the Soviet Union. The CMVF would comprise UNITA and MPLA members and external observers (including UNAVEM representatives).

All implementation and monitoring of the agreements was to be done by these groups, but all of the bodies just mentioned had to be formed, to decide upon their specific mandates and verification procedures, and to establish their own monitoring forces during the postagreement phase. These issues, unresolved at the start of the implementation process except for the general mandate and timetable, resulted in the various monitoring bodies' being constantly behind schedule and relatively ineffective in many of their activities. These bodies could not be formed prior to a cease-fire, but they would have been more effective ultimately had they been formed before the commencement of the implementation phase of the agreement, which included a cease-fire. The detailed implementation issues could therefore not be resolved before the start of the process, which was thus crucially hindered by the necessity to create the requisite mechanisms while it was under way. Supervision of the monitoring teams, in turn, was to be done by UNAVEM II. However, UNAVEM II often found itself assuming—with the parties' permission—several of the tasks the parties were to have carried out themselves. The specific electoral timetable, also left ambiguous in the main agreement, was decided later after heavy UN and other international pressure (and assistance in providing electoral specialists and monitors). These ambiguities were a flaw in the overall settlement package and laid the basis for inadequate verification of force demobilizations before the elections, as well as contributing to the resumption of factional fighting afterwards.

As we will see, various disputes erupted regarding the assembly points and demobilization procedures outlined in the agreement. In September 1991 UNITA temporarily withdrew from the CCPM in protest over disputes with the MPLA about the speed of political reform, the confinement of government troops, and the electoral timetable. Although the commission resumed its activities, the various elements of implementation continued to be points of dispute as each side alleged the other was violating the accords. Furthermore, isolated incidents of violence continued to occur, although the general cease-fire held. Electoral timetables also remained in dispute for a significant period of time, as did the requirement for the government to extend its control to UNITA-held areas as part of the pre-election process. UNITA continued to hinder the process of extending government administration, and by March 1992 Savimbi had become much more virulent in his antigovernment rhetoric, prompting concerns that violence would resume. This problem grew as Savimbi retreated to his Jamba headquarters in the face of increased dissent within his party over the alleged murders of children and several popular members of his party. Savimbi later returned to the peace table, but only after U.S. pressure and a demand for an investigation into UNITA human rights abuses.

Third Parties and the Implementation of the Peace Settlement

Implementation of the Bicesse Accords began auspiciously enough. On May 20, 1991, the UN secretary-general recommended, in response to the Bicesse Accords and requests from the Angolan government, that the existing UNAVEM mandate be expanded to allow the undertaking of the verification tasks set out in the agreement, while still carrying out its primary mandate of supervising the Cuban troop withdrawals. The new mandate would run from May 31 to the day following the elections. The headquarters of the mission would remain in Luanda, with six regional headquarters located as specified in the Bicesse proposals. Furthermore, 350 observers would be deployed both at the mission and regional headquarters (with mobile verification teams); primary emphasis would be put on the operations of 50 five-person field teams operating at the assembly points, with others at "critical points" such as ports, airfields, and border crossings. Ninety police observers would also be deployed, as would an air and medical unit. Troops for the expanded mission were to be drawn from increased contributions by the ten member states already engaged in the UNAVEM mission. The secretary-general also observed that it was extremely important to ensure that the cease-fire was properly implemented and verified now that it had been reached, adding that he felt that the terms seemed fairly sound, provided that the two parties "adhere scrupulously to their commitments."[47]

On May 25, 1991, the Cubans and Angolans announced that Cuban troop withdrawals set to end by July 1 had been completed ahead of the scheduled departure of the final contingent of troops. Three thousand troops had been withdrawn between January and April 1989 as a goodwill gesture, with the first phase of the troop withdrawal completed between April and October 1989. The second phase, due to end in March 1990, had been delayed one month due to UNITA attacks but was resumed in April. The third phase was completed by September 1990, and the fourth phase had been partially completed by mid-September. The last contingent of 1,910 troops, along with their arms and equipment, was withdrawn on May 15, 1991, thirty-six days ahead of schedule. The two parties said that they had moved up the withdrawals "with the aim of making a constructive gesture of peace and demonstrating confidence that the normalization of the internal situation is irreversible."[48] Security Council Resolution 696 (1991) approved the secretary-general's report of May 30 and also announced that the original UNAVEM mandate would be expanded and henceforth known as UNAVEM II, with the new mandate to extend for seventeen months from the date of the resolution. On May 31 the Bicesse Accords were formally signed in Lisbon.

On June 4 the secretary-general reported that he had already taken steps to deploy UNAVEM II, with parties deployed to five of six regional headquarters by June 2.[49] This was followed by the announcement that the proposed contingents for UNAVEM II would be drawn from the following countries: Algeria, Argentina, Brazil, Canada, Congo, Egypt, Guinea-Bissau, Hungary, India, Ireland, Jordan, Malaysia, Morocco, New Zealand, the Netherlands, Nigeria, Norway, Senegal, Singapore, Spain, Sweden, Yugoslavia, and Zimbabwe.[50]

The first glitch in the implementation of the accords was over the release of Angolan prisoners of war. The release was suspended on July 26 because of discrepancies in the numbers of prisoners each side said it held. The government claimed that UNITA held 1,192 POWs, but UNITA said it held only 371, later adding another 126 names.[51]

Other problems also surfaced. On September 10 UNITA withdrew its members from the peace supervision commission to protest the government's failure to put its forces in confinement areas. The government claimed that UNITA's allegations were unfounded, saying it had 22,517 troops in the confinement areas and had readied its proposals for an election timetable, as agreed. UNITA cited several conditions for rejoining the CCPM, including quicker confinement of government troops in the assembly areas, an end to the MPLA's harassment of UNITA supporters, and agreement upon an electoral timetable. The commission resumed its work ten days later.[52]

Further problems were noted by the secretary-general in his October report to the Security Council. On the implementation process, the secretary-general noted that both sides had had problems getting troops into the assembly areas due to poor transportation and logistics. The delays had hindered the establishment of some CMVF groups. Other groups that had been organized had been unable to fulfill the requisite tasks, with UNAVEM observers having to take over the monitoring (a role that had been welcomed by both sides). For example, UNAVEM had begun counting the troops in the assembly areas as of early September. Both sides had failed to fully establish the required police monitors, and there were misunderstandings about the UNAVEM police observer roles—that is, they were there to observe, not to maintain law and order, which was a function of the local police. There was also not yet consensus on what role the United Nations would play in the elections, but there was apparent consensus that it be involved in some measure. In his final observations, the secretary-general noted that the cease-fire had generally held for five months, but, as he had previously reported, incidents of violence or contravention of the cease-fire agreements had occurred on August 7 (Malanje), August 9 (Cuito Cuanavale), September 3 (Cuito Cuanavale), September 13 (Lucapa), and September 21 (Lobito). The most serious had been an incident on September 30 at Malanje, where a UNITA political officer, Colonel Pedro Macanga, had been ambushed and killed. FALA accused FAPLA of the attack even though it had occurred in a FALA-controlled area. The incident had been resolved through CMVF and UNAVEM discussions with the parties. The secretary-general also noted that poor attendance at assembly points, inadequate supervision of collected weapons, and problems with the local monitoring groups were hindering the process and threatening the schedule. The armed forces were starting to reform on schedule, however, with assistance from France, Portugal, and the United Kingdom. The secretary-general said he had attempted to impress upon the parties the need for UN technical assistance in preparing for the elections.[53]

On November 10 dos Santos announced that elections would be held in September 1992, conditional upon state administration being extended to UNITA-controlled areas by mid-November and the confinement of government and UNITA troops to assembly areas by December. Dos Santos said that the government had already drafted various enabling laws, including laws on elections, the media, and political parties. He also pledged to liberalize the economy. Dos Santos transferred some further powers to the prime minister, but he retained personal control of government powers related to security, defense, public order, and foreign affairs.[54] On December 5 Savimbi called on the United Nations to send experts to assist with the elections, proposing that they be held from September 25 through September 27, and also urging Angolans abroad to return for the elections. He warned that UNITA would not remain idle if there were unacceptable delays in the electoral process. The MPLA secretary-general, however, replied that only UNITA would be responsible for an electoral delay, charging that UNITA's strategy was to hinder the peace process and return to the war.[55]

Savimbi and dos Santos met at Futungo de Belas Palace in mid-December to discuss conciliation moves. Savimbi gave assurances that UNITA would neither take part in nor obstruct the upcoming multiparty conference. Clashes between UNITA and MPLA forces continued, however, around the port of Lobito.[56] By January 1992 it was clear that both UNITA and MPLA troops were abandoning their assembly points and returning to the field. Government control of the outlying areas was still not completed and UNITA troops were reported to have reoccupied the district capitals of Dembos, Bula-a-Tumba, and Nambuangongo in Bengo Province, northern Angola, after leaving confinement areas in Uige Province. UNITA announced that it had withdrawn its troops from confinement areas in Cabinda and redeployed them. The MPLA charged that UNITA was still importing arms with South African assistance. UNITA leveled a countercharge that the government was trafficking arms in the south. On January 10 the high command of the new armed forces took up their duties and a new body, the Monitoring Task Group (GAT), was established within the CCPM.[57]

The secretary-general reported on February 7 that Angola had requested UN technical assistance in the elections, along with the dispatch of electoral observers. A technical assistance agreement was signed, and Perez de Cuellar said he would soon report on a plan for electoral observers. At the same time, he recommended the appointment of Margaret Joan Anstee (then the director general of the UN office in Vienna) as his special representative. Her duties would be coordinating the verification of the peace accords and serving as acting chief of UNAVEM II (with the chief military observer [CMO] to retain command of the military and police observers). Both Savimbi and dos Santos had been consulted about Anstee's appointment and had approved. The secretary-general recommended that the UNAVEM II mandate be expanded to include an electoral division.[58] The European Community (EC) vice president Manuel Marin announced that the EC would make $10 million available for the electoral process. Marin also indicated that, following visits to Luanda, the EC had submitted proposals to supply ECU 200 million in reconstruction aid to help with elements such as social reintegration and the unification of the armed forces in Angola.[59]

Following official requests from the Angolan foreign minister for electoral monitoring, on March 3 the secretary-general proposed expansion of the UNAVEM II mandate to include electoral monitoring. He also reported that Anstee had visited Angola in February, been briefed by the CMO, and met with the parties, including the five-party CCPM. The secretary-general noted that most deadlines in the peace accords were behind schedule; the most worrisome aspect was that troops were not being properly contained in the assembly areas. As of February 26, 93 percent of UNITA forces were still in their areas, while the government figure had dropped to 54 percent, evidently due to the poor conditions in the government camps. The police monitors were also still not operating effectively. In terms of the electoral monitoring tasks, the secretary-general recommended a limited scale and approach as already used in Nicaragua (ONUVEN) and Haiti (ONUVEH). The monitors would verify that electoral authorities were impartial during all stages, political parties and forces could operate freely and without intimidation, all parties had adequate access to state media resources, and electoral rolls were properly constructed. They would also report on any complaints and get the authorities to act; observe all activities related to registration, campaigning, and polling; and verify the election results. The electoral division would establish offices in all eighteen provinces, send accompanying registration teams, and provide observers to be stationed at the polls during the voting period. In his final observations the secretary-general noted that there could be no more delays in the process and that the troop containment question had to be addressed. Further work was also needed in deciding voting rules, budgets, and dates in order for the process to get under way by September.[60]

By the end of March, however, diplomats in Luanda were warning that defections within UNITA were increasing and that Savimbi might resume the war in order to maintain his control over his organization. UNITA foreign minister Fernandes and General Miguel N'Zau Puna had defected in February, alleging that Savimbi had committed numerous crimes, including the execution of children and the executions of Wilson dos Santos and Tito Chingundji, the former UNITA spokesmen in Washington. Foreign observers and UN monitors were alarmed by Savimbi's increasingly antigovernment rhetoric. Meanwhile, Savimbi had retreated to his Jamba field headquarters, saying he feared assassination attempts. He had also delayed the army's integration process and had alerted his troops in the assembly areas. Other sources said Savimbi was becoming less optimistic about his chances in the upcoming elections.[61]

The Angolan parliament adopted new electoral laws defining terms for voter registration, setting time limits on the electoral campaigns, and creating the National Electoral Council (CNE) on April 3. Elections were scheduled for September 29 and 30. The parliament would be composed of 223 deputies, 90 elected in eighteen provincial constituencies and the remainder from national lists. UN technical experts were to work with the CNE and 400 monitors to verify the elections. UNITA accepted the electoral timetable but criticized the government for not having conducted adequate poll registration in UNITA-controlled areas. Further amendments to the law on political parties, reducing the required number of signatures from 3,000 to 1,500, were also ratified on April 9.[62]

As preparations for the elections moved forward, however, tensions grew. MPLA supporters killed two people after opening fire on a UNITA rally in Malanje in northern Angola on July 4.[63] By August there were increasing numbers of clashes between UNITA and MPLA forces around Malanje as the MPLA resisted UNITA attempts to establish offices in the city, which was traditionally an MPLA stronghold. UN observers were temporarily moved out of the area; on August 10 the local administration of Kalandula in Malanje Province was forced to flee after UNITA threats.[64] In spite of continued fighting and mutual recriminations, both Savimbi and dos Santos promised a national unity government, saying

that they would make room for opposition members in their governments if they won the elections.[65]

On September 29 and 30 elections were held in accordance with the
Bicesse Accords timetable. On October 17, after a review by electoral
teams under UNAVEM II supervision, Anstee formally endorsed the election
results.[66] In official results, the MPLA received a clear majority of 54 percent over UNITA's 34 percent in the legislative assembly, with the FNLA
coming in a distant third with 2 percent of the popular vote. The MPLA
would have 129 legislative seats and UNITA 70.[67] In the presidential elections, however, dos Santos received just under 50 percent of the vote
against Savimbi's 40 percent, with Alberto Neto of the Angolan Democratic Party (PDA) coming in third with 2 percent and Holden Roberto of
the FNLA finishing fourth with slightly less. By the rules of the new electoral laws, a second round of presidential elections had to be held.

UNITA, the loser, was quick to condemn the results. UNITA radio
accused Anstee of having "sold her honor and dignity for diamonds,
industrial mercury, and United States dollars" provided by the government. Almost immediately, representatives from four countries, including
South Africa, flew to Huambo to hear UNITA's story about alleged electoral fraud and also to make the case for peace and dialogue.[68] Savimbi
and UNITA continued to allege electoral fraud throughout the month of
October, and UNITA troops were withdrawn from the unified armed
forces and returned to strategically encamped FALA units near major
urban centers.[69]

The UN-brokered cease-fire, due to take effect on November 1, broke
down as fighting was renewed in several areas of the country. Fighting
was heavy in and around Luanda, as well as in the areas of Huambo,
Benguela, Lobita, and Lubango; more than 2,000 casualties were reported,
including two UN military observers who were killed. The MPLA killed
several UNITA leaders fleeing Luanda. The Portuguese meanwhile dispatched naval ships and 200 marines to help evacuate some 40,000 Portuguese nationals in Luanda. Portuguese transport aircraft were also
placed on standby alert. Plans to evacuate EC nationals were abandoned
due to the danger of movement through the capital and the closure of
the airport. A negotiated cease-fire was holding by November 3, with the
airport opened for emergency flights on November 4 and the curfew
lifted in Luanda on November 7.[70]

UN officials Marrack Goulding and Margaret Anstee met with Savimbi
in Huambo, after previously meeting with President dos Santos in an

attempt to salvage the peace process. A UNITA communiqué pledged the party's support for the UN cease-fire and mediation attempts. Shortly afterward, dos Santos tried to increase pressure on Savimbi and UNITA by announcing that a government would be formed with or without UNITA. On November 19 Anstee received a letter from Savimbi in which he continued to allege the electoral results had been rigged, but stated that he would accept them.[71]

On November 21 the National Unity Congress was convened by the MPLA government, but UNITA failed to attend. UNITA said it was seeking safety guarantees for its delegates; it would attend only if political prisoners were released and officials in Luanda could participate. UNITA denied UN claims that the delegates had been offered safe passage. Other parties that attended with the MPLA decided that a parliament would convene at the end of November and a unity government would be formed.[72]

Representatives of dos Santos and Savimbi met in Namibe in southern Angola in late November and signed a pledge to abide by the 1991 Bicesse Accords in an attempt to restore the cease-fire and peace process. The agreement followed meetings by Anstee with Savimbi in Huambo on November 24, in which she tried to persuade him to end the military campaign begun after the election. Dos Santos announced that Marcolino Marco, the secretary-general of the MPLA, would become prime minister of a transitional government to be sworn in on December 1.[73]

On December 1 President dos Santos appointed his new cabinet with five portfolios for UNITA members: minister of culture (Vitorino Hossi); deputy minister for material resources, Defense Ministry (General Demosthene Amos Chilingutila); a deputy minister at the Agriculture Ministry; a deputy minister at the Public Works and Urbanization Ministry; and a deputy minister at the Ministry of Assistance and Social Reintegration. The posts of the chief of the army general staff and deputy chief of the general staff were also slated as UNITA posts. All other major posts were reserved for MPLA members.[74]

The UNITA electoral office and electoral task force admitted that they had made mistakes during the election, saying that UNITA had resumed violence and an undemocratic posture in the belief that Savimbi would win. It also said a second round of elections would be disastrous for Savimbi and UNITA, and that UNITA had not played an effective role in the election process and in news management.[75] By the middle of January the tide seemed to be turning in the government's favor. UNITA troops were driven out of Lubango, 400 miles southeast of Luanda, and UNITA commander General Padrinhe Petartes was captured. UNITA claimed that its forces in the city were no threat and that government attacks had been unprovoked.[76] Counterclaims continued about the fighting in and around Huambo, with questions about whether the government could win or sustain a battlefield victory. Artillery fire continued in Cuito Cuanavale and Ngiva; army spokesmen said most troop movements were occurring in the provinces of Cuando Cubango and Moxico. The government instituted a state of emergency and launched attacks using new weapons supplied by Spain. Huambo was captured on January 10 after air strikes and armor attacks. UNITA claimed that it still controlled Huambo and enjoyed the support of the populace, but observers felt that that support had been eroded by UNITA excesses and by dwindling military support following Russian and Cuban troop withdrawals. The government also rejected Savimbi's calls for a cease-fire, saying that peace would require the removal of UNITA. The MPLA was also threatening to ban UNITA by law if the fighting around Huambo continued. Savimbi called for UN intervention and meetings with dos Santos, but the government said there would be no cease-fire until UNITA was out of the cities.[77]

On January 23 the administration of newly elected U.S. President Bill Clinton accused Savimbi of escalating the war and urged him to take part in a new round of UN-sponsored peace talks.[78] Shortly afterward, in the lengthy Security Council Resolution 804 (1993), the United Nations condemned persistent violations of the peace accords, particularly UNITA's rejection of the electoral results, and demanded that the two parties reach an immediate cease-fire and restore meetings in Addis Ababa. In addition to calls for the parties to show some progress in their talks, the Security Council reiterated its demand for all parties to cease sending military supplies to combatants, either directly or indirectly. The council condemned attacks on UNAVEM II personnel (a police observer had recently been killed in cross fire) but also decided to renew the UNAVEM II mandate until April 30, 1993, with the proviso that the secretary-general be able to concentrate the force as he saw fit, pending redeployment to outlying areas. The council also said it would be ready to expand the mandate further, should there be evidence of suitable conditions and progress toward peace.

By the end of January UNAVEM II was forced to evacuate teams from thirty-eight troop assembly and other key areas, as well as the regional headquarters in Huambo, due to the increased violence and the poor security situation.[79] In early February Boutros-Ghali urged the Security Council to withdraw all but 30 of UNAVEM II's 600 military observers due to the flare-up in violence. Some observers would stay in Luanda, but he recommended that all should leave by April 30 unless the cease-fire and genuine peace talks were restored. At the same time, diplomats and UN observers were attempting to organize meetings in Addis Ababa between the warring sides.[80]

Talks took place in Addis Ababa on January 10, but they produced nothing concrete. UNITA took an extreme posture, calling for a restaging of the entire electoral process. The government's position was to restore the Bicesse Accords and to continue blaming UNITA's retention of FALA and the outbreak of violence as hindrances. MPLA members claimed that UNITA had used the preelectoral cease-fire period to consolidate its forces, while UNITA demanded that the government disband the riot police force it had created following the Bicesse Accords, reputedly by transferring FAPLA members to the force.[81]

The Angolan government reinstated the draft for all males between the ages of eighteen and thirty on February 15; the draft had previously been eliminated following the Bicesse Accords.[82] Fighting in Huambo continued into late February, with both sides claiming imminent victory. UN representative Anstee appealed to both sides to conclude a cease-fire, citing severe food and water shortages. The International Committee of the Red Cross, which had to withdraw its personnel from Huambo due to the fighting, also called for peace. Portugal, the United States, and Russia issued a communiqué to UNITA on February 13 to stop fighting by February 17, but it was ignored. Anstee continued to try to broker talks, but the MPLA was talking of using force. Some observers were concerned that Savimbi was now beyond international control, even though UNAVEM said the talks in Addis Ababa revealed several areas of agreement. Savimbi was rumored to be seeking the capture of Huambo before he resumed talks in order to strengthen his bargaining situation. The MPLA government also continued to express its disappointment that the Clinton administration had not yet extended diplomatic recognition to Angola.[83]

President dos Santos, in a March 11 letter to the secretary-general, alleged that South Africa was continuing to supply UNITA through a company called Wonder Air, flying from an airport near Pretoria. Dos Santos said that food and arms had been sent in the last five months, noting evidence arising from meetings between senior SADF and Angolan foreign ministry officials on February 26. He further alleged that the company president, Gert de Klerk, had ties to Foreign Minister Botha and the former defense minister Malan. He asked the United Nations to call on South Africa to cease its shipments.[84]

On March 12 the Security Council passed Resolution 811 (1993), condemning UNITA for its persistent violations of the cease-fire and its rejection of the election results, as well as its refusal to enter into new negotiations with the government. The resolution also demanded that UNITA recognize the results and abide by the 1991 accords, and called upon both parties—especially UNITA—to show tangible proof that progress had been made toward peace by March 30. The council stated that it would hold responsible any party that refused to engage in dialogue. The council also called for a new cease-fire, condemned several acts of violence and propaganda (including the kidnapping of a UNAVEM observer near Cabinda on February 23), and encouraged the parties to resume UN-mediated talks before the end of April. But the resolution was ignored and fighting continued. By mid-April UNITA forces were said to have accomplished as much in two months of renewed fighting as they had in the previous two decades. Diplomatic sources expected Savimbi to continue with the military campaign. Savimbi had captured the oil and diamond regions of the country, giving him both access to resources to sustain the military campaign and control over almost two-thirds of Angolan territory.[85]

The Role of Ripeness

Ripeness existed at the regional level at the time of the signing of the Angola-Namibia accords. The challenge, however, was to sustain the momentum of the peace process so that it carried over into an internal settlement of the civil war in Angola. Achieving an internal settlement, nevertheless, was problematic because of the highly unstable military situation on the ground and the constantly shifting military balance between UNITA and the MPLA. To the extent that a hurting stalemate existed at the time of the Bicesse Accords, it was an unstable one. The MPLA seemed intent on achieving total victory through either military or political means, and the UNITA side had strong incentives to defect because it did not trust the way the process was being handled. In the absence of effective third-party monitoring and verification of the accords, the incentives for both sides to defect from the peace process were considerable.

The parties were still engaged in heavy fighting when the Bicesse Accords were signed. Although the parties were under heavy pressure from their respective sponsors to negotiate and conclude an agreement, they did so reluctantly. President dos Santos and the MPLA refused to recognize UNITA prior to the agreement, and UNITA continued to dispute the MPLA's political legitimacy. The accords allowed for the MPLA to continue to rule Angola with increased input from UNITA and others in the stage preceding formal elections, but the ultimate success of the peace process would, of course, depend upon the active and positive participation of all parties—a condition that remained unfulfilled.

By their participation in the negotiations, the parties gave formal recognition that a military solution to the situation was not possible, but their actions suggest that both still felt that all military options might be as yet unexplored, or that continued military action might lead to a breakthrough that would strengthen their bargaining position and yield real political dividends. This perception seemed more prevalent in the UNITA camp, but recurrent MPLA offensives to take UNITA strongholds suggested that the government also felt that military action might still lead to success.

With the withdrawal of the final Cuban forces timed to coincide with the implementation of the peace accords, the military situation in Angola did change to an important degree. So long as Cubans remained, UNITA was politically as well as militarily constrained from widespread offensives against the government. In the period 1988–91 the military situation had remained largely equal, with no clear advantages being won despite repeated MPLA and UNITA offensives in various regions (the MPLA had several times attempted to crush UNITA-held areas before the Cuban withdrawal, but UNITA, using weapons supplied by South Africa and the United States, had held on). This relative stalemate at the time of the peace agreements began to change, however, as the implementation process bogged down due to ineffective monitoring provisions. While the United Nations recognized that UNITA had sent more troops into the demobilization assembly areas than the government had, the troops were not fully disarmed and very few were actually demobilized and integrated into the unified armed forces as planned. Poor government attendance in the assembly areas was characterized by constant reports of poor troop morale, inadequate food and clothing, and a subsequent high rate of desertion from the assembly points, with troops often leaving armed. No real effort was made to deal with the problems of demilitarization and reintegration of demobilized forces into Angolan society.

As the process continued, UNITA troops began to leave the designated assembly points, retaining their weapons. UNITA also charged that
the government was turning the newly formed riot police into a politi-
cized paramilitary force, dominated by FAPLA members. UNITA troops in
the secessionist Cabinda enclave also left their assembly areas and
returned to the south, deploying to the field. Prior to the elections, therefore, UNITA troops remained under a fair degree of control from UNITA
headquarters and moved to take positions in the field near key strategic
targets and provincial capitals, with some troops resuming the fighting
against MPLA forces. These factors were constantly highlighted by the
UN monitors as a dangerous development in the phases leading up to
the elections. When the elections were finally announced, UNITA was in
a position almost immediately to launch widespread offensives against
the government forces, capturing a good deal of territory in the process.
The military situation began to shift to UNITA's side in early 1993. Political assumptions about the viability of the negotiated peace process were
changed, given continued UNITA violence in the face of what was now
a democratically elected government. This aggression continued; UNITA
remained on the offensive and achieved several significant victories
throughout 1993, even though UNITA spokesmen continued to stress
that a military solution to the Angolan situation was not possible.

High levels of mistrust characterized relations between UNITA and the
MPLA during both the negotiation and implementation phases of the
Bicesse Accords. The fact that previous cease-fires had been recklessly
broken did not augur well for developing even minimal trust. Some cooperation was evident between the two parties in formulating preelection
timetables, but this was largely due to strong and sustained international
pressure from the United Nations, Portugal, the United States, and Russia
to continue with the peace process. In much of the preelectoral period
there were sporadic instances of cooperation between the two parties,
and in August 1992, increased clashes. When the electoral results were
announced, Savimbi reneged on his agreement to accept them, claiming
that they were fraudulent. Savimbi prevented several UNITA members
from assuming their elected positions, saying they would be assassinated,
but some later defied his authority and took up their posts anyway—a
further indication of dissent within the party. After the election UNITA
resumed fighting and escalated the war despite various UN and other
international efforts to restrain it. The benefits of an electoral settlement
were therefore of limited value to Savimbi unless he won, and he was

prepared to resume the war and attempt a military victory. Despite African-sponsored talks in February 1993, in which neither side took a conciliatory position, fighting continued.

In view of all of this, why did the parties agree to a settlement that they seemed intent on breaking? The motivations of UNITA and the MPLA in accepting the accords appeared to center on recognition that the military situation was bogged down (even if it was not perceived to be totally exhausted) and that the agreement offered each party the basic conditions it had been demanding for a settlement. The major elements of their respective demands were satisfied in principle and in sufficient detail to allow a settlement, with the weak point being the implementation procedures so crucial to the success of the agreement. That so much was made of the rapid and efficient demobilization of FAPLA and FALA forces and their integration into a central military and that there was so much dissatisfaction subsequently with the process indicated the high level of mutual mistrust that still existed between the two and their mutual concern that the other would use the demobilization procedures to stall and create a military advantage as the other disarmed. MPLA moves to pass the requisite electoral enabling laws indicated on the surface a willingness to accomplish the provisions of the peace accords, but the government was widely cited by the UNAVEM II monitors for having the poorer attendance record in the assembly points.

While UNITA had a better attendance in the assembly areas, its troops did not demobilize; both MPLA and UNITA defectors repeatedly alleged that troops were being withheld from the official counts verifying the numbers of troops to be demobilized. UNITA troops in Cabinda, for example, were openly redeployed to UNITA areas in the north and not into assembly areas. As dissatisfaction with the process grew on both sides, defections increased, and UNITA openly resumed hostilities in the preelectoral phase. UNITA members later said this was due to confidence that they would win any vote, but the continued fighting served instead to alienate the party from crucial electoral support. The profusion of political parties in the preelectoral phase—many of them splinter groups of the main MPLA, UNITA, and FNLA parties—indicated that there were varying levels of support for the peace process as managed by the key leaders. UNITA suffered a number of criticisms from high-level defectors about its undemocratic stance in the preelection phase and the rumored killing of popular members (including the UNITA representative to the United States) by Savimbi.

Both parties seemed to feel initially that they could win the election and thus supported the process as a means of gaining power in the face of a relative military stalemate. As support shifted in favor of the MPLA, however, UNITA reverted to force and tried to exploit advantages that seemed to have been consciously gained by withholding troops and not surrendering weapons during the demobilization process. Despite international calls for an end to military supplies from outsiders, external support in the form of materiel continued to flow, although in reduced amounts, to both sides during the process, ostensibly so that neither side would gain a military advantage that might prompt a full-scale return to the battlefield.

Assessment and Conclusions

The reasons for the success of the Angola-Namibia peace accords and the failure of the Gbadolite and Bicesse Accords are complex and tangled. Not only were the latter settlements flawed because they lacked proper power-sharing mechanisms, but also third parties that had primary responsibility for helping to implement the agreements displayed little commitment and staying power in a difficult situation. Unlike the Angola-Namibia accords, in which third-party involvement in implementation was substantial, third-party involvement in this case was quite limited and is a principal reason the settlement failed and the civil war in Angola continued.

The peace process was marked by a shifting cast of mediators and third-party intervenors over nearly two decades. In the negotiation and implementation of all three Angolan accords the key players were the OAU, Portugal, the United States, and the Soviet Union (later Russia). The most significant role was played by the United States, which became more involved in the situation during the late 1970s, when Cuban and Soviet involvement increased in the area. There were low-key but sustained diplomatic efforts by the Carter administration as part of the Western Contact Group initiative (see chapter 3). These were followed in 1980 by a considerably more activist approach to the region's problems under Reagan's policy of constructive engagement, which sought to exert a positive influence on South Africa to reach a political accommodation with its neighbors. The United States and to a lesser degree the Soviet Union were actively involved in the negotiation process, as was the United Nations. However, the United Nations, with its antiapartheid stance, was generally viewed by South Africa as too partial to the interests of the African frontline states. Thus, effective mediation could be conducted only by the United States.

Substantial involvement in the peace process also came from the OAU and the frontline states, mostly in the form of their support for Namibian independence. Specific initiatives by President Sassou-Nguesso of Congo in supporting and helping to organize the Brazzaville meetings, which were part of the peace process leading to the Angola-Namibia peace accords, were also crucial to the success of negotiations.

In the internal Angolan conflict, the United States, the Soviet Union, Cuba, and South Africa were substantially involved. Initially they provided military support for their various client factions in the civil war; however, once these powers became committed to a political settlement, they lent their support to African-mediated talks. These talks were headed by President Mobutu of Zaire under the auspices of the OAU and the eight-nation Committee for Reconciliation in Angola headed by Zambian president Kaunda. In addition, a series of bilateral initiatives was launched by South Africa to support the process through separate talks between Savimbi and dos Santos. Following the breakdown of the 1989 peace process and the faltering of the African mediation efforts, the United States stepped in to try to reaffirm Mobutu as mediator. Key to subsequent agreements, however, was the renewed role of Portugal in arranging and facilitating peace talks with the strong backing of the United States and the Soviet Union in what came to form the "troika." These meetings varied in their composition and membership but included provisional talks between high-ranking delegations from UNITA and the MPLA, shuttle missions by Portuguese mediators between leaders who refused to meet face to face, and later direct talks between Savimbi and dos Santos that eventually led to the Estoril agreement. Importantly, the Bicesse Accords were reached with external assistance from the troika. Additionally, the troika agreed to form the core of a monitoring and verification arrangement separate from but complementary to the UN involvement already in place through the UNAVEM and later the expanded UNAVEM II mandates.

The implementation of the Bicesse Accords was conducted with the assistance of the troika nations, the United Nations, the EC, and the OAU. Following the elections, the United Nations and the troika continued to try to broker a cease-fire. South Africa and other regional states launched their own unilateral or limited, multilateral mediation efforts—largely uncoordinated—in an attempt to restore the peace process. By

January 1993 the Clinton administration was involved in urging the parties to enter into new dialogue sponsored by the United States and the United Nations. UN-mediated talks were held in several neighboring African countries as well, but they met with little success.

Outside parties were called upon to perform all of the above-mentioned roles, with the major powers involved in setting up meetings, pressuring clients for settlements, and providing support and assistance to the peace process. The United States and the Soviet Union were called upon to help monitor the implementation of the 1988 accords along with the United Nations. During the 1991 talks, the troika was an essential element within the coordinating CCPM body, assisting the entire process and attempting to keep it on track by promoting adherence to the provisions set out and formulating acceptable electoral timetables and rules. The United Nations was heavily involved in both instances, verifying Cuban withdrawal in the UNAVEM mandate, and to a degree in the UNAVEM II mandate as of May 1991, and bearing primary responsibility in the 1991 accords for verifying national implementation of the peace plan and assisting, after subsequent talks, in electoral supervision and assistance. UNAVEM troops continued to be involved in monitoring roles as of April 30, 1993, but the mandate proved difficult to carry out due to the escalating violence. The International Committee of the Red Cross (ICRC), the UN Development Programme (UNDP), the UN High Commission for Refugees (UNHCR), and various other UN and regional aid agencies were also involved in the 1991 process (as well as earlier) to monitor and verify prisoner exchanges (ICRC), assist with elections (UNDP), and address refugee questions (UNHCR). Other assistance was provided by individual states and agencies.

Third-party assistance seems to have accomplished little if anything, because of continuing conflict between the parties. African attempts at mediation and reconciliation collapsed quite quickly because of excessive ambiguity, a lack of attention to details on implementation, and the support of some African states for the MPLA government. The result was that African mediation efforts were undermined by UNITA's fears of bias (Mobutu fell out of favor after he cut UNITA supplies that were being sent through Zaire from the United States). The troika mediation was more successful, apparently because the powers had ties to the respective parties through their military and financial support. Weapons supplies were a key source of leverage for the United States and the Soviet Union, which held control over the military balance. Both countries, however, were reluctant to use this threat for fear of giving the other side an advantage that could lead to military victory and to a settlement imposed by force rather than through negotiation. While arms shipments were reduced and provisions made for their suspension, transfers continued to both parties.

UN monitoring attempts within the scope of the UN mandate proved to be almost totally ineffective. Part of the problem was that Angola was a low-priority mission, given other UN monitoring and peacekeeping commitments in 1991 and 1992. The United Nations sent only 350 unarmed military observers, 125 unarmed police observers, and 100 electoral officers (400 during the voting) to Angola. This small contingent was clearly overwhelmed by the size of its task. But the United Nations was also hindered by the fact that its role was to monitor the implementation of the peace process by local forces, not to carry out the actual implementation of the accords. In fact, UN forces did take over some crucial troop monitoring functions that the parties were unable to conduct themselves. From an operational standpoint, however, the UN mission was undermined by its all-too-narrow mandate and the parties' obvious lack of compliance with the main provisions of the accord. UNAVEM also lacked the capability and resources to take effective corrective action to violations beyond minor action and diplomatic pressure. The troika was unable to ensure full implementation through its position within the CCPM and with the parties directly.

The civil war in Angola was a tragedy. The negotiation of the Angola-Namibia accords provided a solid foundation for the May 1991 accords to build upon. But this structure was not completed because the United Nations failed to supervise the disarmament and demobilization of the MPLA and UNITA forces. In the climate of mutual mistrust and hostility that existed, it was also important to ensure that elections were free and fair and that a process of political reconciliation would follow nationwide elections. This was not achieved. Furthermore, the inability of the United Nations to take corrective action in the face of noncompliance meant that the organization could only document violations and failures. This documentation was later used to challenge UNITA's rejection of the electoral results and MPLA charges that UNITA had used the electoral results to build up its military advantages in hope of a military settlement. UN action could not have been much more efficient unless UNAVEM II had been given a substantially wider mandate to implement the peace process and put more personnel on the ground. The parties were reluctant to accept an expanded UN role until major difficulties with implementation occurred, but by then it was almost too late to expect the United Nations to do more. The narrow and poorly executed UN mandate contributed to the failure of the accords, as did the accords themselves. The winner-take-all provisions in the elections agreement gave the losers little incentive to comply with the outcome. The parties themselves are also to blame for undermining the peace process and not living up to the commitments they had agreed to earlier. In this regard, the Angolan experience demonstrates, tragically, how a lack of staying power by third parties and poor or weak implementation procedures can destroy the possibilities of achieving ripeness and undermine a peace settlement.

Epilogue

In November 1994 in Lusaka, Zambia, the Angolan government and rebel UNITA forces signed a new peace agreement. Unlike the Bicesse Accords, the new agreement contains explicit power-sharing provisions as well as an enlarged role for UN peacekeeping forces. The Lusaka Protocol guarantees UNITA four cabinet posts in the government, three provincial governorships, and scores of local offices. The demobilization plan also calls for a unified army of up to 90,000 soldiers to be created as soon as rival troops are deployed to quartering areas, rather than at the end of a long period in which they remain in separate sites as in the Bicesse Accords.

Under the interim coalition government arrangement, elections for the presidency are to be postponed for several years. There is no position for UNITA leader Jonas Savimbi in the new government, leaving him the flexibility to remain an opposition leader.

On February 8, 1995, the Security Council voted to send to Angola a 7,000-member peacekeeping force—the largest peacekeeping operation in Africa since that in Somalia in 1993.[86] This new operation is intended to profit from past mistakes. The presence of many more peacekeeping troops—with the possible addition of aerial surveillance—will also make cheating more difficult. The first peacekeepers deployed in Angola come from Brazil, India, Pakistan, Romania, Uruguay, and Zimbabwe. Under the resolution establishing the force, a limited number of observers have been dispatched to set up quartering centers for rebel soldiers. Several hundred nonmilitary observers have also been sent to Angola, along with military observers, a civilian staff, and a team of mine-clearing experts.

Part of the costs of the operation will be paid by Angola. At the time of this writing, it is still too early to assess whether the new settlement will hold and whether the peacekeeping operation will be successful. But there are grounds for optimism. A cease-fire is holding and for the first time the two sides appear to be committed to a genuine dialogue that is allowing the peace process to move forward.

In the next chapter we turn to a discussion of the peace process in El Salvador and explore the reasons the process there succeeded as well as it did. The outcome in El Salvador stands in marked contrast to that in Angola. Not only did the peace accords take root, but Salvador today is a very different country from what it was ten or even five years ago. The civil war has ended and the prospects for democratic governance have greatly improved. As the next chapter argues, third parties played a key role in bringing the peace accords to fruition and helping with their implementation. Peace in El Salvador was indeed nurtured with the assistance of third parties. The case illustrates the effective role third parties can play in helping to advance the peace process in an unstable situation in which the potential for renewed conflict and violence remains high even after a peace agreement is signed.

5 EL SALVADOR

On March 24, 1994, democratic elections were held at national and municipal levels in El Salvador. Because no party had been able to secure an absolute majority in the first round, these were followed a month later by runoff elections for the office of the presidency. Although both sets of elections were marked by some irregularities and anomalies, for the most part they were conducted in an atmosphere free of violence and intimidation. Such an outcome would have seemed inconceivable a mere two or three years before. More significant, however, was the fact that candidates of the FMLN (Farabundo Marti National Liberation Front) were participating in the elections alongside the ruling governing party, ARENA (the Nationalist Republican Alliance). These two parties had been deadlocked in a bloody and bitter armed struggle lasting more than a decade and costing the country more than 75,000 in lost lives.[1]

What brought about such a dramatic transformation in the political and social setting of El Salvador? Why was the peace process able to advance as far as it did? In addressing these two questions, we must recognize at the outset that many problems in the implementation of the original peace accords signed by the government of El Salvador and the FMLN at Chapultepec Palace in Mexico City on January 16, 1992, remain unresolved. These remaining problems relate to public security, including the deployment of the new National Civil Police and the phasing out of the old National Police; the reintegration into society, through transfers of land and other programs, of estranged groups, including former combatants; and the constitutional reforms recommended by the Commission on the Truth.[2] Notwithstanding these difficulties, most observers are prepared to acknowledge that the peace process is well advanced and that a truly remarkable transformation has occurred in Salvadoran society.

The peace process would not have advanced as far as it did without the active involvement of various third parties, foremost among them the United Nations, in both the negotiation and subsequent implementation of the Salvadoran peace accords. It was not simply their presence that mattered, however, but the critical resources they provided at key turning points that helped to deescalate the conflict, bring the parties to the negotiating table, and, once negotiations were under way, move them forward. At the same time, once a settlement was reached, third-party involvement was absolutely crucial to ensuring that the peace process stayed on track. More than once implementation was threatened by recalcitrant behavior, outright violations, and the high levels of mistrust that characterized relations between the FMLN and the government even after they had signed the peace accords. Had the United Nations not been there, relations could easily have worsened to the point at which fighting and violence would have resumed. The staying power of the United Nations in a difficult situation and its willingness, along with other actors, to commit diplomatic, technical, and financial resources helped maintain the dialogue between the parties and encouraged them to exercise moderation and restraint.

The first part of this chapter examines the history of the conflict and background of the peace talks that were mediated by the United Nations. The chapter then considers whether the conflict was indeed ripe for resolution when the talks began. Third-party roles in cultivating ripeness are then examined, along with the regional context of the peace process. The terms of the agreement and the impact of systemic factors on the peace process are also explored. In assessing the impact and influence of these various factors on the peace process, the chapter argues that third parties played a critical role in advancing the settlement and ensuring that the implementation of the peace accords was not undermined by the latent potential for violence, which could easily have led to the resumption of armed conflict and renewed civil war.

History of the Conflict

The UN-brokered settlement ended a protracted and brutal civil war during which neither the Salvadoran army (the Armed Forces of El Salvador, or FAES) nor the FMLN guerrilla resistance movement had managed to accomplish much in the way of political goals. During the war, the Salvadoran government had expanded the FAES to about 70,000 military and paramilitary personnel, an impossible feat but for the considerable assistance provided by the United States. No amount of military and economic assistance, however, could buttress the senior command's poorly conceived and unevenly implemented strategy of "sporadic infantry attacks supported by aerial bombings across extensive 'free fire' zones" for which "any military success . . . was gained at high cost to the civilian population." With less impressive resources, including outside support from Cuba, Nicaragua, and the Soviet Union, the FMLN sustained for ten years a well-organized campaign of "dispersed ambush attacks, urban terrorism and economic sabotage."[3]

Perhaps even more than the resources of the guerrilla movement, the difficult terrain of El Salvador helps account for the length of this war. El Salvador is a tiny country, slightly smaller than Massachusetts in area and in population (5.3 million people living in about 8,100 square miles). Its five largest cities are only a few miles from remote and inaccessible mountainous terrain, which provided convenient cover and the possibility of virtually undetectable bases to which retreat was quick and reliable. Maneuvering through the northern El Salvador uplands, which stretch down to the coastal lowlands, makes a slow and difficult journey, especially for heavy equipment and armed forces. Enormous portions of the country could be monitored by the military only by air.

Within this environment, then, the right-wing military "death squads" (with which the government and the conservative ARENA party were accused of colluding) and FMLN terrorist cells engaged in ceaseless retaliatory attacks on key figures associated with the opposing party. In a campaign intended to embarrass, delegitimize, and expose the vulnerability of the government, the FMLN assassinated the attorney-general, the minister of the presidency, local election officials, and other highly visible public officials. The death squads, for their part, sought to terrorize the civilian population, especially the peasantry, to frighten them away from supporting the FMLN. However, their campaign of assassinations, mass killings, disappearances, and torture of political activists, trade unionists, church leaders, local village leaders, and other suspected "sympathizers" with the guerrillas probably alienated as many government supporters as it intimidated FMLN supporters.

Thus the results for most Salvadorans were disastrous, as they watched city after city, town after town, village after village transformed into bleak battlefields. At least 75,000 civilians and combatants were killed. As the fighting dragged on, the war and the military consumed about half of the annual government budget. Per capita income and other measures of economic development rolled back to levels not seen since the 1960s. The war destroyed crops, communication and transport infrastructures, and other essential components of the agrarian and export economies, which were also besieged by a severe earthquake in 1986, a drought shortly thereafter, and persistent problems of governmental corruption and incompetence. Most foreign businesses left the country, and the combined rate of unemployment and underemployment rose to over one-half of the entire adult population. Many observers believe that without U.S. assistance the economy would have collapsed. Not surprisingly, enormous numbers of people fled their homes as refugees, searching for jobs and in fear for their lives. According to one estimate, about half of them (550,000, or more than 10 percent of the population) relocated internally, while the same number abandoned the country altogether, escaping to the United States or to neighboring countries in Central America.[4]

The Role of Ripeness

By the late 1980s the people and government of El Salvador had clearly grown weary of a civil war that was destroying the social, political, and economic fabric of their country. As Terry Karl argues, this war between the U.S.-backed Salvadoran government and the communist-backed guerrilla forces of the FMLN had reached a hurting stalemate by the mid-1980s.

> The stalemate consisted of a set of mutually reinforcing vetoes. The Reagan administration was committed to the defeat of a communist revolution on its watch, which ruled out a military victory for the FMLN. Congress, however, refused to condone either an open alliance with the violent ultraright or intervention by U.S. troops, which ruled out both the full restoration of the old Salvadoran regime and the FMLN's total defeat. Finally, the FMLN demonstrated that it was too strong to be defeated by the Salvadoran military alone or excluded from the consolidation of a new order. In sum El

Salvador faced gridlock in a set of international and domestic circumstances that prevented either an authoritarian or a revolutionary outcome.[5]

Joseph Sullivan similarly notes that by the mid-1980s neither side had the ability to wrest a military victory out of the conflict.

The Salvadoran armed forces (consisting of more than fifty-five thousand men) were the stronger of the combatants but had been unable to defeat the FMLN forces decisively . . . for its part, the six-thousand-member FMLN (organized into five guerrilla armies), after its failed November 1989 offensive, had no prospect of prevailing militarily or of inspiring a civil uprising against the Salvadoran government. The FMLN had substantial popular support in several rural areas but little support in the rest of the country.[6]

Though a necessary condition, military gridlock was not sufficient to propel the parties to the negotiation table. There were repeated efforts— all during a time of military stalemate— to start negotiations, first in 1984 and then again in 1986 and 1987. But the parties remained deadlocked over incompatible political goals and objectives. Whereas the government wanted to see a complete demobilization and disarmament of the FMLN, the FMLN wanted the government to agree to power-sharing arrangements in a transitional government that would reorganize El Salvador's political and constitutional order.

Other factors were responsible for helping to turn the tide. Foremost among these was the March 1989 presidential election in El Salvador. Alfredo Cristiani was elected to the presidency and the moderately based Christian Democratic Party was replaced by the more conservative ARENA party, which enjoyed the strong backing of the armed forces. As William LeoGrande observed at the time,

Cristiani and the moderate right may be seriously interested in reaching such a settlement. They represent a "modernized" segment of the private sector that, unlike the traditional oligarchy, believes its economic interests can be safeguarded in a democratic system. . . . If Cristiani could manage to both end the war and begin economic recovery, ARENA's political fortunes would be bright indeed. If the war goes on, ARENA risks the same fate as Duarte's Christian Democrats—continued economic crisis and eventual defeat at the polls.[7]

During the election campaign the FMLN had indicated that it would lay down its arms if the elections were postponed and it was allowed to participate. Its offer was rebuffed and its efforts to disrupt the electoral campaign were thwarted by El Salvador's armed forces, which continued to receive aid from the United States. However, in November 1989 the FMLN launched a major new offensive that demonstrated it was still a formidable force to be reckoned with. The armed forces were unable to stave off the FMLN's attacks, which were carried right into the heart of the nation's capital, San Salvador. The offensive by the FMLN thus made the military stalemate more stark. However, this was not a stalemate between two parties equally matched in military power, but a stalemate between two parties matched as in a chess game—one had the power to check the other and to deny it the possibility of achieving a total military victory.[8]

In September and again in October 1989 a series of inconclusive discussions were held in Mexico and Costa Rica between the government of El Salvador and the FMLN on the matter of formal negotiations. One key development was that the parties agreed at the Mexico meeting that a credible third party should help move the process forward and that that third party should be the United Nations.[9] A third meeting scheduled for November in Venezuela was canceled as a result of an FMLN attack on the offices of the National Trade Union Federation of Salvadoran Workers (FENESTRAS) and the subsequent all-out FMLN offensive. At the December 1989 Central American summit in San Isidro, Costa Rica, the participants called for the FMLN to begin talks with Cristiani's government to end the conflict in El Salvador. At the same time, UN Secretary-General Javier Perez de Cuellar, Canada, and the "Group of Three"—Mexico, Venezuela, and Colombia—urged the FMLN to immediately cease military hostilities in order to get negotiations under way.

By 1990 the FMLN's support in the general population was declining because of growing public weariness with the civil war. On January 31, 1990, President Cristiani met with the UN secretary-general in New York and formally asked him to use his good offices to persuade the FMLN to agree to the initiation of peace talks under the terms of the agreement, "Procedures for the Establishment of a Firm and Lasting Peace in Central America," which had been signed by the Central American presidents at the Esquipulas II summit meeting on August 7, 1987.[10] Secretary-General Perez de Cuellar agreed to do so. The groundwork for the formal onset of peace talks was thus laid.

On March 13, 1990, the FMLN declared a partial suspension of its attacks on government officials and employees with no ties to the army or paramilitary groups, and of its sabotage operations against public transport vehicles, commercial establishments, and telephone lines, as a goodwill gesture to the UN secretary-general. This action was followed a week later by an announcement by El Salvador's minister of information that the government was prepared to resume talks with guerrilla forces immediately, without preconditions. At the end of March, President Carlos Andres Pérez of Venezuela met separately with senior government officials, leaders of the FMLN, and leaders of the Democratic Convergence party at Caracas, to review the possibilities of setting the dialogue in motion.

Superpower and Regional Interests

The peace process in El Salvador was also a direct beneficiary of the end of the Cold War between the United States and the Soviet Union and their desire to end proxy wars in regions like Central America. From 1981 until 1989, U.S. policy toward El Salvador followed one track—a military one. During Ronald Reagan's presidency, the United States had provided massive aid to the Salvadoran government to defeat what the U.S. administration saw as a communist-led insurgency. The election of George Bush to the presidency, however, witnessed an important shift in U.S. policy to a less obsessive focus on Central America. The United States began to reduce its aid to the Salvadoran military. Bush threatened to cut off military aid after the brutal murder in El Salvador of six Jesuit priests and began to cooperate with efforts to find a negotiated settlement to the conflict. Although the United States was strongly supportive of UN efforts, it was not directly involved in the negotiations and did not offer mediated solutions. The negotiations were, in that sense, "autonomous." However, the United States did help to nurture President Cristiani's stature as a moderate conservative who could retain the support of the nation's strong right-wing forces while winning the trust of rebel leaders. U.S. diplomats also exerted useful influence on Cristiani during the final round of negotiations in New York by pressuring Cristiani to make the concessions necessary to clinch the deal.[11] Moreover, the United States, through its bilateral aid programs, continues to be a crucial player in the implementation of those aspects of the peace accords dealing with military, social, and economic reform.[12]

The FMLN clearly received varying levels of military support not only from the Soviet Union but also from Nicaragua under the Sandinistas and Cuba. However, as the Cold War began to wind down and Nicaragua experienced its own change in regime with the ousting of the Sandinistas in national elections, the FMLN's list of external sponsors began to shrink. At the same time, the FMLN had developed a rather formidable guerrilla fighting machine able to continue its campaign of armed struggle against the government on its own. This autonomy also meant that Soviet influence over the FMLN was quite limited, even if the Soviets were interested in bringing about a negotiated settlement to the conflict. Political relations between the Soviets and the FMLN also were not especially close. For example, when Soviet foreign minister Eduard Shevardnadze visited Managua in 1989 and indicated his desire to meet with the FMLN, the FMLN refused and sent a clear signal to the Soviets that it was not prepared to allow the Soviets to negotiate on its behalf. According to a senior FMLN member, "the Soviets were not a factor in the negotiations."[13] When the FMLN launched its November 1989 offensive, the Soviets protested in vain.

The United States was more important to the peace process in El Salvador for the reasons just mentioned. But the capacity of either superpower to exercise leverage over negotiations and the peace process itself was limited. The civil war in El Salvador was a proxy affair in only a limited sense; it had its roots in a domestic insurgency unprovoked from the outside. Thus internal conditions had to change before a settlement could be reached.

The regional security environment was also supportive of the peace process in El Salvador. Democratic governance took hold in country after country in Latin America in the 1980s, providing a base for regional support of real democratization in El Salvador. As a result of the Contadora-initiated peace process that led to the Esquipulas II peace accords, the civil war in Nicaragua had been brought to a peaceful end, and El Salvador's neighbors were keen to see an end to its civil war as well. Once negotiations were under way, the leaders of the countries of the region continued to express their strong support for a negotiated settlement. In the same manner, officials from Colombia, Mexico, Spain, and Venezuela, known as the "four friends of the secretary-general," worked with both sides in support and at the behest of the secretary-general to prevent a breakdown of talks.

Third-Party Efforts to Negotiate a Political Settlement

Although a military stalemate and a supportive regional and international environment helped to propel the parties to the negotiating table, the parties' fundamentally conflicting political objectives meant that a political settlement was not preordained. The government's main goal was to end the war, whereas the FMLN's goal was to change Salvadoran society, initially by demobilizing the armed forces. Because there was no straight or easy quid pro quo, it would take an outside mediator to help the parties reach a negotiated agreement. Although the conflict in El Salvador was in one sense ripe for resolution, ripeness was not a sufficient condition in laying the foundations for a durable settlement. Given the considerable mistrust and suspicion between the Salvadoran government and the FMLN, the potential for violence was high even after a cease-fire had been negotiated. The foundations of the peace settlement therefore had to be laid with the assistance of third parties that could help to define the terms of a negotiated settlement and ensure that, once the settlement was negotiated, the disputants adhered to its terms and lived up to their commitments.

The United Nations was chosen to be the mediator because it was able to "neutralize" outside parties and build on the new U.S. and Soviet interests in defusing regional conflicts. The secretary-general discussed the situation with interested neutral states and dealt separately with governments that had taken sides. He tried to obtain a commitment very early on from the United States, the Soviet Union, and Cuba that they would support the negotiations and avoid taking positions that would jeopardize them. He also tried to invest the negotiations with such prestige that it would be seen to be bad form to undermine them.[14] Among the warring parties in El Salvador, however, many thought it was impossible for the United Nations to be an effective interlocutor. The FMLN wanted the United Nations to be just a mediator, and initially the government did not want a mediator at all. However, once the UN secretary-general became involved, the United Nations came to be viewed as a more effective and desirable mediator than, say, the Organization of American States (OAS). Through the United Nations the two superpowers would have an indirect seat at the table, and therefore they would support the initiative.[15] As a mediator, the United Nations helped overcome key barriers in the negotiation by being a source of proposals, reframing the meaning of concessions, creating a sense of urgency, imposing deadlines, and offering side-payments, assurances, and the threat of sanctions if progress was not forthcoming. In undertaking these tasks it enjoyed the support of the "four friends," who lent their encouragement when negotiations appeared to be floundering.

A formal agreement to begin talks was signed on April 4, 1990, in Geneva, under the auspices of the secretary-general, by a government delegation headed by the minister of the presidency, Oscar Alfredo Santamaría, three ambassadors accredited to European countries, and an FMLN delegation comprising Commanders Shafik Handal, Ana Guadalupe Martínez, and Roberto Canas. The meeting was an important breakthrough insofar as (1) the parties agreed that the conflict was "political" and not ideological, (2) they reached a basic understanding on the need to promote the democratization of the country, and (3) they agreed that negotiations would have to be concluded within a reasonable period of time.[16]

The first round of full-fledged talks, held in Caracas in May, set the agenda and a tentative timetable for negotiations. It was decided that the first phase of the talks would deal with issues such as human rights, the Salvadoran armed forces, the judiciary, the electoral system, constitutional reform, socioeconomic reforms, a cease-fire, and the UN role in verification. The second phase would focus on a cease-fire. Once a cease-fire was in effect, negotiations on implementation of the political agreements would follow. The phased integration of these two aspects of the peace process, in the words of one observer, "cut the Gordian knot" and allowed the negotiations to move forward.[17]

The second round of negotiations, held in Oaxtepec, Mexico, in June, dealt with the armed forces and human rights. The government proposed to restructure the army, while the FMLN proposed that the army be purged, its troop strength reduced, and its control placed entirely in civilian hands. The FMLN also insisted that paramilitary groups, civil defense forces, and the death squads be disbanded; that a single police force be established under civilian control; and that penalties be imposed against military personnel implicated in human rights violations. The government responded positively to some of these demands. At the Oaxtepec session, the issue of human rights was also broached with the possibility of setting up a Commission on the Truth as a way to address problems of impunity.[18]

A human rights agreement was subsequently reached at the third round of negotiations in San José, Costa Rica, in July. Both sides agreed to a draft UN proposal calling for each to pledge respect for human and civic rights and to allow for the establishment of a UN human rights monitoring mission once a cease-fire went into effect. The mission would monitor the situation for one year and would have the authority to investigate specific cases of alleged human rights violations, to make recommendations, and to report to the secretary-general. The powers of the mission would be broad and would include the right to visit any place or establishment freely and without prior notice; to receive communications from any Salvadoran individual, group, or entity; and to conduct direct investigations.[19]

In mid-August a fourth round of negotiations took place at San José that dealt with the armed forces. Factional differences within the FMLN prompted its negotiators to present a new eighteen-point proposal calling for the disbanding of the Salvadoran armed forces (the FAES), to take place simultaneously with dissolution of the FMLN army. At the same time, the FMLN asked that the September 15 target date for a cease-fire be set aside.

On September 19, 1990, an electoral agreement was signed in El Salvador by all political parties, including the three left-wing parties. This agreement had been worked out by an interparty commission appointed for this purpose, which Cristiani had set up in April. Electoral rules governing March 1991 legislative and municipal elections were revised, and the number of seats in the legislative assembly was increased from sixty to eighty-four.

Negotiations resumed on October 31 following failure to meet the September 15 cease-fire target date. Unresolved issues on the negotiating table included the composition and procedures of the ad hoc commission that was to identify and discharge armed forces officers accused of human rights violations and determine whether the security forces should be completely disbanded. When talks appeared on the verge of floundering, the "four friends" offered encouragement to the parties in El Salvador and the UN representative to reach an agreement as soon as possible.

Both sides then asked that human rights verification begin without awaiting a cease-fire. In December 1990 the secretary-general informed the UN Security Council that he intended to propose the establishment of a United Nations Observer Mission in El Salvador (ONUSAL) that would verify any peace agreement that was negotiated by the parties.[20] In March 1991 a preliminary mission consisting of human rights experts and technical advisers was sent to El Salvador to help determine the extent of verification activities feasible before the cessation of armed conflict. The preliminary mission reported widespread desire in all sectors of opinion in El Salvador that UN monitoring activities should begin immediately, without waiting for a cease-fire. On May 2 both the government of El Salvador and the FMLN reiterated their request that the mission be established before a cease-fire. The secretary-general endorsed the mission's conclusions and transmitted them to the Security Council.[21] The decision to deploy a human rights observer mission before a cease-fire went into effect was unprecedented in the history of UN peacekeeping. But it was a bold move that was to have a major impact on curbing violence and instilling confidence in the peace process.

A partial agreement was signed in Mexico City on April 27, 1991. It did not deal with all aspects of the Caracas agenda; however, it provided for certain constitutional reforms on which the parties had reached agreement and that would have to be submitted to the National Assembly before its term expired on April 30.[22] The reforms subordinated the armed forces to civilian authority; removed from the armed forces its autonomous role to defend the constitutional legal order; established a National Civil Police (PNC) and a State Intelligence Agency that would be independent from the armed forces; reorganized the Supreme Court of Justice and established new procedures for the election of Supreme Court justices; created a Supreme Electoral Tribunal to replace the Central Electoral Tribunal; and established a Commission on the Truth entrusted with the task of investigating incidents of violence that had occurred since 1980 and about which the public should know the truth.[23]

On September 17, 1991, a new round of negotiations began in New York City. The secretary-general proposed the creation of a peace commission to oversee the peace process, particularly during the implementation phase. On September 25 the parties signed the New York Accords, which set conditions and guarantees to ensure the full implementation of previous agreements. Agreement was reached for the establishment of the National Commission for the Consolidation of Peace (COPAZ), which would oversee implementation of all the political agreements reached by the parties. COPAZ would include two representatives of the government, one of them from the armed forces, two from the FMLN, and one each from the other parties or coalitions represented in the National Assembly. The archbishop of San Salvador and a delegate of ONUSAL would serve as observers to the commission. COPAZ's broad authority included "the power to issue conclusions and recommendations of any kind relating to the implementation of the peace agreements and to make them public"; the power "to prepare the preliminary legislative drafts necessary for the development of agreements which have been reached, both on the subject of the armed forces and . . . other items";

and access to and the power of inspection of "any activity or site connected with the implementation of the peace agreements."[24]

In addition, the parties agreed to a process of "purification" of the armed forces that would see the removal of all officers or enlisted personnel who had committed human rights abuses; a reduction in the size of the armed forces and a redefinition of it role, limited to defending the sovereignty of the state and the integrity of its territory; and professional training that emphasized the "pre-eminence of human dignity and democratic values, respect for human rights, and the subordination of such forces to the constitutional authorities."[25] The parties also agreed to a compressed agenda for negotiations "and to secure, at one go, political agreements to: (a) coordinate an end to the armed conflict and to every act that violates the rights of the civilian population . . . [and] (b) establish the guarantees and conditions needed to reintegrate members of the FMLN into the civilian, institutional, and political life of the country in absolute legality." The subjects for negotiation would include doctrine, training, and purification of the armed forces; replacement of all public security forces by the single PNC; disbanding of the military-controlled National Guard, Treasury Police, and intelligence services; judicial and electoral reforms; ratification of the constitutional reforms agreed to in Mexico on April 27, 1991; economic and social questions; and conditions for the cessation of armed confrontation.[26]

During these talks Washington held behind-the-scenes meetings with the FMLN and indicated that the United States was prepared to provide training for a new civilian police force to assist with national reconstruction. The FMLN informed Washington that FMLN combatants had to be included in a new civilian police force.

On December 4, 1991, as negotiations dragged on and Perez de Cuellar's tenure as secretary-general was about to end, he again proposed that talks be moved to New York, which was done on December 16. To the surprise of the other parties, the FMLN suddenly introduced into the negotiations new demands on land reform. The government responded that it wanted an agreement on a cease-fire before addressing broader social and political issues.

The FMLN agreed to cease-fire talks under the chairmanship of UN under secretary-general Marrack Goulding on December 24. This encouraging move motivated Cristiani to travel to New York for negotiations, although he did not meet directly with the FMLN. During the course of the negotiations, the United Nations played a key role in offering compromise formulas on key issues. One UN formula provided that the number of former FMLN members in the new PNC not exceed the number of former National Police officers drawn into the new organization; it was accepted by both sides. The United Nations also offered a proposal on socioeconomic issues, which would make land available to former combatants and to former landholders in conflict zones (who had long since been forced to flee the fighting). Cristiani informed the secretary-general that he intended to reduce the size of El Salvador's armed forces by 50 percent within two years and to immediately dismantle the army's notorious Immediate Reaction Infantry Battalions as the FMLN began to demobilize. The parties also reached an agreement on a cease-fire. The final agreement was initialed at midnight December 31, 1991, with a view to the formal signing of the peace accord on January 16, 1992.

The cease-fire agreement provided that the process of ending armed confrontation would begin on February 1, 1992, and would be completed by October 31, 1992.[27] Any alleged violation of the cease-fire would be investigated by ONUSAL. Separation of forces would be carried out in two stages, the first ending on February 6, 1992, and the second on March 2, 1992, with the FAES redeploying progressively to the positions it would maintain in normal peacetime deployment, and the FMLN forces concentrating progressively in agreed "designated locations" in the areas of conflict. During the two weeks of informal cease-fire between January 16 and 31, the chief military observer of ONUSAL, in consultation with the two sides, would define the locations for redeployment of FMLN forces, work out the movement of forces of both sides to their designated locations, and supervise these redeployments. After signing the agreement, both sides would convey to ONUSAL detailed information about the strength and armament of their forces.

As part of the overall agreement, two of El Salvador's existing security bodies would be disbanded early in the process and the third—the National Police—would be phased out over a longer period as the PNC took shape. The UN role would entail more than mere verification—it would include direct involvement in maintaining the public order, in particular by monitoring the operations and conduct of the existing National Police until the new PNC was deployed throughout the country.

The final peace accords, which were signed in Mexico City on January 16, 1992, represented the culmination of the negotiations on all substantive items of the Caracas agenda and of the New York Accords of September 25, 1991. The agreements comprised five chapters dealing with (1) the armed forces, (2) the PNC, (3) the judicial system, (4) the electoral system, (5) economic and social questions, (6) political participation by the FMLN, and (7) cessation of the armed conflict. It also contained numerous annexes and articles and came to some ninety-five pages in total. The key provisions in the accord, building on the previous settlements, entailed the following:

- redefining the mission of the armed services to defend the sovereignty of the country and its territory;
- bringing the armed forces under strict civilian control;
- establishing a new basis for training members of the armed forces;
- purifying the armed forces "with a view to the supreme objective of national reconciliation";
- reducing and reorganizing the armed forces;
- creating a new national civilian police force and State Intelligence Agency;
- establishing a new National Public Security Academy;
- reforming the judicial system to include a new judicial training school and Office of National Counsel for the Defense of Human Rights;
- establishing new economic and social instruments covering land reform, loans to the agricultural sector, measures to alleviate the social cost of structural adjustment programs, a forum for economic and social consultation, and the National Reconstruction Plan;
- transferring agrarian lands, with preference given to former combatants of both parties and landholders in conflict zones;
- adopting measures to guarantee former FMLN combatants full exercise of their civil and political rights and their reintegration into society; and
- ceasing armed conflict by means of a cease-fire, separation of forces, end of the military structure of the FMLN, and UN verification of these activities.

In sum, the most difficult issue in the negotiations between the government and the FMLN concerned the FMLN's reintegration into Salvadoran society. The FMLN wanted to see the armed forces completely abolished; this the government strongly resisted. Negotiations centered on limiting the role of the armed forces to external defense and eliminating their role in the internal affairs of the country. In Mexico City in April 1991 the government agreed to make the necessary constitutional changes to

exclude the armed forces from internal security management and to place
the military under civilian control. Although the FMLN was not satisfied
with this arrangement, it agreed in New York in September 1991 to accept
a more restrictive set of constitutional provisions on the military and the
establishment of a new civilian police force to deal with internal security
affairs. In addition, under the New York Accords signed on December 31,
1992, the armed forces were to be reduced in size and purged of officers
who had committed egregious human rights violations. New programs
would be set up for the military to train its personnel to have a greater
respect for human rights and democracy. COPAZ was also established to
monitor and verify compliance of the parties to the peace accords and
ensure that FMLN members could enlist in the newly created civilian
police force. Many of these specific proposals and recommendations,
including the creation of COPAZ, came from the UN mediator.

The Settlement Package: Strengths, Weaknesses, and Ambiguities

One explanation of the general success of the Salvadoran peace process
is that the terms of the final settlement were essentially sound. The settlement included provisions not only for free and fair elections and the
reinvigoration of El Salvador's democratic institutions, but also for far-
reaching reforms of the judiciary and security institutions. Several key
elements of the accords aimed at bringing about a fundamental change
in civil-military relations by placing the Salvadoran military under firm
civilian control. As Condoleeza Rice notes, one of the biggest problems
in making a transition to democracy is placing civilian control of the
army on the agenda early in the peace negotiations. According to Rice,
institutions of violence can be a source of stability in transitions provided
that they are brought under democratic control. To achieve this goal,
four conditions must be met: (1) institutions of violence must be subordinate to civilian control; (2) there must be institutional mechanisms that
preserve this subordination; (3) a clear, functional division of responsibilities has to be maintained between the army and the police—the
police exist for internal control, the army for external control; and (4) new
norms have to be established through training and professionalization so
that the military stays out of the political process.[28]

Generally speaking, the peace accords intended to bring about a far-
reaching reform of civil-military relations in the direction noted by Rice.
However, the accords did contain a number of deficiencies, some of

which contributed to the difficulties that surfaced during the implementation of the settlement. Knut Walter and Philip J. Williams argue that the accords failed to address adequately several important areas in which the military retained political influence.[29] First, the accords did not mention the military's administration of key state institutions. These include such entities as the National Administration of Telecommunications (ANTEL), the National Administration of Water and Sewers (ANDA), the Executive Commission for Ports and Harbors (CEPA), the General Directorate of Land Transport, the General Directorate of Statistics and Census, Customs, Civil Aeronautics, and the Postal Service.[30] Second, Walter and Williams contend that the accords did not do enough to dismantle the military presence in the countryside. They failed to abolish the territorial service (a paramilitary body) in the countryside in spite of calling for the creation of a new system of military reserves, and they continued to allow the military to establish recruiting offices around the country.[31] Whether these weaknesses are the Achilles' heel of the accords remains to be seen and can only be a matter of conjecture. The more serious problem has been the government's failure to implement properly those sections of the accords calling for the creation of a national civilian police force free of military control.

The COPAZ national mechanism to verify the peace accords also suffered from major weaknesses. COPAZ was an unwieldy body because of the size of its membership. And, as a report by David Holiday and William Stanley notes, COPAZ members also "lack[ed] technical expertise to deal effectively with some of the issues they [addressed]. The end result [was] that COPAZ's role [was] only to provide inputs into the process of implementing the accords, rather than to verify final outputs through actual field investigations." COPAZ was "incapable of enforcing compliance with the accords when major delays or violations . . . occurred. . . . COPAZ might have functioned better if ONUSAL had been allowed to mediate during COPAZ meetings the same way it has in direct bilateral discussions between the government and the FMLN, rather than serving only as an observer to COPAZ."[32] COPAZ, however, was meant to be a national mechanism to strengthen the Salvadoran government; UN mediation would have defeated this purpose.

On the political-juridical side, the accords were weak in specifying reforms to the judicial system. The procedures for selecting new judges, justices, and prosecutors were not as clearly spelled out as they might have been. As noted by Holiday and Stanley,

The reforms leave untouched the extremely hierarchical structure of the courts that enables the Supreme Court to control the jurisdiction, legal decisions and administration of all lower courts. In the past, this concentrated power has been used to block investigations that might harm the interests of leading political parties or the military. The attorney general's office suffers from a similar vertical structure, which leads to political control over prosecutor's investigations. During the prolonged legislative battle over how to structure the National Council, ARENA pushed through legislation extending the terms of incumbent judges, thus perpetuating ARENA control of the judiciary in a period when critical human rights and land questions might come before the courts.[33]

But again, these were the key dilemmas of reform. Had the reforms gone further they would have been knocked down by the Salvadoran Supreme Court. Luckily, as we will see, the Commission on the Truth picked up where the negotiators had left off. In the short term, however, the accords' lack of specificity about ONUSAL's oversight of the judiciary and police clearly hindered ONUSAL's effectiveness in dealing with these bodies during the implementation phase of these agreements,[34] although the problem was not fatal to the peace process.

Perhaps the central weakness of the Chapultepec Accords is that they provided for a land-for-arms exchange to former combatants. This deal was based on a hastily arranged compromise reached during the final stages of the negotiation, with little apparent regard for the broader social and economic implications of such an arrangement.[35] By September 1992, however, land transfer had become the most contentious issue in the implementation of the peace accords; it threatened to scuttle the whole peace process. In a survey conducted in October 1992, people were asked which issue was the most difficult to implement; 37 percent said the transfer of land, 20 percent said the demobilization of the FMLN, and 13 percent said the purification of the armed forces.[36] The UN proposal of October 13 was intended to break the impasse; the lack of an agreement on land transfers was jeopardizing the demobilization of the FMLN, which in turn was preventing reform of the armed forces. "The proposal was designed to ensure both the early and rapid transfer of substantial quantities of land to ex-combatants of the FMLN and the Armed Forces and the formalization of tenure, or, if necessary, the relocation, of landholders in the zones of conflict."[37] Although the proposal kept the peace process on track in the short run and allowed the demobilization of the FMLN to go forward, it required large infusions of domestic and foreign financing that have not been forthcoming.[38] Failure to resolve this particular issue could have far-reaching implications for the long-term success of the peace process and El Salvador's movement toward democratization.

Plainly, some of the difficulties experienced during the initial implementation of the peace agreements in El Salvador lie with the accords themselves. The peace settlement that was signed by the government and the FMLN at Chapultepec Palace was not perfect. That said, the agreements were quite sound on the key issues of military reform, demobilization of the FMLN, and the establishment of a national police force that would be independent from the armed forces. The difficulties and delays in implementation that occurred were rooted in a politically unrealistic timetable for implementation. Time and time again, the timetable had to be renegotiated between the parties with the help of UN officials. However, in spite of these failings, the accords themselves did not represent a fundamentally flawed settlement package. In fact, the immediate success in bringing about an end to armed violence and confrontation in El Salvador is partly attributable to a settlement package that was essentially sound. But other factors also contributed to the overall success of the peace process.

Third Parties and the Implementation of the Peace Settlement

The need for third-party assistance did not end once the settlement was reached. The implementation process required the continuing contributions of the United Nations and others. First, the deployment of human rights workers before the final agreement had been negotiated helped to create a local climate of confidence in the United Nations, the accords, and the seriousness of the signatories. Second, the cease-fire that went into effect subsequent to the signing of the accords also lent much-needed stability to the peace process. Participants have called "the cease-fire the most successful part of the whole peace process." There was not one violation, and ONUSAL's verification of the cease-fire and subsequent demobilization of forces by both sides contributed to this result. However, the linking of the cease-fire with other political factors created its own problems, and demobilization was slow because of this linkage. Nonetheless, the "cease-fire brought about a level of maturity; parties saw that without armed conflict they could advance in different areas. The cease-fire thus helped to contain the conflict."[39]

Although the cease-fire was a crucial confidence-building measure, major problems emerged during the implementation of the peace accords that threatened to upset the peace process. These problems included (1) a growing crime wave during the demobilization process that led the government to deploy its forces in certain regions of the country, contrary to the peace accords, ostensibly to secure public safety; (2) the entry of former members of the armed forces into the new PNC; (3) difficulties in implementing land transfer provisions in the agreement; (4) continuing shortages of the funding necessary to implement key provisions; and (5) the difficulty of conducting free and fair elections. ONUSAL played a critical role in addressing these and other problems, all the while ensuring that they did not become serious enough to derail the peace process. Each of these aspects of the peace process and of ONUSAL's involvement is discussed below.

ONUSAL was launched at the end of July 1991, headed by Chief of Mission Iqbal Riza, special representative of the secretary-general. (Riza served until March 1993, after which he was succeeded by Augusto Ramirez-Campo.) ONUSAL's military personnel functioned under the command of the chief military observer, Brigadier-General Victor Suanzes Pardo (Spain), who had previously been the chief of the United Nations Observer Group for Central America (ONUCA).

By September 15 a total of 101 international civil servants from twenty-seven countries had joined the mission, which comprised 5 senior management staff members; 42 human rights observers and advisers, legal advisers, educators, and political affairs officers; 15 military advisers; 16 police advisers; and 23 support and communications staff members. Regional offices were set up in San Salvador (central region), San Vicente (paracentral region), San Miguel (eastern region), and Santa Ana (western region), with suboffices in Chalatenango and Usulután. The mission embarked immediately on an extensive program of visits both to official institutions and to nongovernmental organizations working in the field of human rights, as well as to marginal populations, communities of returnees and other vulnerable sectors of Salvadoran society, and eventually to populations living in conflict zones.[40] During the first phase of its operations, ONUSAL also made contacts in the field with the FMLN and established its own internal structure and channels of communication.

In the first report by ONUSAL's human rights division on the situation in El Salvador, the division's director, Phillipe Texter, noted several difficulties experienced by the mission. First, the absence of a cease-fire was complicating the mission's verification task in parts of the country. Second, the San José agreement was only a partial one; no other agreements had been reached on issues that affected the human rights situation. In addition, there were structural problems related to the judiciary and the armed forces; the parties had originally intended human rights monitoring to take place only after a cease-fire and in the context of institutional reforms designed to ensure respect for human rights. Moreover, extremist groups were launching efforts to intimidate mission members. Shortly after the mission was set up, groups such as the self-styled Salvadoran Anti-Communist Front and the Crusade for Peace and Work—offshoots of groups that had been active in the 1980s and that surfaced during the April 1991 negotiations on constitutional reform—began to arouse hostility towards ONUSAL and to question its constitutionality. In addition, the mission was suffering from the problem of raised expectations. "Vast numbers of Salvadorans, right across the political spectrum, believe the Mission will be able to prevent, or at least punish, human rights violations in spite of the fact that its powers are limited to verification; the mission had neither the power to prevent violations nor the power to punish violators."[41] Nonetheless, the mission lent an element of stability to the peace talks by opening up an important channel of communication between the combatants and in areas of the country that hitherto had been wracked by violence and war.

On October 1, 1991, ONUSAL entered its second phase of operations, in which it began to investigate cases and situations involving human rights violations and to follow up on these cases with relevant bodies in the government. ONUSAL also maintained an ongoing dialogue with the FMLN concerning its violations of the San José agreement. During this phase ONUSAL significantly expanded its contacts with the parties by holding regular working meetings with an interagency group in the Salvadoran government coordinated by the executive secretary of the governmental human rights commission. The group consisted of representatives of the Supreme Court of Justice, the armed forces general staff, the Office of the Attorney-General, and the Ministry of Foreign Affairs. In addition, ONUSAL expanded its contacts with local and regional political, judicial, and military authorities, making frequent visits to the mayors' offices, departmental governments, military and police units, law courts, and other public entities. It also held periodic meetings at Mexico City or Managua with the FMLN political and diplomatic commission and maintained ongoing contact with FMLN leaders inside the country.

The mission also began its educational activities and an information campaign designed to publicize its function as widely as possible. The team of ONUSAL educators worked in consultation with human rights organizations to design a program to engender respect for human rights that was directed mainly at the armed forces, the FMLN, and social organizations. From the time it was set up, the mission received over one thousand complaints of alleged human rights violations and was able to confirm that a number of summary executions by unidentified individuals or paramilitary groups had taken place. It noted that no special investigation had been made by security forces or the judiciary and that this heightened the feeling of insecurity in El Salvador. The mission recommended that the government of El Salvador, the Office of the Attorney-General, and the judiciary establish mechanisms to ensure that attacks on the life of persons be systematically investigated in order to find and punish the perpetrators. ONUSAL also recommended that vigorous action be taken to end the practice of intimidation and threats by clandestine groups and that regulations be adopted to prohibit those groups broadcasting (on radio or television) threatening messages.[42]

Although the political situation remained tense, November brought some encouraging developments. COPAZ, having just been set up, was still in an "informal phase in which delegates from all the political parties represented in the National Assembly came together to discuss and establish guidelines for the preliminary drafting of secondary legislation enabling the political agreements adopted at the negotiating table to be incorporated into El Salvador's legal system."[43] However, some parties had strong reservations about the direction and rate of negotiations, as well as apprehension about the political, legal, and social insecurity that might arise as a result of the end of the conflict: while the National Assembly was ratifying the constitutional reforms emanating from the negotiations, the fighting had intensified. However, tensions eased when the FMLN announced a unilateral cessation of offensive operations in mid-November 1991.

On January 14, 1992, just before the formal signing of the El Salvador peace agreement on January 16, the UN Security Council enlarged ONUSAL's mandate to include verification and monitoring of the agreement. ONUSAL would thus verify all aspects of the cease-fire and separation of forces, in addition to verifying the implementation of the 1990 human rights agreement. ONUSAL would also be responsible for monitoring the maintenance of public order while the new national civil police force was set up.

Once the agreement was signed in Mexico City, the United Nations moved swiftly to deploy ONUSAL's military contingent and to implement its military and public security monitoring and verification activities.[44] During the informal cease-fire (January 16–31, 1992), the military division received its first personnel, who came both from ONUCA and from a number of contributing countries directly.[45] Military observers were deployed at all the verification points on January 31 and one day later, as agreed, began their verification activities. Under UN supervision, the first stage of the separation of forces proceeded without incident. As of February 25, the military division had 368 of 373 authorized observers deployed. At the beginning of February the police division was established under the command of Colonel Pierre Gastelu (France), within the framework of the agreement on the establishment of the PNC. Its job was to facilitate the transition in public security until the new police corps became fully operational, which was scheduled for the middle of 1994. The division had deployed 147 of 631 authorized police observers, with 120 more observers slated to arrive the first week of March. The military division of ONUSAL, as stipulated in the agreements, was responsible for monitoring FAES and FMLN troops at the locations stipulated by the peace agreements. This task included verifying the inventories of weapons and personnel furnished by the two parties, authorizing and accompanying the movements of both forces, and receiving and investigating complaints of violations. ONUSAL observers were deployed among four regional military offices and fifteen verification centers.

Difficulties soon arose with regard to the definition of the fifteen locations designated for the concentration of FMLN combatants and FAES troops. Where it was impossible to agree upon a definition, both sides accepted the delimitation determined by the chief military observer. The majority of troops from the armed forces were concentrated at the designated locations. However, forces remained at about sixteen additional locations because the government claimed that they were necessary to protect installations of national importance, and at twenty others on the grounds of a lack of space. ONUSAL pressed the government troops to withdraw, which they gradually did. By May 25, they remained at only one disputed location.

Difficulties also arose over the two public security bodies—the Treasury Police and the National Guard—which, under the peace agreement, were supposed to be abolished by March 1, 1992, with their members incorporated into the army. The government's failure to carry out the disbanding of these two bodies by that date contributed to the failure to complete the concentration of the two sides' troops as agreed. For several weeks after their incorporation into the army, the former members of these two bodies remained in their original barracks, even though these were not included in the sixty-two locations designated for the armed forces. The FMLN denounced this as a violation of the peace agreement and refused to complete concentration of its own forces until the problem was resolved. Although the majority of former personnel of the Treasury Police and National Guard were relocated, some 3,500 continued to remain in their barracks in San Salvador in violation of the agreement.

The FMLN had concentrated its forces at the fifty locations designated for the first stage, but the second stage of concentration scheduled for March 2 was not completed because of a lack of infrastructure at the agreed-upon locations and the government's noted failure to comply with the agreement. Further deadlines were established only to be broken. Concern also grew that the inventory of arms presented to ONUSAL by the FMLN was inaccurate and that the FMLN was secretly retaining caches of arms and ammunition. These fears proved to be justified.

On the positive side, the signing of the peace agreement and the cessation of military hostilities had a major, beneficial impact on the activities of ONUSAL's human rights division.[46] Difficulties linked to armed conflict generally disappeared and freedom of movement was restored. The number of complaints about human rights abuses also declined. However, summary executions and violent deaths were still occurring in certain regions of the country, and no action was being taken either to end these murders or to root out their perpetrators. There were recurring threats against nongovernmental organizations, trade unions, churches, and political leaders. The mission made a number of specific recommendations to government authorities concerning these incidents and the state's duty and responsibility to prevent and investigate them, but these recommendations were not heeded in the manner prescribed in the San José agreement. However disturbing, these violations were not serious enough to throw the peace process off track.

As 1992 came to a close, implementation of the peace accords advanced steadily. The cease-fire held without incident. The FMLN engaged in political activities in anticipation of its full legalization as a political party, suggesting to the United Nations that the government and

FMLN both intended to consolidate peace. "The peace process in El Salvador shows every sign of being irreversible," reported ONUSAL.[47] However, major compliance problems remained. The most serious threat was the failure of both parties to comply with the October 31 date for ending the conflict. Related to this problem was the government's failure to comply with the schedule of the ad hoc commission on the purification of the armed forces as called for by the Chapultepec Accords. The government also had reservations about the inventory of weapons submitted by the FMLN and the FMLN's compliance with the demobilization schedule.

These delays and each party's reactions to them were clearly leading the peace process into a cul-de-sac as each party held the other responsible for the delays while insisting on its own interpretation of key clauses in the accords. To break the impasse, the secretary-general sent Marrack Goulding and Alvaro de Soto, his senior political adviser, to San Salvador on October 30 to mediate a solution. De Soto conducted extensive discussions separately with the government and with the FMLN. The result was an adjustment in the Chapultepec timetable and an exchange of letters stipulating that compliance with specific undertakings by one side would be contingent upon compliance with specific undertakings by the other side. Under the new schedule, the dismantling of the military structure of the FMLN would begin on October 31 and be completed by December 15, 1992.[48]

There were also delays in the constitution of a new State Intelligence Agency and of the National Public Security Academy that would train the PNC. The latter began its activities four months behind schedule on September 1, 1992. It had funding problems, despite financial support from the governments of Norway, Spain, and the United States. Two groups totaling 622 students joined the academy on September 1. Although the accords required that applicants from the National Police be evaluated by the director-general of the PNC before they took admission examinations, this requirement was not met and evaluations continued to remain behind schedule.

Contrary to the peace accords the government had been transferring personnel from the Treasury Police and National Guard into the National Police. Following ONUSAL's intervention, the government halted the transfer. However, units from the demobilized Immediate Reaction Infantry Battalions, including officers, were also integrated into the National Police, in spite of ONUSAL's position that such transfers were contrary to the spirit of the agreements. The government defended the practice on the grounds that it needed the personnel to deal with an increase in crime in rural areas where the former National Guard and Treasury Police had functioned.[49]

On December 15, 1992, the armed conflict between the government of El Salvador and the FMLN formally came to an end in accordance with the adjusted UN timetable for implementing the peace accords that the two sides had accepted. This event was preceded by legalization of the FMLN as a political party. [50]

A continuing difficulty was the phasing out of the National Police force, which was meant to be phased out gradually as the PNC was deployed, but which was in fact increasing in size as a result not only of transfers but also of the monthly graduation of some sixty to one hundred police officers from the National Police training school, which continued to operate. While the agreement did not expressly establish that the reduction of the National Police should be synchronized with the deployment of the PNC, it stated clearly that new police force should replace the old one. ONUSAL requested that the government provide its plan for the reduction of the National Police and that it inform ONUSAL of its plans for closing the National Police training school.[51]

The accords allowed a small number of former FMLN and National Police members to be admitted to the new civilian police, but purposely excluded members of the armed forces. However, the transfer of several hundred former members of the army and Treasury Police to the National Police in early 1992 raised concerns that these individuals might find their way into the new PNC. ONUSAL tried, albeit unsuccessfully, to secure personnel records to identify these individuals. More serious was the discovery that eleven superior-level candidates who were presented by the government as former National Police force members in the academy had actually come from the army, Treasury Police, and National Guard, in direct violation of the peace accords. Following extensive discussions in a subcommission of COPAZ and with the parties to the accords, the officers were permitted to remain in the training program because they were relatively young and had spent no more than three years in military service. ONUSAL secured a pledge from the government not to enroll any more former military personnel in the training academy and civilian police force.[52]

The land-tenure problem was also a major source of disagreement and conflict. The peace agreements did not sanction an overall land redistribution program of the sort that many postrevolutionary regimes implement after a civil war. Rather, the peace accords specified a land transfer program as "the main venue . . . through which ex-combatants and supporters of the FMLN would be reintegrated into the productive life of the economy."[53] Land-tenure questions were especially sensitive issues, given the importance of agriculture to the economy and the fact that arable land was in short supply and unevenly distributed. Ownership of land also made available other potential benefits, like housing credits and assistance for agricultural production. Additionally, because the peace accords themselves reflected only broad principles, the actual details of land transfer had to be worked out during implementation with ONUSAL's help.

The peace accords stipulated that, pending agreement on various issues, the current land-tenure situation would be respected in former conflict zones and current landholding occupants would not be evicted. They also assigned COPAZ the task of verifying implementation of these provisions through a special commission. The special commission, which had the same composition as COPAZ, took up the problem of land tenure one week later than called for in the implementation timetable. One of the difficulties it faced derived from the peace agreement's failure to define the conflict zones. February and March 1992 saw tensions rise in the countryside after various peasant groups seized properties, only to be evicted by security forces. These actions were also of concern to FMLN combatants who were waiting to move into designated concentration areas. COPAZ's appeal to peasants and landowners to allow the dispute settlement provisions of the peace agreements (those involving evictions and property rights) to go into effect was only partially heeded. As conditions failed to improve, the secretary-general sent Under Secretary-General for Peacekeeping Marrack Goulding to El Salvador to meet with the parties, including Cristiani and the general command of the FMLN. On March 13, 1992, it was agreed that land seizures and evictions would be suspended to facilitate the processing of cases submitted to the special commission of COPAZ. In his report the secretary-general noted that "ONUSAL is operating in an atmosphere of deep distrust, which may be an inevitable consequence of a long and bitter conflict. Its insistence on maintaining its impartiality is sometimes misperceived by each side as being partiality towards the other." Threats against ONUSAL personnel again became a problem.[54]

The accords required that arrangements for transferring land to ex-combatants of both sides and for legalizing wartime occupations of land be completed by July 31, 1992. Before then COPAZ had to verify the inventory of affected lands presented by the FMLN, define the conditions of transfer (determine potential beneficiaries, their entitlements, terms of payment, and so forth), and make the actual transfer of land titles. There were delays in meeting each of these goals. The FMLN's inventory was incomplete and had to be revised several times before a complete inventory was submitted to COPAZ in June. Discussions in COPAZ about the inventory caused further delays and the conditions for land transfer were presented to the government only at the end of August. The government itself, unhappy about the transfer conditions, dragged its feet. ONUSAL became involved in the issue because of these delays and the fact that land transfers were supposed to have begun on May 1, 1992. The secretary-general commissioned a group of experts from the International Monetary Fund (IMF), the World Bank, and the UN Food and Agriculture Organization to visit El Salvador and work with ONUSAL on this issue. On October 13, 1992, the secretary-general submitted a proposal of his own to both sides in order to break the deadlock.[55]

The question of implementing the recommendations of the Commission on the Truth was also a source of major controversy. The commission, established in accordance with the Mexico Agreements of April 27, 1991,[56] was entrusted with the task of investigating serious acts of violence that had occurred since 1980 and whose impact on society was deemed to require an urgent public knowledge of the truth.[57] The commission was set up on May 15, 1992, and was to transmit, within six months of starting its work, a final report with conclusions and recommendations to the parties and to the secretary-general. The report, entitled *From Madness to Hope* and numbering more than two hundred pages, with annexes of several hundred pages, was delivered to the secretary-general and President Cristiani on September 22, 1992. It was originally scheduled for public release in January 1993, but as a result of an agreement between the FMLN and government, its appearance was postponed until March 15, 1993. The commission received 22,000 complaints of serious acts of violence that had occurred between January 1980 and July 1991, of which 60 percent referred to illegal executions, 25 percent to "forced disappearances," and more than 20 percent to instances of torture. The commission was able to confirm 7,312 specific cases of human rights abuses, including 6,566 deaths and disappearances, and indirect evidence of 13,562 victims of abuses, including 11,130 deaths and disappearances. The statistical results of the report suggested that the rightist military, paramilitary, security forces, and death squads were responsible for 97 percent of human rights violations and the FMLN the remaining 3 percent.

Cristiani implored the commission not to release the names of perpetrators of human rights abuses. He argued that if names were made public he would not be able to guarantee the personal safety of those who had testified before the commission. FMLN leader Joaquin Villalobos also reportedly requested that the names of violators be suppressed. These pleas went unheeded. Following the experiences of Argentina and Brazil, the commission went public with names on the grounds that the purpose of the exercise was to enable the country to come to grips with its past as a vital first step in national reconciliation.[58]

The commission offered recommendations requiring a wide range of administrative, legislative, and constitutional measures, including a recommendation that the entire Supreme Court step down. The National Assembly was asked to adopt new laws and to ratify and approve these new constitutional amendments. Cristiani indicated that he was willing to comply with those recommendations falling within his competence, but other government officials accused the commission of having exceeded its mandate and of assuming judicial functions. A leading member of the FMLN, Shafik Handal, indicated that although he harbored a number of reservations about the commission's report, the FMLN accepted its recommendations in their entirety.

Although there was no violence directly attributable to the release of the report, five days after its release El Salvador's National Assembly, controlled by Cristiani's ARENA party, passed legislation granting total amnesty to all those guilty of extrajudicial crimes during the war, thereby rejecting one of the principal recommendations of the report. The head of the Salvadoran military, General Rene Emilio Ponce, who resigned as defense minister just before the report's release, also went on national television to repudiate the report's findings, arguing that many cases of human rights violations had been left out of the report. Mauricio Gutiérrez Castro, the chief justice of the Supreme Court of El Salvador, whose immediate resignation was called for by the report, also condemned its findings.[59]

Progress in implementing the recommendations of the truth commission report was slow. The recommendation to dismiss from their posts and discharge from the armed forces officers who were named in the report, and who were personally implicated in the perpetration or cover-up of cases, was delayed for several months. The recommendation to dismiss civilian officials who covered up or failed to investigate serious acts of violence was also not carried out immediately. The recommendation that current members of the Supreme Court of Justice resign their posts to enable constitutional reform proved difficult to implement because of the separation of powers in the Salvadoran Constitution. Gutiérrez Castro was not inclined to go, and Cristiani was powerless to compel him and the thirteen other judges to step down. Implementation of other recommendations was delayed or not carried out.[60]

With the cease-fire and demobilization firmly in place, the job of the United Nations might have ended there. But it did not. On January 8, 1993, the government of El Salvador formally requested UN observation of the elections for the presidency, the National Assembly, the mayoralties, and the municipal councils to be held in March 1994.[61] This request for further assistance was formally accepted by the Security Council on May 27, 1993.

A technical mission visited El Salvador from April 18 to April 28, 1993, to define the terms of reference, concept of operations, and financial implications of expanding ONUSAL's mandate to include electoral monitoring as requested by the government. The mission identified a number of serious problems concerning the inadequacies of the existing electoral roll and difficulties encumbering the timely issue of electoral documents. Key among these were the large number of names belonging to expatriates and dead persons and insufficient national controls to avoid double registration of voters; discrepancies between the names on the electoral rolls and those on electoral cards; and large numbers of citizens—possibly as many as one-third of potential eligible voters—whose names were not on the electoral roster.

With these problems in the background, the electoral division of ONUSAL was established in September 1993 under the following terms of reference: (1) to observe that measures and decisions made by all electoral authorities were impartial and consistent with the holding of free and fair elections; (2) to observe that appropriate steps were taken to ensure that eligible voters were included in the electoral rolls, thus enabling them to exercise their right to vote; (3) to observe that mechanisms were in place effectively to prevent multiple voting, given that a complete screening of the electoral rolls prior to the election was not feasible; (4) to observe that freedoms of expression, organization, movement, and assembly were respected without restrictions; (5) to observe that potential voters had sufficient knowledge about how to participate in the election; (6) to examine, analyze, and assess criticisms made, objections raised, and attempts to delegitimize the electoral process, and, if required, to convey such information to the Supreme Electoral Tribunal; (7) to inform the tribunal of complaints received regarding irregularities in electoral advertising or possible interferences with the electoral process, and to request information on corrective measures taken by the tribunal; and (8) to place observers at all polling sites on election day to verify that the right to vote was fully respected.[62]

The electoral division decided to conduct its operations in five stages: (1) preparatory organization at the central and regional level; (2) verification of citizens' registration; (3) observation of the electoral campaign; (4) observation of elections, counting of votes, and announcement of results; and (5) observation of a second round of elections for the presidency to be held in the event that the first round did not yield a definitive result.[63]

The electoral division functioned for more than six months with a staff of thirty-six professionals working out of six regional offices. It was able to perform its duties, despite its small staff, by working closely with other elements of ONUSAL. In addition to observing the Supreme Electoral Tribunal, the political parties, other public organizations, and the media, ONUSAL provided technical and logistical support to the registration of voters throughout the entire country.

Initially, the electoral division focused on observing voter registration, which was to close on November 20, 1993, and on monitoring the election campaign. It also assisted in drawing up electoral rolls, in keeping with the appeal made by the Security Council on November 5, 1993.[64] The division held regular joint meetings with the Supreme Electoral Tribunal, the Board of Vigilance (made up of representatives of all political parties), and the party campaign managers to solve any problems that arose during the campaign. The division asked the parties to provide a schedule of their campaign activities. It also set up a system to receive and process allegations of violations of the electoral code. These allegations were transmitted to the Supreme Electoral Tribunal, which had to report on follow-up action taken. The division also prepared a plan for the deployment of international observers who, working with mission staff, would bring the total number of monitors up to nine hundred for election day.[65]

Six parties and one coalition registered to run in the presidential election: Armando Calderon Sol for ARENA; Fidel Chavez Mena for the

Christian Democratic Party; Ruben Zamora for the coalition composed of
the National Revolutionary Movement (MNR), the Democratic Conver-
gence (CD), and the FMLN; Eduardo Rodríguez for the Movement of
National Solidarity (MSN); Jorge Martinez for the Unity Movement (MU);
Rina de Rey Prendes for the True Christian Movement (MAC); and
Roberto Escobar García for the Party of National Conciliation (PCN). The
number of parties running in the elections for the National Assembly and
municipal councils was reduced to nine following the merging of the
Popular Social Christian Movement (MPSC), the Social Democratic Party
(PSD), and the National Democratic Union (UDN) into a single party
called Democratic Convergence, and the failure of the Free People's
party (PL) to put forward any candidates.[66]

A number of reforms in electoral legislation were introduced during
the campaign period intended to facilitate the participation of political
parties and Salvadoran citizens. The deadline for the close of voter registration was extended to January 19, 1994, to facilitate the issuance of
voter registration cards. The deadline for registering candidates running
for the office of deputy in the National Assembly and for the municipal
councils was extended from January 19 to 31. Publishing the results of
surveys or projections of possible voting outcomes was prohibited from
fifteen days before the election until the final results were made public.

As a result of pressure from ONUSAL, a major reform of the electoral
code succeeded in resolving a dispute between the Supreme Electoral
Tribunal and the parties comprising the MNR/CD/FMLN coalition with
regard to the composition of the departmental and municipal elections
boards. The dispute arose from the tribunal's decision to reduce the number of representatives of the coalition parties from three to one. ONUSAL
asked that the problem be resolved by means of a broad interpretation of
the law that would allow all parties running in the four elections to participate. The legislative reform of January 19 unequivocally called for all
parties registering candidates to be represented on the departmental and
municipal election boards.

Major improvements had been made in the voter registration process
before the closure of voter registration on January 19 and the drawing up
of provisional electoral rolls. The tribunal made its own procedures more
flexible. The U.S. Agency for International Development (USAID) played
a major role in equipping the electoral tribunal to register voters, while
ONUSAL provided strategic and logistical support for registration.
ONUSAL teams made at least nine observation visits (more than 2,350 in

total) to each of the country's 262 towns and 3,700 mobile team visits to other sites around the country. By January 19, 1994, 2,653,871 voter registration cards had been issued, of which 2,171,805 replaced voter registration cards issued in previous years and 482,066 were temporary cards that could be converted into permanent cards once they were claimed at distribution centers. All told, voter registration cards had been issued to 80 percent of the estimated population of voting age; and once the temporary registration cards were converted, 85 percent of the voting population was registered to vote. However, there was a discrepancy of 400,000 registrations between the electoral division's estimate of 2.3 million potential voters and the 2.7 million listed on the rolls. This was due to (1) an indeterminate number of deceased persons holding voter registration cards who remained on the rolls; (2) some 300,000 temporary cards that had been issued but not claimed; and (3) Salvadorans possibly residing outside the country who still possessed registration cards.[67]

Locating birth certificates in order to validate some 154,000 requests for registration posed another set of problems. El Salvador does not have a civil registry, and there is great latitude in the use of surnames. This problem was compounded by rural-urban migration and displacements caused by armed conflict, which made it difficult to verify place of birth. There were two planned efforts, implemented by ONUSAL, the UN Development Programme (UNDP), and USAID, to recover more than 360,000 birth certificates from municipal offices, particularly in former conflict areas. As a result of those efforts, nearly 60,000 applications were validated. Some 80,000 remained invalidated when the voter registration period closed.

By late 1993 there were "disturbing signs of the reappearance of some ugly features of El Salvador's past" including politically motivated murders and assaults by death squads.[68] On November 23, 1993, the secretary-general reported that although the government was taking necessary steps to comply with the provisions of the peace accords relating to purging the armed forces of human rights offenders, several other key aspects of the peace accords "were suffering from serious delays."[69] The program for land redistribution was falling behind the targets agreed in October 1992. Delays were also affecting the programs of reintegration for ex-combatants and war disabled. There were startup problems with the National Public Security Academy and delays in the deployment of the PNC because new recruits were still not available. The collection of weapons previously issued for exclusive use by the armed forces also remained far from complete.

Civilianization of the police was a crucial element of the whole peace settlement and necessary to create a propitious climate for the elections. It was essential that the armed forces be structured to limit their role to external defense and that they be placed under full control of civilian authorities. In furtherance of these objectives, the government undertook to adopt laws on the possession of weapons and the regulation of private security services; to submit a plan for phasing out the National Police; to ensure the civilian character of the PNC and its autonomy from the FAES; to deploy the new force; to appoint former FMLN combatants to executive senior posts at the National Public Security Academy; and to accelerate both the transfer of land and the reintegration programs. The government and the FMLN also agreed to cooperate in eradicating illegal armed groups and pledged to refrain from mutual accusations when serious incidents occurred. ONUSAL devised a timetable for implementation of these commitments and joint government-ONUSAL working groups were created or reinforced to deal with them.[70]

As a result of increasing crime and growing security problems, the government unilaterally decided to deploy the armed forces in several areas of the country in a deterrent capacity. Under the peace accords the FAES was to be used for public security functions only in exceptional circumstances, which were to be reported to the National Assembly. ONUSAL pressed the government to issue such a report as required by the Salvadoran Constitution, but the government failed to comply with this request.

The growing number of murders and assaults raised fears about the possible resurgence of illegally armed groups, including the death squads. In October ONUSAL's human rights division raised this issue with the government and stressed the need to establish an independent authority to investigate these incidents. The killing of two senior FMLN leaders (Francisco Velis, a member of the FMLN national council and candidate in the forthcoming elections, and Eleno Castro, another member of the national council), along with the discovery of bodies of several FMLN supporters, a member of ARENA, and two former municipal officials, further underscored the problem and led ONUSAL to call for the creation of an interinstitutional commission to investigate these crimes. At a meeting between President Cristiani and the FMLN leadership with ONUSAL present, it was decided to invite foreign experts to cooperate in the investigation of the murder of the two FMLN leaders. A subgroup of this commission, the Interinstitutional Investigation Group (IIG), was created for that purpose. On October 29 ONUSAL informed the government that the IIG did not meet UN criteria for the investigation of summary executions.

In February 1994 new problems surfaced that some observers feared would jeopardize the peace process and the upcoming elections in March. There was a great deal of concern that the former head of the Anti-Narcotics Unit, army captain Oscar Pena Duran, who was appointed deputy director of the PNC, was violating the letter and spirit of the peace accords by monitoring the activities of ex-FMLN colleagues in the PNC and appointing old cronies to key posts in the organization. In January 1994 the government also suspended the demobilization of National Police on the grounds that it needed extra forces to address the growing crime wave in the country. The government informed ONUSAL that it would complete the demobilization by the end of 1994, thus breaking the July 1994 deadline it had earlier agreed to. The PNC also stopped accepting technical assistance and logistical support from ONUSAL and began to limit its overall contact, thus preventing ONUSAL from carrying out its human rights verification activities. According to one report, "Human rights violations attributed to PNC units . . . increased . . . with a sharp upturn in October [1993] after the discontinuation of the PNC's close collaboration with ONUSAL's Police Division in the field."[71]

Despite such problems, the presidential electoral campaign began on November 20, the campaign for the National Assembly elections on January 20, and the campaign for municipal elections on February 20. All proceeded without major incident, although uneven compliance with electoral rules prompted remedial efforts by ONUSAL and the tribunal. The political parties signed pacts of honor about the conduct of the campaign in all of the fourteen departments of El Salvador. On March 10, at ONUSAL headquarters, all presidential candidates signed a declaration of their rejection of violence and their commitment to respect the results of the elections and to comply with the peace accords. The parties held joint meetings at regular intervals under ONUSAL auspices to discuss the campaign. The electoral division also held regular joint meetings with the Supreme Electoral Tribunal, the Board of Vigilance, and the party campaign managers to solve problems that arose during the electoral process. The division met with some seventy delegations from governments, nongovernmental organizations, universities, and media seeking information about the electoral process. ONUSAL helped to mobilize some two thousand international observers in addition to its own nine hundred election observers.[72]

On March 20, 1994, national elections were held for the presidency, the 84 seats of the National Assembly subject to proportional representation, and the office of mayor in some 262 municipal districts. Although ARENA won a plurality in the first round, it did not have the majority of votes necessary to secure the office of the presidency; a runoff election for the presidency was therefore called for April 24. The presidential candidates in the runoff were Armando Calderon Sol and Ruben Zamora, for ARENA and the MNR/CD/FMLN coalition, respectively.

Voter records indicated low turnout in the election, with only 53 percent of those registered voting. Although this number was substantially higher than in previous elections, it fell well below expectations. Part of the problem was attributable to the cumbersome nature of the Salvadoran voting system. First, the complex system of registration meant that citizens had to invest a considerable amount of time to obtain a voter card. Second, the limited number of polling stations meant that voters in rural areas had to travel great distances to cast their ballots. These problems were by no means entirely remedied in time for the elections.[73] Although UN chief of mission Ramirez-Campo stated that only 25,000 people were unable to vote, other international observers charged that up to 300,000 citizens were not allowed to vote because their names did not appear on the voting lists. International election observers reported serious electoral anomalies but not sufficiently serious to have changed the outcome of presidential voting. In his report on the conduct of the elections, the secretary-general stated that ONUSAL observers experienced no interference in their work by monitors of the main political parties, also present at the main polling sites. There was no evidence of ballot rigging, nor were there any serious incidents of violence on election day that could have affected the outcome. The difficulties cited were problems with organization of the voting and preparation of the electoral roll, insufficient public transport to the voting sites, citizens who had voting cards but whose names did not appear on the register of voters at the time of the vote, and citizens who were unable to vote because others had already used their names to vote. This confusion in the election process created considerable tension and led to bitter feuding among the parties over the election results.[74]

To overcome some of the serious problems detected in the first round of elections, ONUSAL's electoral division on March 24 recommended to the Supreme Electoral Tribunal improvements in the number of polling centers, transport for voters, guidance and training of electoral officials on the polling station teams, and electoral publicity. The division posted observers to monitor the three areas of work that the contending parties and the Supreme Electoral Tribunal designated as most important: voter registration, compilation of voter lists, and the training of election monitors and polling attendants. Thirty-five additional polling centers were established and, with the assistance of USAID and UNDP, arrangements were made to provide free transportation to polling places in rural areas and in the San Salvador metropolitan area. Some 15,000 names were added to the electoral roll and voters were given more information about how to find their proper polling stations.

On runoff election day, ONUSAL posted approximately nine hundred observers around the country to cover all polling centers from the time the stations opened until they closed and the first vote tally was completed. ONUSAL also observed the official vote-counting process in the Supreme Electoral Tribunal, concluding that the runoff election was largely free of serious incidents affecting law and order or involving ballot rigging, and that there was "a distinct improvement in the organization of the election, including the layout of the polling centers, the stationing of personnel to direct voters to the proper polling places, the finding of names on the electoral roll," transportation of voters to polls, and early broadcasts of the election results. There were some minor irregularities; for example, some polling stations closed before they were supposed to, some party members campaigned at polling centers in violation of the electoral code, and, as in the first round, "a considerable number of citizens were unable to exercise their right to vote even though they had voter cards."[75] But these incidents were not considered serious enough to call into question the final result. Conservative candidate Armando Calderon Sol won the presidential runoff election with 68.3 percent of the vote. His leftist opponent Ruben Zamora received 31.7 percent. Of the 2.7 million eligible voters, slightly more than 50 percent cast their ballots.

With the approaching end of the ONUSAL mission's mandate, Secretary-General Boutros Boutros-Ghali sought to maintain the capacity of the United Nations to verify compliance of aspects of the Chapultepec peace accords that remained to be fulfilled, especially in the areas of land settlement, reintegration of the former combatants, and legislative and juridical reforms. In the midst of lingering discontent with the incomplete implementation of the peace agreements, the secretary-general envisioned that a small force of approximately eight UN officials with support staff would verify the fulfillment of the peace process, provide good offices for future disputes, and supply the UN Secretariat with reliable information on the situation in the country. This force, designated as the United Nations Mission in El Salvador (MINUSAL), was approved by the Security Council on February 17, 1995, for an initial period of six months from the date of the ONUSAL operation's termination. Boutros-Ghali stated that the new mission would work in close coordination with UNDP in El Salvador, but it was necessary for MINUSAL to maintain a separate identity due to the political nature of its tasks and responsibilities.[76]

Assessment and Conclusions

How are we to assess the contribution of the United Nations and other third parties to the peace process in El Salvador? Did peace come by itself or was it indeed nurtured with outside help? If it was nurtured, which third parties played key or leading roles? Although the conflict in El Salvador in 1989 was, in one sense, ripe for resolution, the ripeness had to be cultivated and sustained by external actors, including the United Nations, the United States, and various countries in the region. This was because the conflict in El Salvador had deep roots in the country's history and long-standing social and economic inequalities. To be sure, these grievances had been fueled by the Cold War and intervention by the United States and the Soviet Union in the affairs of the region. Thus, support by the United States was crucial to advancing the peace process in El Salvador. But a transformation in the fundamental relationship between the government and the FMLN was also required to end the civil war. This could only be achieved if the parties to the conflict came to realize that it was in their own long-term interests to end the campaign of armed violence and pursue their objectives through negotiations and a peaceful transformation of the political system. Much of the third-party effort in the peace process, especially UN effort, sought to persuade the parties to relinquish the use of force and settle their differences through peaceful political means. By bringing the parties to the table and convening a dialogue to address unresolved and outstanding issues, particularly during the implementation phase, third parties were able to keep the peace process on track. This was no mean feat, and on more than one occasion it appeared as if the process might fail. That it did not was due to the important mediation services provided by the United Nations and its contributions to the implementation of the Chapultepec Accords. These contributions went well beyond traditional peacekeeping and observation to include electoral monitoring; human rights observation; and assistance with political, judicial, economic, and social reform. The early deployment of a human rights monitoring team by ONUSAL before the fighting had ended and final accords were signed was especially important to instilling in the parties a sense of confidence in the peace process.

Other aspects of direct ONUSAL involvement in the peace process included observation of voter registration, deployment of international observers during the electoral campaign, mediation and resolution of various disputes between the Supreme Electoral Tribunal and the parties involved in the election, assistance with improvements to the system of voter registration, continued monitoring of the human rights situation, voter education, and help in overcoming the serious problems experienced in the first round of elections.

What factors account for the widely observed success of the ONUSAL mission? Undoubtedly the groundwork laid by a serious process of negotiations greatly reduced the problems of implementation. That the negotiations directly and specifically addressed issues of human rights and political and military reform minimized the threats posed by these contentious issues to collaboration between former disputants. Along these same lines, the ongoing availability of UN mediation services during the implementation phase preempted the emergence of unforeseen grievances or uncertainties about the accords, further affirming the perceived stability and appropriateness of the agreement.

The early deployment of human rights workers also created a local climate of confidence in the United Nations, the accords, and the seriousness of the signatories. The ONUSAL human rights bureaucracy aimed the international spotlight directly at the Salvadoran government, putting it on the defensive as it tried to explain the appalling evidence of state-sponsored brutality. The government was compelled, one might even say shamed, by the intense international scrutiny to compensate for past atrocities by complying with the terms of the agreement and proving its commitment to a reinvigorated democracy. However, there was an obvious tension between the degree to which the United Nations could push for human rights and its ability to keep the Salvadoran government and military on task and committed to the peace process.

For the FMLN, demobilization proved to be thorough, stable, and permanent—an accomplishment that effectively ended the guerrilla war and created a fresh climate for cooperation. A successful ONUSAL mission was inconceivable without disarming the FMLN, but demobilization had its double edge, eliminating as it did the FMLN's single greatest source of leverage against the government. At the same time that the demobilization secured cooperation from the government, it drastically reduced the ability of the FMLN and other domestic groups to bring pressure on the government to treat them seriously, to reform its practices, and to stick to the agreement. Throughout its mission, ONUSAL was forced to address this inequity in power between the two parties.

Finally, the relatively small size of the UN force in El Salvador actually worked to the advantage of the peace process. Unlike the UN operation in Cambodia, for instance, with its far larger and more cumbersome bureaucracy, ONUSAL did not experience major delays in deploying its workers, setting up its offices, acquiring the necessary equipment, or generally going about its business. As the peace process gathered momentum, ONUSAL was in position to exploit the initial euphoria and the sense of urgent goodwill as the parties were striving to cultivate the results of their negotiations. ONUSAL's logistical efficiency enhanced the perception that the peace accords could work.

Although the United Nations was instrumental in ensuring that the peace process stayed on track, some critics have charged that ONUSAL did not make sufficient use of its "moral authority" and "status as an objective interpreter of the accords." Holiday and Stanley argue that ONUSAL failed to criticize the government for its performance on human rights "in a timely fashion," and failed to distinguish adequately between state violations of human rights and "common crime" violations.[77] They also point out that the ONUSAL personnel responsible for implementing the accords were not those who had negotiated them. Disputed points of interpretation between the parties were therefore not easily or quickly resolved; the mediators were sometimes forced to wait instead for clarification from UN headquarters.[78]

The mission ran into other problems as well. ONUSAL's budget did not finance activities such as the reintegration of ex-combatants into society and the promotion of democratic institutions beyond electoral monitoring and assistance. Furthermore, as noted by Alvaro de Soto and Graciana del Castillo, there was a "lack of coordination and transparency within the UN system": the IMF and the World Bank did not keep the United Nations abreast of the economic programs they sponsored, and the United Nations neglected to inform the Bretton Woods institutions of the peace accords. As a consequence, El Salvador's economic stabilization program worked at cross-purposes with the peace program. El Salvador found itself ineligible for concessional financing under its structural adjustment program because its per capita income was higher than the ceiling allowable for concessional financing.[79]

These are fair criticisms; certainly, aspects of ONUSAL's involvement in the implementation of the peace accords could have been carried out better than they were. On the other hand, these criticisms should not detract from the more basic point that without ONUSAL's active and constructive involvement in the implementation the peace process would surely have come unstuck. Too many outstanding issues and points of contention in the agreement had to be negotiated—in some instances, renegotiated—between the parties. Outright violations of the accords by both sides engendered mutual feelings of hostility and mistrust. These could have easily escalated had the United Nations not been there to deal with them and secure the parties' continuing commitment to the peace process. Finally, the parties clearly were incapable, or unwilling, to perform entirely by themselves many tasks and functional activities related to the peace process. In the management of the elections, rehabilitation and integration of ex-combatants into society, and military and police reform, the United Nations found itself having to respond to appeals from the parties to do more. ONUSAL's mandate was therefore constantly redefined and expanded so that it could take on the additional responsibilities being requested by the parties. Whether this kind of dependency relationship is ultimately healthy for a society in the long run remains to be seen, but without it, in the short run, the peace process could not have been sustained.

Alvaro de Soto has expressed concern about the durability of the peace agreement in El Salvador. Since the withdrawal of the United Nations in the early months of 1994, a number of developments have suggested a flagging commitment by both sides to the peace process. The government's "sluggish" attempt to dismantle the National Police has suggested a "lingering reluctance to see it disappear."[80] The revelation that the FMLN hid large stockpiles of arms from ONUSAL monitors fueled a long-standing "root fear that the undertakings of the Government coupled with international verification were insufficient to ensure compliance" with the accords.[81] Both the FMLN and the government have been responsible for "serious delays" in the implementation of the land-transfer program and other strategies for reintegrating former combatants into the economy—a failure that, according to de Soto and del

Castillo, results mainly from the "lack of political will among lower-level government officials."[82] The *Washington Post* reported in March 1995 that "former combatants from both sides of the war"—armed with automatic weapons and rocket-propelled grenades—were overwhelming the PNC in its efforts to ensure public order in postsettlement El Salvador.[83] While the specter of political murders and disappearances has not yet been revived, this new criminal violence randomly terrorizes all of El Salvador's major cities.

These challenges to the peace process, however, have little to do with deficiencies in the peace accords or flaws in the ONUSAL operation itself and more to do with the question of timing and withdrawal from the field. In fact, the most significant lesson that de Soto draws from the ONUSAL experiment is that "deciding how and when to end such an operation . . . may well be as difficult and as important as deciding [when] to begin the operation." Judging the appropriate moment for exit after the implementation of a settlement should not be based on "whether things seem quiet or elections have taken place, but whether peace-related reforms have advanced enough to make the process durable, indeed irreversible."[84] To make that judgment, we may have to wait a number of years.

CAMBODIA

$\mathbf{O}$n October 23, 1991, the Paris Peace Agreements were signed, providing for a comprehensive settlement of the civil war in Cambodia. The agreements were signed by the four members of the Supreme National Council: the Cambodian Peoples' Party (CPP), which headed the government in Phnom Penh, led by Hun Sen; the Khmer People's National Liberation Front (KPNLF) led by Son Sann; the National Front for an Independent, Neutral, Prosperous, and Cooperative Cambodia (FUNCINPEC) led by Prince Norodom Ranariddh; and the Khmer Rouge headed by Khieu Samphan and Pol Pot. The president of the council was Prince Norodom Sihanouk, who had ruled Cambodia from the time of its independence in 1953 to his overthrow in a right-wing coup in March 1970.

For over twenty years Cambodia had been wracked by civil war and a series of brutally repressive governments that had cost the country millions of lives. It now looked as if the civil war might come to an end if the terms of the new peace settlement could be effectively implemented.

Under the terms of the settlement, the United Nations would disarm 70 percent of each of the four armies—the Cambodia People's Armed Forces (CPAF), Kampuchean People's National Liberation Armed Forces (KPNLAF), National Army of Independent Kampuchea (NAIK), and National Army of Democratic Kampuchea (NADK)—and supervise the activities of the remaining forces. The coalition government would return from exile to Phnom Penh, the NADK would be disbanded under strict supervision, the Khmer Rouge would be given minor positions in the interim government, a UN force would supervise elections to a constituent assembly based on proportional representation, and Cambodian refugees would be returned for the elections.[1]

The Cambodia peace accords were the first cooperative agreement among the five permanent members of the Security Council (the United Kingdom, France, the United States, the Soviet Union, and China) of the post–Cold War era. Although the essential provisions of the settlement were implemented, the implementation process was plagued by great difficulties, and the long-term future of democracy in Cambodia is still in doubt. But even critics of the Cambodian peace process are forced to concede that Cambodia now has the prospect of building a democratic future—a prospect it did not have when the peace talks were first launched some six years ago. The government in Cambodia today is one that has been democratically elected by the people of Cambodia. That in itself, given the recent history of Cambodia, is no small achievement. It is the argument of this chapter that this result would have not come about had there not been extensive third-party assistance and involvement in both the negotiation and implementation of the Paris Peace Agreements.

This chapter explores the factors and forces that shaped the peace settlement and the difficulties experienced by the United Nations and other third parties in implementing the settlement's key provisions. Financial constraints hindered the UN operation in Cambodia and influenced its degree of success in monitoring and implementing the accords. The forces of the United Nations Transitional Authority in Cambodia were also deployed at a slower pace than they should have been. This weakened the United Nations' credibility with Cambodian factions intent on disrupting the peace process. In addition, a number of unanticipated issues posed major difficulties during the implementation phase. These concerned refugee resettlement and immigration, infrastructure and support for cantonment and demobilization, and the need for presidential elections to provide stability during the transition period. But because the electoral and political components of the peace plan were carried out so successfully, the United Nations succeeded in spite of the fact that it was not able to implement some of the provisions in the peace plan for a cease-fire and the demobilization of forces.

Opportunities for a settlement were also influenced by shifting power balances at the regional and international levels. Although improved great-power relations at the end of the Cold War—in particular, the Soviet Union's interest in ending the conflict—played a key role in the settlement process by promoting the conditions for a hurting stalemate, these circumstances were not sufficient to promote the elements of a durable and lasting peace. This is because China had an interest in continuing its support for the Khmer Rouge as long as Vietnam threatened to dominate the region. Thailand also wanted to see the conflict continue, for reasons similar to China's. The dynamics of regional power politics thus crucially affected the negotiation and implementation of the peace settlement. Only when Thailand and China decided to limit their involvement in the internal affairs of Cambodia—in favor of stabilizing the region for economic growth and development—did the peace process move forward. Vietnam also gave up its efforts to control Cambodia through the CPP in order to turn to economic development.

This chapter begins with a brief history of the conflict in Cambodia—an account that shows how the existence of both civil and regional elements within the conflict greatly complicated the prospects of achieving a viable negotiated settlement. An examination of the run-up to the Paris Peace Agreements then explores whether the conditions for ripeness were satisfied at the time the agreements were signed. Attention then moves to the implementation phase of the agreements and the role of third parties in peace building. The influence of third parties—notably, the United States, the Association of Southeast Asian Nations (especially Indonesia), Japan, Australia, and the United Nations—in nurturing and sustaining the peace process during implementation is shown to have been positive and substantial. There were elements that could have worked better than they did, and the United Nations failed to anticipate some of the serious problems that threatened to scuttle the implementation of the accords. On balance, however, the process worked to give Cambodia the political opportunity to determine its own future.

History of the Conflict

Cambodia's civil war began some ten years after Cambodia attained its independence from France. In 1963 Pol Pot led the Khmer Rouge in insurrections against Prince Sihanouk, who had governed the country since independence.[2] The U.S. intervention in Vietnam after 1964 created further difficulties for Sihanouk, especially as the war led North Vietnam to develop infiltration routes and safe areas in Cambodia, and the United States began to bomb these targets. To prevent the North Vietnamese army from supporting the communist insurrection against his regime, Prince Sihanouk allowed Hanoi to run supply lines through eastern Cambodia and China to supply North Vietnam from Cambodian territory. Later, he severed Cambodia's diplomatic relations with the United States following the full-scale deployment of American troops in South Vietnam. But the more immediate threat to Sihanouk came from the right instead of the left; in March 1970 he was overthrown by Lon Nol in a right-wing coup. One of Lon Nol's first actions on taking power was to resume full diplomatic relations with the United States.[3]

Under Lon Nol, Cambodia soon found itself dragged more deeply into the quagmire in Vietnam. American and South Vietnamese troops undertook military incursions into Cambodia to remove North Vietnamese and Khmer Rouge communist bases. These incursions were supported by the Lon Nol regime. They were not successful, however, as the communists simply moved farther into Cambodia, prompting an intensification of the U.S. bombing campaign. In November 1970 Lon Nol proclaimed the Khmer Republic. Suffering politically as a result of the effects of the civil war, Lon Nol began to rule by decree in October 1971.

The signing of the 1973 Paris Peace Agreements between the United States and North Vietnam brought little relief to war-torn Cambodia or South Vietnam. As the U.S. bombing of Cambodia continued, peasant support for rebel Khmer Rouge forces grew. Cambodian refugees flocked to neighboring Thailand as the economic and political situation deteriorated.[4] In April 1975, however, the U.S. Congress cut off funding for the bombing, and an isolated Lon Nol was ousted by the Khmer Rouge and "Democratic Kampuchea" was formed. Once in power, the Khmer Rouge, led by Pol Pot, began to forcibly implement its ideology of deurbanization. As part of the process, perceived traitors, religious opponents, foreigners, intellectuals, professionals, and members of the governing classes were eliminated in mass executions. Fearing that Vietnam had designs on Cambodia, the Khmer Rouge began purging Vietnamese settlers who had moved across the border during the Vietnam War.[5] Pro-Vietnamese elements in Khmer Rouge ranks (or those perceived to be so by the paranoid Pol Pot) were also purged. As a result, many of them left Phnom Penh for Hanoi. Many other Cambodians began to seek refuge in Thailand, prompting the

Thai government to attempt to discourage the refugees with policies of forced repatriation.[6]

In January 1977 Khmer Rouge forces crossed into Vietnam and massacred hundreds of Vietnamese. Vietnamese forces retaliated by crossing the border and attacking the Khmer Rouge. Although the Vietnamese troops withdrew shortly thereafter, they remained at the border in a defensive position. Relations between the two countries continued to worsen to the point where Cambodia decided to formally break its relations with Vietnam.

On December 25, 1978, Vietnamese forces invaded Cambodia and overthrew the Khmer Rouge. The Khmer Rouge escaped westward from Phnom Penh to the Cambodian jungle and refugee camps on the Thai border. From these locations, the Khmer Rouge planned and carried out insurrections against the Vietnamese puppet regime with Chinese assistance channeled through Thailand. Vietnam's motivation for the invasion included continued armed provocations by the Khmer Rouge, the threat of a Chinese-backed regime in Phnom Penh, the genocidal policies of the Khmer Rouge, the uncontrollable refugee situation, and unstable domestic conditions in Cambodia.[7] To protect its interests in Cambodia, Hanoi installed a pro-Vietnamese communist government under the presidency of Heng Samrin. The People's Republic of Kampuchea (PRK) was thus formed. The new government consisted mainly of former Khmer Rouge members who had escaped to Vietnam during the anti-Vietnamese purges in Cambodia. Viewed as a Vietnamese-backed puppet regime, the new government in Phnom Penh was not recognized in the West and was supported only by the Soviet Union and the Eastern bloc countries.

During the period 1980–85 the civil war for control of Cambodia continued. The PRK government was unable to establish total dominance. The Khmer Rouge was determined to retake power, using as its mobilizing strategy the message that the goal of the Vietnamese was to annex Cambodia as a province of Vietnam. The Khmer Rouge forces pursued guerrilla warfare aimed at undermining the pro-Vietnamese regime. This provoked Vietnamese forces to attack the Khmer Rouge military bases located among the refugee camps at the Thai border. Three noncommunist factions—the armed forces of FUNCINPEC, the National Army for an Independent Cambodia, and the KPNLF (a "republican" faction consisting largely of supporters of Lon Nol and led by Son Sann)—participated in armed hostilities against the Vietnamese and PRK armed forces. All three resistance factions controlled several refugee camps and maintained them as military bases. The resistance was financially and militarily supported by Thailand and China and had the moral support of the West and of other states that opposed the Vietnamese invasion.[8]

From the early 1980s the Association of Southeast Asian Nations (ASEAN) tried several times to initiate diplomatic talks that would end the conflict in Cambodia. But whereas the Vietnamese government took the view that the conflict in Cambodia was an internal matter that could only be settled by the PRK government and the opposition, ASEAN focused on Vietnamese military occupation of Cambodia, which ASEAN saw as the greater threat to regional political stability.[9]

In June 1982, with the assistance of ASEAN, the Coalition Government of Democratic Kampuchea (CGDK) was formed as the Cambodian government in exile, in an effort to unify and strengthen opposition to the Vietnamese-backed PRK. The CGDK consisted of Prince Sihanouk's FUNCINPEC and the KPNLF as the noncommunist factions and the Khmer Rouge (People's Democratic Kampuchea). It was supported by the West (excluding the United States, which opposed the inclusion of the Khmer Rouge), ASEAN, and China as the legitimate government of Cambodia. This group of supporters believed that, in light of its bloody record, the Khmer Rouge could not by itself secure viable support for a diplomatic effort to oppose the Phnom Penh regime—hence the noncommunists were apparently pressured into joining an alliance with the Khmer Rouge. Prince Sihanouk was persuaded by the United States and China to become head of state of the CGDK and its president.[10] Khieu Samphan, the nominal head of the Khmer Rouge, became vice president. Son Sann, leader of the KPNLF, became prime minister.[11]

Superpower and Regional Interests

With Mikhail Gorbachev's accession to power in the Soviet Union, the situation in Cambodia began to change. In August 1985 the governments of Vietnam, Laos, and Cambodia announced that Vietnam was prepared to consider a withdrawal of its troops from Cambodia if certain conditions could be met. This was followed in March 1986 by a CGDK announcement of an eight-point proposal calling for the withdrawal of Vietnamese forces from Cambodia and the possible formation of a quadripartite government consisting of PRK and CGDK officials. Some interpreted the proposal as no longer making the complete withdrawal of Vietnamese troops an absolute precondition for talks with the Phnom Penh government.[12]

Other developments were to have an important impact on diplomacy as well. In 1987 Hun Sen, a less dogmatic leader than Heng Samrin, became president of the PRK. As part of its overall effort to normalize relations with China, the Soviet Union began to step up its own efforts to resolve the conflict, by encouraging Vietnam to withdraw its main army units from Cambodia and by raising the prospect of an abrupt termination of its military, economic, and strategic aid to Vietnam.[13] Prince Sihanouk announced that he, personally, was ready to meet with Hun Sen to discuss a five-point proposal put forward by Phnom Penh. Feeling pressured by these developments, China also decided to support the idea of national reconciliation under the leadership of Sihanouk. And ASEAN agreed to an Indonesian proposal of an informal "cocktail" meeting of the parties.[14]

In several respects, shifting regional and international power balances played a decisive role in the Cambodian peace process. As regional and international systemic conditions began to change, so too did the interests of key actors in a political settlement in Cambodia. To begin with, as the region's major power, China was interested in preventing Vietnam from dominating the region. This dictated its involvement and support for the resistance in Cambodia, primarily the communist Khmer Rouge. Chinese support for the Khmer Rouge also served to counter China's adversary, the Soviet Union, which supported Vietnam and the Phnom Penh regime. As long as Vietnam posed a threat, China continued to assist the Khmer Rouge militarily in its war against the Vietnamese troops and, after their withdrawal, against the Phnom Penh regime headed by Hun Sen. Beijing's strong support for the Khmer Rouge influenced the negotiation process insofar as Beijing rejected any proposal that excluded the Khmer Rouge from an interim government.

Thailand was also interested in continuing the conflict, for reasons similar to China's. In particular, the Thais feared a Vietnamese expansion across Indochina from Cambodia's western border. Thailand was a critical route for Chinese supplies reaching the Khmer Rouge, and also served as the base for several refugee camps controlled by the three resistance factions and used as military bases for incursions against the Phnom Penh regime. An additional problem was posed by rogue Thai military officers who were making enormous profits from trade with Khmer Rouge in gems and timber and would benefit from a continuing conflict.

The hard-line positions maintained by China, Thailand, the Soviet Union, and Vietnam began to soften by 1987. First, Vietnam, facing a

worsening domestic economic situation and suffering from the international isolation that hindered any prospects for economic growth,
slowly lost its political will to remain in Cambodia and began to withdraw
its troops. Second, following the 1987 democratic election of Chatichai
Choonhavan as prime minister, Thailand emphasized economic reconstruction, which depended largely on a stable region and thus an end to
the conflict in Cambodia. Thailand grew less willing to support the
Khmer Rouge and the resistance, and came to play an influential role in
the negotiation process.[15] Third, Gorbachev became leader of the Soviet
Union and redirected its priorities toward domestic economic reform. His
policy of "new thinking" implied a need to decrease Soviet foreign commitments and to settle regional conflicts in which the Soviet Union was
involved. Moscow felt it had nothing further to gain by remaining
involved in Cambodia or in continuing the conflict. Once Vietnamese
forces began to withdraw from Cambodia, relations between Moscow
and Beijing began to improve.

Agreement among the United States, China, and the Soviet Union on a
framework agreement for an eventual settlement of the Cambodian conflict affected the long-term cost-benefit analyses of the Cambodian parties they supported. The different factions could no longer rely on their
foreign allies for assistance to continue the conflict, and they quickly
came under pressure to settle it.

Third-Party Efforts to Negotiate a Political Settlement

A multiplicity of third parties played various roles in initiating formal
negotiations and promoting conditions for a peace settlement. Initially,
negotiations were held under the auspices of ASEAN, which overcame
several obstacles and succeeded in bringing the interested parties
together for discussions. The main issues discussed were the legitimacy
of the Phnom Penh regime and the nature of the conflict—that is,
whether it was an internal one between the Cambodian factions, a view
maintained by the Phnom Penh regime and Vietnam, or an international
one between the CGDK and Vietnam, a view maintained by the CGDK,
ASEAN, China, and the West.

ASEAN's initial mediation efforts were followed by those of Indonesia,
France, and the five permanent members of the Security Council. France
worked with Indonesia in the spring of 1989 to convene the first Paris
conference on Cambodia. Those talks failed. Then the United States led

eight months of negotiations among the Permanent Five, which culminated in August 1990 in agreement on a framework that provided the basis for the second (and successful) Paris conference in October 1991. The proposal featured a neutral transitional authority to govern Cambodia while preparations were made for elections. Similar to the process in Namibia (see chapter 3), the four warring factions were to disarm to prevent intimidation during the election process. The framework agreement was developed within the context of great-power negotiations because the interests of the Cambodian factions were represented by their allies among the Permanent Five. The Soviet Union represented the Phnom Penh regime and Vietnam; China and the United States represented FUNCINPEC, KPNLF, and, in some measure, Thai interests.

Although the external dimension of the Cambodian question was settled by August 1990, agreement among the Cambodian parties remained to be worked out. Further negotiations were held by the Cambodian parties with the cochairs of the Paris Peace Conference—France and Indonesia—until a final settlement was reached and an agreement was signed by the warring parties, major regional powers, and great powers at the second Paris conference in October 1991. In the discussion that follows, we briefly trace the evolution of the Cambodian peace negotiations and the roles played by different mediators in those negotiations.

On July 25, 1987, the first Jakarta Informal Meeting (JIM I), hosted by the Indonesian government, was held between the four Cambodian parties (the PRK, FUNCINPEC, the Khmer Rouge, and the KPNLF). Also in attendance were representatives from Vietnam, Laos, and ASEAN. China, however, did not attend. The meeting failed to produce a joint declaration. The major stumbling block was the issue of national reconciliation. The parties disagreed over who should organize Cambodian elections and act as an interim authority. Also at issue were the status and the role of the Cambodian parties in the interim period.[16] Supported by ASEAN, the CGDK put forward a proposal based on a three-stage Vietnamese troop withdrawal program. At the first stage, some of the troops would have been withdrawn. At the second stage, more troops would have been withdrawn at the same time that a provisional quadripartite government was established to organize the elections. At the third stage, all Vietnamese troops would have been withdrawn and elections held in Cambodia.

The PRK representatives rejected the proposal, proposing instead the formation of a national reconciliation council that represented all factions, with Prince Sihanouk as its chair. The PRK also proposed that China cease assistance to the Khmer Rouge once the Vietnamese troops were withdrawn in order to prevent the Khmer Rouge from taking advantage of the withdrawal and strengthening its military position. By August the Khmer Rouge had agreed to discuss national reconciliation and the creation of a provisional four-party government to oversee the elections.[17]

In early December 1987 and again on January 20, 1988, the first substantive negotiations on Cambodia were held between Prince Sihanouk and Hun Sen in Paris. The Khmer Rouge and the KPNLF did not participate in this first round of talks. During the negotiations Prince Sihanouk and Hun Sen agreed in principle that a postsettlement Cambodian government would involve the PRK and the three factions of the CGDK. In essence, they agreed to national reconciliation and the need for an international conference to guarantee Cambodia's independence and neutrality. They also agreed to free elections in Cambodia. The two, however, could not agree on whether the elections would be held before or after a settlement was reached. They were also deadlocked on a timetable for Vietnamese troop withdrawal and on the formation of an interim government to stay in office until elections were held. The Khmer Rouge and the KPNLF rejected the validity of the principles agreed upon because they were not present at the negotiations.

In November 1988 Sihanouk and Son Sann met with Hun Sen in Paris under French auspices for discussions on Cambodia. The Khmer Rouge publicly announced that it no longer demanded reparations from Vietnam. The Khmer Rouge also declared that it did not reject the government in Phnom Penh and was willing to take part in a four-party coalition government to prepare Cambodia for elections under a UN supervision group. The same month the UN General Assembly passed a resolution calling for the withdrawal of all foreign troops from Cambodia under the supervision and control of an international commission. It also called for the creation of an interim administrative authority to govern Cambodia in the period after foreign troop withdrawal and before elections. It further urged the promotion of national reconciliation in Cambodia under the leadership of Prince Sihanouk. The resolution supported an international conference under the auspices of the secretary-general for peace negotiations on Cambodia, and it declared that Cambodia should not return to the condemned policies of its recent past—a reference to the activities of the Khmer Rouge.

On January 6, 1989, Vietnam announced that it would withdraw its troops from Cambodia by September 1989 if a political settlement were reached by then.[18] Several reasons have been offered for Vietnam's decision to withdraw. Not only were economic conditions in Vietnam deteriorating, but Hanoi was being pressured to withdraw by Moscow, which had its own agenda dictated by "new thinking."[19] Moscow could not improve its relations with Beijing while the situation in Cambodia forced the Soviet Union and China to support opposing sides. At the same time, Moscow's policy emphasized an end to support for and involvement in regional conflicts. The occupation of Cambodia isolated Vietnam politically and economically. To develop its economy, Vietnam required assistance from the West and an end to the West's economic blockade; it could not expect either while its military forces occupied Cambodia. Hanoi may have also believed that the meager offensives by the resistance forces indicated that they no longer posed a military threat to the pro-Vietnamese regime in Phnom Penh.[20] The PRK government in Phnom Penh was considered to have sufficient military strength to control the resistance forces following a Vietnamese troop withdrawal. Although its security interdependence could no longer be realized through its presence in Cambodia, Vietnam kept open the option of reintervention in the event that the military resistance to the PRK and foreign assistance were to continue. Vietnam understood that the PRK could not be completely abandoned; as a condition of its withdrawal, Vietnam let it be known that there would need to be a political settlement of the situation in Cambodia.[21]

Negotiations were given additional impetus when Soviet foreign minister Eduard Shevardnadze visited China in February 1989. The Soviet Union was eager to end its hostility toward China and to cease financial support of regional conflicts. China was convinced that the Soviet Union had been pressuring Vietnam to get out of Cambodia and was feeling less threatened because of the Soviet reorientation to domestic problems. Moscow had also been pressuring Phnom Penh to compromise on including the Khmer Rouge in an interim government. During the visit a nine-point Sino-Soviet statement on Cambodia was formulated. It indicated agreement between the two states on the need to withdraw Vietnamese troops by September 1989, cease the delivery of foreign military aid to warring factions, and hold free national elections. They also agreed that the implementation of these points required an effective control mechanism, such as an "appropriate" role for the United Nations in the peace process and the convening of an international conference on the situation. Disagreement remained on the nature and composition of the government that would stay in office until elections were held.

Moscow supported the PRK government currently in Phnom Penh, while Beijing supported a coalition government representing all four Cambodian parties.[22]

At about the same time the second Jakarta Informal Meeting (JIM II), again hosted by Indonesia, was attended by all concerned parties from Indochina and ASEAN. Several issues were discussed, including the proposal for a quadripartite coalition to govern as the interim authority during the elections, options for the international supervision of the foreign troop withdrawal, a cease-fire, and elections. No concessions were made by the parties, and disagreement remained on other issues, such as the composition and size of a peacekeeping/control mechanism, a timetable for the withdrawal of Vietnamese troops, and the administration of the elections. ASEAN and the CGDK continued to stand by their demands for an unconditional and verified Vietnamese withdrawal from Cambodia, the establishment of a quadripartite provisional coalition government before elections were held, the dismantlement of the Phnom Penh regime, and the need for a UN peacekeeping force.[23] Sihanouk also demanded that a new Cambodian constitution create and preserve a multiparty system and that a cease-fire be in force at the time of implementation of the settlement. In response, the PRK and Vietnam maintained that Sihanouk should chair a national reconciliation council that would organize elections for November 1989, that the PRK regime was to remain in place in the interim, and that Vietnamese troop withdrawal was conditional on achieving a political settlement. Having ended the meeting with no significant movement, the negotiators agreed to continue in the context of an international conference.

The first Paris Peace Conference, held from July 30 through August 30, 1989, was attended by the four Cambodian factions, as well as Vietnam, Laos, Japan, Canada, Australia, India, Zimbabwe, the five UN Security Council permanent members, and the six members of ASEAN.[24] These discussions were marked by deep mistrust and suspicion. One particularly controversial issue was the involvement of the Khmer Rouge in a future Cambodian government. Prince Sihanouk proposed a quadripartite inclusion of all parties equally, including equal-sized armies and a four-way power-sharing plan for key government ministries. This ultimately implied a ratio of the CGDK to the State of Cambodia (or SOC, as the PRK was now known) of 3:1. The SOC, however, wanted to remain in the current administrative structure of government and allow the quadripartite group to look after the elections only. If the Khmer Rouge were excluded, a settlement on Cambodia would not be comprehensive and would risk a continuation of the civil war. If the Khmer Rouge were included, it would effectively be rewarded for its policy of genocide. At the same time, the SOC perceived the conflict as a civil war against the Khmer Rouge, while the Khmer Rouge viewed it as a national resistance movement against the Vietnamese invasion. The SOC wanted Khmer Rouge leaders excluded from any position of authority; the Khmer Rouge maintained its contempt toward the SOC because of its close association with Vietnam.[25]

A second controversial issue was the role of the United Nations in an international control mechanism. Given UN support for the CGDK and UN recognition of the CGDK as the legitimate occupier of Cambodia's seat at the United Nations, the SOC was leery of a strong role for the United Nations. At the same time, securing the involvement of the United Nations would legitimize the concerns of those elements that claimed that the problem was an internal one and thus did not require international supervision.

A third issue was the presence of large numbers of Vietnamese settlers in Cambodia. The Khmer Rouge argued that the participation in the elections of more than one million Vietnamese would distort the election results.

The Khmer Rouge also adamantly opposed the inclusion of the word "genocide" in a possible settlement agreement because it would justify the 1978 Vietnamese invasion, whereas Phnom Penh and Hanoi demanded that a statement be included in the settlement that condemned the past policies and practices of the Khmer Rouge. A proposal for a UN fact-finding mission to Cambodia to consider the possibility of a UN observer mission and a peacekeeping force was at first opposed by the Khmer Rouge, which later relented after pressure from China.

Whereas the major factions in Cambodia remained at loggerheads on these key issues, the major powers showed a willingness to "strike a balance of interests." China was interested in improving its international image following the Tiananmen Square massacre by pursuing a conciliatory approach on the Cambodian question.[26] The Soviet Union was also eager to make a contribution to resolving regional conflicts in order to improve its relations with the West. The United States was not keen to see Pol Pot return to power in Cambodia, but it was prepared to defer to Sihanouk's wishes to include the Khmer Rouge in an interim government if this would enhance the prospects of achieving a successful settlement. U.S. negotiators understood that the Khmer Rouge was too strong a guerrilla group to ignore and that China would not accept anything less than Khmer Rouge participation in an interim government.

Because no agreement was reached in Paris, the Vietnamese troop withdrawal from Cambodia was completed without international supervision or verification. As expected, the withdrawal was followed by an escalation of the civil war between the resistance and SOC forces.

At the end of 1989 various efforts were made to jump-start the peace negotiations that had floundered in Paris. Representative Stephen Solarz of the U.S. Congress, a supporter of Prince Sihanouk, proposed that Cambodia, like Namibia (see chapter 3), be given a UN interim administration to ensure that cease-fires be observed and that free and fair elections be held. Australian foreign minister Gareth Evans, after consulting with the various parties, presented a detailed peace plan based on Solarz's ideas. It addressed the contentious issues of an interim government for Cambodia, as well as how to guarantee free and fair elections. Under Evans's plan, a UN interim administration would be supplemented by a Supreme National Council (SNC) comprising representatives of all four Cambodian parties. The CGDK would vacate the Cambodian seat at the United Nations and be replaced by the SNC. The government in Phnom Penh would hand over its powers of government to the UN interim administration, placing the country under UN administration until elections were held. The proposal established the momentum for a stronger UN presence in the process while sidestepping the issue of Khmer Rouge involvement. It also became the basis for further consultations.

The UN Security Council agreed that a Supreme National Council consisting of representatives from the four Cambodian factions be established to serve as a national reconciliation council and the interim provisional government. At the third Jakarta Informal Meeting (JIM III), on February 26–28, 1990, the Cambodian factions agreed to an enhanced UN role in the process.

The Permanent Five met in Paris on March 12 and 13 to discuss further the modalities of a comprehensive political settlement. At an earlier meeting in New York, it was decided that the Cambodian question would best be resolved by a comprehensive political settlement that addressed both military and administrative aspects during a transitional period. The need for effective measures to guarantee human rights and fundamental freedoms was also stressed. The primary purpose for the United Nations was to ensure that free and fair elections were held under UN authority and in a neutral political environment. The elections would choose a constitutional assembly that would approve a new constitution and transform itself into a legislative assembly. The four Cambodian parties were invited to establish the SNC as the legitimate body and source of authority during the transition period. The parties themselves could decide its composition. The SNC would then delegate to a United Nations mission the necessary powers to conduct elections and to advise and consult on electoral organization.[27]

On April 9, 1990, in an effort to resume discussions, the Sihanouk plan was released. Prince Sihanouk proposed the establishment of an SNC consisting of six representatives from each of the two existing Cambodian governments: the CGDK and the SOC. The SNC chair would be elected by unanimous vote. The formation of this body implied that the SOC accepted the participation of the Khmer Rouge in the CGDK in return for Prince Sihanouk's retracting his demand for a quadripartite power-sharing arrangement. The Khmer Rouge objected to the proposal, however, because its power would be reduced and because the CPP administration would remain.[28]

In early June Japan hosted further negotiations among Cambodian parties except for the Khmer Rouge, which boycotted the meeting. At the meeting Sihanouk and Hun Sen signed a cease-fire and an agreement based on the Sihanouk plan. The participants also called for the reconvening of the Paris Conference, and the establishment of a Supreme Council. The agreement, however, was boycotted by the Khmer Rouge, which claimed the agreement was invalid because all three resistance groups had to be signatories. The CPP proposed that Prince Sihanouk become chair of the SNC, and Hun Sen vice chair, with no leadership role for the Khmer Rouge. There were to be twelve positions on the SNC, divided between the CPP and the CGDK, leaving the Khmer Rouge with only two seats. The arrangement was not confirmed because of Chinese and Khmer Rouge pressure on Prince Sihanouk to remain with the CGDK.

Sihanouk was elected president of the SNC in early July. And on July 18, 1990, the United States announced that it would no longer recognize the CGDK as the Cambodian representative at the United Nations or as Cambodia's legitimate representative. This change in policy allowed for a great deal of progress in the Permanent Five negotiations for a Cambodian settlement because it meant the United States now shared the view that a Cambodian settlement would involve the participation of the Khmer Rouge in the negotiations.[29]

After eight months of discussions, the five permanent members of the Security Council agreed on August 26, 1990, on a framework for a comprehensive settlement.[30] The framework had five parts:

- the creation of an SNC to represent Cambodia in the preelection period, with administrative authority and responsibility to organize free elections transferred to a United Nations Transitional Authority in Cambodia (UNTAC);
- the establishment of civilian and military components of UNTAC to supervise, monitor, and verify the cease-fire agreements, as well as to monitor the withdrawal of all foreign forces and the cessation of foreign aid to the factions;
- the organization and holding of free and fair elections by the United Nations to choose a parliament that would draw up a new constitution and appoint a new government;
- the protection of human rights in light of "Cambodia's tragic past" as the basis of the settlement of Cambodia; and
- the declaration of Cambodia as an internationally guaranteed neutral state.

The framework agreement appeared to have resolved the power-sharing dispute, "based on the contention that there could not be a settlement through the participation of all the factions without a change in the political status quo."[31] The Khmer Rouge was included to avoid the likelihood of the continuation of the civil war.

On September 9–10, 1990, the four Cambodian factions accepted the framework agreement reached by the Permanent Five as the basis for settling the Cambodian conflict. The CPP withdrew its objection to participation in a political settlement by the Khmer Rouge, which for its part was obliged to reconsider its previous opposition to a settlement given that its ally, China, and the other members of the Permanent Five had adopted the framework agreement. The SNC was formed, with the CGDK parties together getting six seats and the CPP getting six. All four Cambodian parties committed to accepting the entire peace plan as the basis for a Cambodian settlement.

On November 23–26 a meeting was held in Paris with Indonesia and France (the cochairs of the Paris Conference), the UN secretary-general, and the five permanent members of the Security Council to draw up a detailed draft comprehensive agreement.[32] The four Cambodian factions met again in Paris in December with France and Indonesia to consider the draft agreement.[33] Although the meeting ended inconclusively, it was recognized that before the Paris Peace Conference could reconvene all parties had to restrain themselves on the battlefield. On May 1, 1991, a voluntary cease-fire was agreed to by the Paris Conference cochairs and the UN secretary-general.

Another important breakthrough came June 24–26, 1991, in Pattaya, Thailand, when all the Cambodian factions agreed to Sihanouk and Hun Sen's joint proposal for a twelve-member SNC that would become fully operational in Phnom Penh, a continuation of the voluntary cease-fire, and arms transfer reductions. In the background of these and subsequent negotiations were the purge of the North Vietnamese foreign minister, Nguyen Co Thach, who was virulently anti-Chinese, and a deal between Beijing and Hanoi to normalize relations and to base the Cambodia settlement on the Permanent Five framework.

On September 30, 1991, the secretary-general released his report on Cambodia in which he outlined the purpose of the United Nations Advance Mission in Cambodia (UNAMIC). UNAMIC would exist until UNTAC could be established, approximately six months after the signing of the agreement, then it would be absorbed into UNTAC. UNAMIC would facilitate communication between the military factions of the Cambodian parties. UNAMIC would also train civilians on how to avoid injury from mines or booby traps; priority would be given to those areas covering repatriation routes, reception centers, and resettlement areas.[34] The Security Council gave its approval to UNAMIC's establishment and mandate less than a month later.

SNC agreement on the UN comprehensive settlement plan for Cambodia was finally reached on October 23, 1991. The terms of the Paris Peace Agreements were as follows:

- The United Nations would demobilize and disarm 70 percent of each of the four armies and supervise the activities of the remainder.
- The coalition government would return from exile to Phnom Penh.
- The Khmer Rouge would be given minor positions in the interim government.
- The Khmer Rouge army would be disbanded under strict supervision.
- A UN force would be deployed to supervise elections to a constituent assembly based on proportional representation.
- Cambodian refugees would be returned for elections.[35]

At the signing ceremony Secretary of State James Baker announced that the United States would lift its embargo against Cambodia once UNAMIC began to implement the peace settlement. He also proposed that all five permanent members of the Security Council maintain an active presence in Cambodia to ensure that the settlement was effectively implemented.[36]

On October 31 the UN Security Council approved Resolution 718 expressing the council's full support for the final settlement reached in Paris. In accordance with the terms of the settlement, the resolution called for the secretary-general to designate a special representative for Cambodia and to prepare a plan for implementing the mandate.[37] UNAMIC arrived in Cambodia on November 9 to draw up plans for implementation and to prepare for the deployment of UNTAC. Shortly thereafter Prince Sihanouk returned to Phnom Penh to establish the SNC's headquarters.[38]

The Settlement Package: Strengths, Weaknesses, and Ambiguities

The terms of trade in the peace agreement were based on national reconciliation, self-determination, human rights, and international recognition and guarantee of Cambodia's neutrality. These ideas found their concrete form in free and fair elections, the disarming of all Cambodian factions, the installation of a neutral transitional authority in Phnom Penh, the withdrawal of all foreign troops, and the cessation of foreign military assistance—all in a politically neutral environment. The elections for a new Cambodian government were to be organized by UNTAC. UNTAC was to take control of the administrative structures of the Cambodian government, thus denying any one political party the opportunity to gain an advantage over the others. UNTAC would also supervise, monitor, and verify the cease-fire and withdrawal provisions. UNTAC personnel were to register all Cambodians for the elections and to instruct them on voting procedures—including Cambodian refugees, who were to be repatriated from Thailand and Vietnam and resettled in Cambodia. To ensure that the transition was peaceful and that the returnees were not subject to intimidation, the four Cambodian army factions were to gather in cantonments, demobilize, and disarm. This process would also make available much-needed land for resettlement while the mine-clearing program continued. The elected constitutional assembly would be responsible for a new Cambodian constitution; the assembly then would transform itself into a legislative assembly. In the interim, the SNC would represent Cambodia.

In general, the terms of trade do not appear to have been so broad that the primary basis for conflict was over their implementation. No one party had a dominant or more advantageous position, although UNTAC itself was accused by the Khmer Rouge of working to support the CPP. However, ambiguity surrounding the provision for verification of foreign troops in Cambodia did pose implementation problems. The Khmer Rouge insisted that Vietnamese troops had remained in Cambodia. As we will see, three Vietnamese personnel were in fact discovered upon investigation by UNTAC. However, in its correspondence with the Security Council, the Vietnamese government argued that under the definition of foreign troops outlined by the secretary-general's special representative to UNTAC, the personnel identified did not qualify as foreign troops. Notwithstanding, in an effort to allay any fears that foreign troops were deployed in Cambodia, UNTAC increased the number of checkpoints on the Vietnam-Cambodia border.

Inevitably, however, a number of unanticipated issues arose during the implementation process and had to be dealt with by UNTAC authorities. Though they did not scuttle the peace-building process, these issues did pose major obstacles to the implementation of key provisions of the Paris accords. Among the more serious problems faced during implementation were the following:

- the presence of a large number of Vietnamese immigrants who had entered Cambodia in the expectation of its economic renewal;
- the urgent need for the mine-clearing process to begin under UNAMIC before the deployment of UNTAC, so as to facilitate the repatriation of refugees to areas free from danger;
- the difficulties of repatriating refugees who had become "urbanized" by living in refugee camps for years and who, in any case, did not want to go back to the land;
- the urgent need for infrastructural improvements to support the cantonment, disarmament, and demobilization provisions of the Paris accords;
- the need for presidential elections to provide some measure of stability in a postsettlement Cambodia in light of the failure of the military component of UNTAC to guarantee stability (it was expected that Prince Sihanouk would run for the presidency and would provide this stability, given his popularity among Cambodians);

- the lack of adequate financial support and commitment for implementation; and
- the failure of the UN civilian administration component to adequately supervise (or even understand) SOC power structures—a failure that undermined UN credibility while strengthening some of the Cambodian factions, including the Khmer Rouge.

The last item was potentially the most serious and was handled on a largely ad hoc basis. A meeting to organize financial questions was held in Tokyo in June 1992, more than six months after UNAMIC had been deployed and three months after UNTAC had begun deployment. By October 1992 governments and financial institutions were asked to make their contributions as announced in June. In April 1992 the UN secretary-general had appealed to the international community for $593 million for Cambodia's rehabilitation.

Except for the shortcomings just outlined, the terms of the Paris accords dealt with most of the issues of the Cambodian conflict. The Khmer Rouge was prevented from returning to power, none of the Cambodian factions was placed at an advantage, foreign troops were withdrawn and their withdrawal was verified, and foreign assistance ceased. However, the failure of the Khmer Rouge to comply with its obligations under the terms of the agreement threatened the peace process right up to the elections.

The Role of Ripeness

The defection of the Khmer Rouge from the peace process raises the question of whether the conflict in Cambodia was indeed ripe for resolution at the time the peace accords were negotiated and signed, and whether the situation on the ground did in fact meet the conditions of a hurting stalemate.

A hurting stalemate did exist in the sense that the Cambodian parties found themselves without the foreign support on which their campaigns depended. The withdrawal of Vietnamese troops, begun in 1985 and completed by 1989, left the PRK without its strongest military supporter. China, the Soviet Union, and the United States had reached agreement in August 1990 on a framework for a settlement in Cambodia that included the cessation of foreign military assistance to the Cambodian parties. The four Cambodian parties had no alternative, therefore, but to agree to the terms of the framework. China and the Soviet Union, as part of their policy of rapprochement, had agreed to end military assistance to their proxies, the Khmer Rouge and the PRK, respectively. The United States in July 1990 withdrew its support of the CGDK. The external parties had a strong interest in moving their relationship to a more cooperative footing.

At the same time, the Cambodian parties also experienced their own sense of war weariness. The Khmer Rouge was unable to establish permanent control over any territory or win the support of the people. In particular, the refugees at the camps it controlled were slowly deserting, to the point where the Khmer Rouge prevented them from leaving. Reports circulated that the Khmer Rouge camps were controlled by the same brutal means as those the Khmer Rouge regime had employed. Overall, the membership of the Khmer Rouge was decreasing as recruitment fell and desertion rose. This resulted in a decline in morale and an unwillingness to continue fighting.

However, whether this war weariness and hurting stalemate were sufficiently durable to lay the foundations for a permanent settlement of the conflict is another matter. First among the factors to consider is that the relationship among the parties was militarily and politically asymmetrical, and this created its own set of tensions. The Khmer Rouge and the CPP, on the one hand, were militarily dominant. This strength is documented in reports indicating that despite the cessation of foreign military aid to the Cambodian factions, the Khmer Rouge had enough armaments to last for two years. However, this military strength did not provide these parties with political strength or legitimacy. FUNCINPEC, the KPNLF, and Prince Sihanouk, on the other hand, were more dominant politically and enjoyed greater levels of public support, but they lacked strong military capabilities and thus had to resort to moral and political suasion to back their demands. Asymmetries in political legitimacy and military capabilities, though canceling each other out in the short term, created long-term problems once the parties began to reassess their interests in the period following the Paris Agreements.

Second, each party's motivations for agreeing to sign the peace accords when it did were also driven by the prospect of short-term political gains rather than a desire to achieve a comprehensive or lasting political settlement. Some of the parties seem to have been most intent on using the accords to stall for time until they could strengthen their positions politically and militarily. This attitude was particularly pronounced in the case of the Khmer Rouge, which not only refused to cooperate with UNTAC in implementing the provisions regarding cantonment, disarmament, and demobilization, but also repeatedly violated the cease-fire. The Khmer Rouge refused to participate in the elections as well. The Khmer Rouge's unhappiness with the peace process was inspired in part by the fact that the CPP still held de facto power until the elections, even though UNTAC had supposedly assumed responsibility for the country's civil administration.

Having been abandoned by its external supporters (Vietnam and the Soviet Union), the CPP agreed to the peace accords to avoid being isolated from the process and to make certain that the terms would prevent the return of the Khmer Rouge to power. At the same time, the CPP had improved its military position by June 1991, following several successful advances, and was in a position to negotiate a final agreement and participate in the political process. The motivations of the other two parties, FUNCINPEC and the KPNLF, were to ensure their participation in the settlement process and to prevent a return to power of the Khmer Rouge.

Once it became evident to the Khmer Rouge and the CPP that they could not win the elections scheduled for May 1993, they reassessed the utility of using force to achieve an outcome favorable to themselves. As a result, the CPP began a program of intimidation against members of opposition parties. For its part, the Khmer Rouge refused to cooperate with UNTAC in preparing those areas under Khmer Rouge control for elections and cantonment.

The cost-benefit perceptions of the Khmer Rouge regarding cooperation as opposed to armed confrontation may have been fundamentally altered during the implementation phase of the peace process once it realized that it was not going to win the elections. Having nothing to lose, the Khmer Rouge was in a position to secure whatever control it had and to undermine the settlement process itself. In fact, the Khmer Rouge could gain *only* during the negotiations leading up to the settlement, when it was included in the process. That stage having been completed, the Khmer Rouge could no longer benefit from the outcome of the peace settlement.

Third, the delicate political equilibrium that existed at the time the peace accords were signed was upset by the high levels of mistrust among the parties. The failure of the parties to strengthen their political relationship and move it to a sounder footing based on trust thwarted subsequent efforts to institutionalize the peace process and achieve the modicum of harmony that would ease the difficult transition to democracy. At the time of the Paris Conference, the parties apparently worked together only for reasons of expediency, fearing exclusion from the final settlement. A high degree of mistrust prevailed throughout the negotiation and implementation process. During the negotiations it became clear that none of the parties was willing to allow the others to dominate in an interim government and thus be in a position to influence the outcome of the elections. The CGDK refused to consider a national reconciliation council to organize elections while the CPP remained as the government of Cambodia. Furthermore, Prince Sihanouk threatened to leave the CGDK in protest at Khmer Rouge military action against the other factions of the CGDK. In particular, the CPP initially rejected any proposal that involved the Khmer Rouge and had repeatedly linked Vietnamese troop withdrawal to the withdrawal of the Khmer Rouge from the settlement process. Khmer Rouge proposals to form a four-party Cambodian army were rejected because such an arrangement would have tied up the arms and personnel of the other factions while leaving the militarily stronger Khmer Rouge with extra personnel with whom to continue hostilities and make the bid for power that the other factions feared.

Third Parties and the Implementation of the Peace Settlement

Because the relationship among the Cambodian factions was so volatile at the time of the signing of the Paris Peace Agreements, the United Nations—as a body through which a neutral political environment in Cambodia could be established and free and fair elections conducted—was to play a critical role in implementing the settlement. To facilitate the implementation of the agreements, the United Nations, through UNAMIC and UNTAC, performed functions such as fact finding, mediation, verification, monitoring, humanitarian assistance, refugee relocation and assistance, electoral preparation, electoral supervision and monitoring, civil administration, rehabilitation, engineering and infrastructure reconstruction, cantonment, disarmament, and demobilization.

The implementation phase of the peacemaking process began immediately after the Paris Peace Agreements were signed on October 23, 1991. As recommended by a UN fact-finding mission, the Security Council passed Resolution 717 on October 16, 1991, for the establishment of UNAMIC to prepare Cambodia and the four Cambodian parties for the deployment of UNTAC. UNAMIC's physical presence in Cambodia began on November 9, 1991. UNTAC's deployment was scheduled to begin six

months after the deployment of UNAMIC. Seven components of UNTAC
were to be deployed: human rights, electoral, military, civil administration,
police, repatriation, and rehabilitation. The Security Council passed Resolution 745 establishing UNTAC on February 28, 1992. The council also
decided that Cambodian elections should be held no later than May
1993. The resolution urged the Cambodian parties to demobilize and disarm completely before the end of the registration process, in accordance
with the Paris Peace Agreements. All parties were urged to comply with
their obligations to the Paris Peace Agreements and to take necessary
measures to ensure the safety and security of UN personnel. The initial
deployment began March 15, 1992, with the arrival in Phnom Penh of the
secretary-general's special representative to UNTAC, Yasushi Akashi.[39]

UNTAC human rights officers, responsible for investigating cases of
harassment and intimidation, were deployed in fifteen of twenty-one
provinces; the remaining six were under the control of the Khmer Rouge,
which denied access to UNTAC. In spite of the uncooperative stance of
the Khmer Rouge, the SNC signed instruments of accession to the International Covenant on Civil and Political Rights and the International
Covenant on Economic, Social, and Cultural Rights.

The deployment of the military component of UNTAC proceeded very
slowly. By April 20, 1992, only 3,500 of an expected 16,000 UNTAC military personnel were deployed. By June 12, the day before the cantonment process of approximately 200,000 Cambodian fighters was to begin
under the supervision of the military component of UNTAC, only 10,000
of 16,000 military personnel were deployed. By July 14 the UNTAC military component was almost completely deployed, with 14,300 troops in
the field. In total, UNTAC consisted of 15,738 military personnel, 3,224
civilian police officers, 927 administrative personnel, and 426 volunteers.
UNTAC's civil administration component took over those governmental
bodies or agencies perceived to be vulnerable to outside manipulation
and therefore able to influence the election process. These bodies were
foreign affairs, national defense, finance, information, and public security.

UNTAC's first task was to establish, in consultation with the SNC, electoral laws and regulations to govern the electoral process. Voter registration was to begin in October 1992 and last for three months. The military
component would carry out its verification responsibilities at points on
the Cambodian border where foreign troops would be likely to enter:
seven units on the border shared with Thailand, nine units on the border
with Vietnam, two units on the border with Laos, one unit at each of the

ports of Kompong Som and Phnom Penh, and one unit at each of the airports in Phnom Penh, Battambang, Siem Reap, and Stung Treng. Verification would also be supplemented by mobile teams. In accordance with the Paris Peace Agreements, the armed forces of all four Cambodian parties would provide information on the size and locations of their respective forces. Because of the large size of the Cambodian forces (more than 200,000 in total), the UNTAC military component would have to be massively deployed for an extended period of time. The infrastructure would have to be quickly improved to support the cantonment and demobilization provisions.

The UN High Commission for Refugees (UNHCR) determined that there were more than 360,000 potential returnees, of whom more than two-thirds were living in refugee camps along the Thai border and had been doing so for longer than ten years. Repatriation was to occur over a nine-month period.[40] Again, this timetable proved to be overly optimistic, partly because mine-clearing operations necessary to clear land for repatriated settlers took longer than anticipated. Many refugees also did not want to go back to the land and went to urban areas instead.

By the end of March, repatriation of Cambodian refugees and displaced persons had begun. UNTAC, however, was having problems with the Khmer Rouge, which was failing to live up to its commitments in the Paris Peace Agreements. Although Vietnam confirmed that it no longer had troops in Cambodia, the Khmer Rouge charged that foreign troops were still in the country, and used this an excuse for noncompliance with the Paris accords. When UNTAC decided to look into these allegations, the Khmer Rouge failed to provide the personnel UNTAC had requested to help it carry out its investigations.[41]

The secretary-general released a special report on UNTAC on June 12, 1992, in which he indicated that the Khmer Rouge was neither cooperating nor honoring the assurances it had given to the commander of the military component of UNTAC.[42] The secretary-general noted that the Khmer Rouge had not complied with the provisions because of the alleged presence of foreign military personnel. Until the withdrawal and non-return of such personnel had been verified by UNTAC, the Khmer Rouge maintained that its own security required that it defer fulfillment of its obligations. UNTAC, however, had already taken action to ally any fears, such as establishing an added checkpoint at the border between Cambodia and Vietnam and allowing all four parties to send representatives to the border checkpoints. But these measures were clearly insufficient

from the point of view of the Khmer Rouge. The implementation of the
Paris Agreements was at a critical stage. The secretary-general's report
underlined the importance of Phase II for success in the provisions
regarding repatriation and constitutional elections. Given that only 10,000
UN personnel had been deployed in Cambodia, it was unlikely that the
balance of UNTAC's military component would be deployed in time to
meet the June 13 deadline. Regardless, the secretary-general decided that
Phase II should begin on June 13, 1992, otherwise the momentum of the
process might be lost and UNTAC's ability to conduct elections jeopardized. The other three groups were consulted to ensure that their cantonment, disarmament, and demobilization would be conducted in such
a way that any military disadvantage they might suffer because of the
noncompliance of the Khmer Rouge would be minimized.

The United Nations had set June 13 for Cambodia's various armed factions to begin implementing Phase II of the peace settlement by assem-
bling in cantons and preparing for disarmament. The Khmer Rouge
chose to simply ignore the date, charging that because the settlement
provisions on verification of withdrawal and the role of the SNC had not
been implemented, it was not obligated to proceed with Phase II until its
concerns had been addressed. Other factions were also reluctant to disarm if the Khmer Rouge did not. Fighting resumed between the Khmer
Rouge and the Hun Sen government forces three days later.[43]

The regroupment and cantonment process was to have ended by
July 11. However, because UNTAC had to maintain a military balance
among the four parties, progress was slow and only 5 percent of an estimated 200,000 military personnel were cantonized by that date. In deliv-
ering his second special report on UNTAC, the secretary-general con-
veyed both good news and bad news. He noted that the Khmer Rouge
was standing behind its claim that the withdrawal of foreign troops and
the provisions relating to the role and power of the SNC had not been
implemented. He pointed out that UNTAC was doing what it could to
implement quickly and fully the provisions on verification of foreign
troops. It was also giving top priority to recruiting and training civilian
administrative personnel to direct the five agencies as stipulated in the
Paris Peace Agreements. The report stated that the CPP's administrative
structures could not be dissolved as requested by the Khmer Rouge
because this would be contrary to the terms of the Paris Agreements,
which stipulated that UNTAC was to exercise control through existing
administrative structures. The secretary-general also noted that the

military component of UNTAC was now almost completely deployed, with 14,300 troops in the field along with approximately 1,780 police monitors. Some 50,000 Cambodian refugees had been repatriated.[44]

By the end of August more than 100,000 Cambodian refugees and displaced persons had been repatriated—an indication that this aspect of UN operations was proceeding well. The same was not true of the cantonment process. Clearly, Khmer Rouge fighters were strengthening their control over pockets of territory previously controlled by other factions, and as of September 10 only 52,292 of the estimated 200,000 troops were cantonized. Some 50,000 weapons had also been retrieved by the military component of UNTAC.[45]

In October Japan and Thailand held unsuccessful consultations with the Khmer Rouge on solutions to problems relating to the implementation of the Paris Peace Agreements; they determined that tripartite consultations were not appropriate and that a larger meeting should be held instead. However, the domestic political situation continued to deteriorate. Artillery fire was exchanged by Khmer Rouge and CPP forces in central and northern parts of Cambodia. Attacks on UNTAC personnel located in Khmer Rouge–controlled areas of Cambodia also increased.

In response to the deteriorating situation, a meeting was held in Beijing on November 7 and 8 between representatives of France, Indonesia, Prince Sihanouk, the SNC, the Permanent Five of the Security Council, Australia, Germany, Japan, Thailand, and the United Nations. The Khmer Rouge was again criticized for not cooperating with the implementation of the Paris Agreements. The representatives of the Khmer Rouge stated that it intended not to participate in the elections because of the absence of a neutral political environment. The Paris Conference cochairs, France and Indonesia, replied that no party could withdraw from its obligations on the pretext of a complaint regarding the implementation of the Paris accords. It was decided at the meeting that, with the suspension of the demobilization, disarmament, and cantonment provisions of Phase II, the activities of the military component needed to be adjusted. A decision was also made to hold a presidential election at the same time as the national elections for Cambodia, in the hope that Sihanouk, as a symbol of Cambodian nationhood, would be the likely winner, thereby forcing the Khmer Rouge to comply with the peace settlement.[46]

With the end of the rainy season, violations of the cease-fire by the armed forces of the CPP and the Khmer Rouge increased. Attacks on UNTAC personnel also increased. Although 200 members of the Khmer

Rouge armed forces spontaneously presented themselves to UNTAC, the Khmer Rouge leadership continued to refuse to participate in the peace process. The UN deadline for the Khmer Rouge to disarm and agree to take part in national elections was also ignored. The United Nations ultimately suspended Phase II of the implementation program, leaving almost half a million Cambodians still armed.[47] Many concluded that elections would be held in an environment that was politically partial and intimidating.

But other aspects of the peace process remained on track. By the end of December, some twenty political parties had registered and some 4.2 million voters had been registered for the upcoming May elections. The deadline for voter registration was extended to January 31, 1993, to allow returning refugees to register, even though approximately 100,000 refugees remained in transit camps. UNTAC was also expanding human rights education and training programs and promoting the development of an independent judiciary.

The military component of UNTAC was redeployed to assist with weapons control, repatriation, engineering, mine clearing, logistics, communications, patrolling, observation, and confidence building. Its priority was to protect voter registration and the electoral process. The checkpoints initially established to monitor the withdrawal of foreign forces were given the added responsibility of regulating the petroleum supply and the moratoriums on log exports. As part of its civil administration role, UNTAC drafted guidelines for the operation of a free and responsible press. Quick-impact projects were also proceeding under UNDP management, key areas of activity being infrastructure, health, water, agriculture, and education.[48]

On January 28, 1993, the SNC met in Beijing. At this meeting the Cambodian parties agreed to the Security Council proposal for presidential elections to be held at the same time as the national elections. The SNC also agreed to hold elections in May. Ignoring the protests of the Khmer Rouge representatives, Prince Sihanouk issued a declaration calling for self-restraint by all Cambodian parties.[49]

As the deadline for voter registration approached, the cease-fire was violated on numerous occasions. Hostile intimidation by CPP and Khmer Rouge guerrillas also threatened efforts to register approximately 40,000 eligible voters at border camps. Many Vietnamese settlers, immigrating to Cambodia to take advantage of improving conditions, were being killed by the Khmer Rouge, which continued to see them as economic and social threats to Cambodia. Secretary-General Boutros Boutros-Ghali warned that UN troops might remain in Cambodia following the elections in light of the continued fighting among Cambodian guerrillas. There were also reports that the CPP, which expected to lose the May elections, was killing members of FUNCINPEC, which was expected to win.[50]

The Khmer Rouge was escalating its campaign of violence. On March 9, 1993, Khmer Rouge fighters entered a floating village populated by Vietnamese settlers and killed thirty-eight people. The same month, the Khmer Rouge killed three Bulgarian peacekeepers.[51] On April 8, just after the election campaign was officially under way, a Japanese UN volunteer was killed in Kompong Thom.[52] Although initial reports suggested that the Khmer Rouge was responsible for the killing, a formal investigation revealed that he was probably killed by a disgruntled SOC soldier who had not been hired as a polling official.

Suggestions that the May elections be postponed, however, were rejected, as the credibility of the United Nations and UNTAC was at stake.[53] But the United Nations was clearly experiencing serious difficulties. By the end of April, 19 out of 420 volunteer electoral officers had resigned. Boutros-Ghali noted that the process in Cambodia was not going as well as originally hoped.[54]

Nevertheless, from May 23 to May 28, UNTAC held national elections for Cambodia. Much to everyone's surprise, almost 90 percent of the 4.7 million eligible Cambodians voted in the elections.[55] UNTAC reported that the elections were free and fair, prompting Yasushi Akashi to proclaim them a success.[56] Despite the Khmer Rouge boycott of the elections, some Khmer Rouge fighters did vote.[57] Although a number of polling stations were attacked and forced to close, for the most part the elections were carried out in an atmosphere remarkably free of violence.

As expected, on June 1 FUNCINPEC was announced the winner of the national elections. In accordance with the Paris Peace Agreements, its leader, Norodom Ranariddh, commenced efforts to form a coalition government.

On June 3, Prince Sihanouk attempted to form a new government and assume full executive powers. His action, which departed from the terms of the Paris Peace Agreements, did not receive support from the United States, China, Britain, Australia, UNTAC, and FUNCINPEC. Sihanouk's bid failed. Ten days later, Norodom Ranariddh rejected the CPP declaration that seven Cambodian provinces under its military control were autonomous. Many feared that civil war would break out once again. But on June 16 Norodom Ranariddh formed a coalition government with his party, FUNCINPEC, and the ruling CPP. Thus began the difficult road to democratic governance and Cambodian self-rule.

Assessment and Conclusions

The Cambodian peacemaking and peace-building process was a success in the sense that a transitional authority was installed in Phnom Penh, foreign troops were withdrawn, refugees were repatriated, and a relatively neutral environment was created to allow for free and fair elections. However, elements of failure were also present because all of the parties were not disarmed and the fighting did not cease.

Part of the reason the fighting did not stop is that the conflict was only partially ripe for resolution, as the Khmer Rouge continued to believe it could pursue its objectives through the use of force. The Khmer Rouge opted out of the political settlement process once it concluded that the elections would lead to a result inimical to its interests. However, the Khmer Rouge was not strong enough to prevent elections from taking place. Thus, in a curious way, there was enough ripeness to pursue a negotiated option and a political settlement, but not enough to end violence and ensure that all the provisions of the peace settlement plan were fully implemented.

The rather delicate military and political equilibrium at the time of the Paris accords was also influenced by the actions of neighboring regional powers and interests. Chinese involvement was crucial to both the agreement and implementation phases of the peace settlement process. Chinese support for the Khmer Rouge, along with that of the Thai government, prevented the peace process from advancing in the early stages of negotiations. But as Chinese and Thai fears of Vietnamese dominance in Indochina diminished and their support for the peace process grew, the possibility of achieving a durable peace settlement increased. Had there been greater pressure on these two countries to withdraw their support from the Khmer Rouge earlier, the peace process might have moved forward more quickly than it did. At the same time, we should not overestimate the Khmer Rouge's dependence on its allies; it had access to independent sources of arms and finance through its secret trade in timber, gems, and arms with the Thai military.

The preceding narrative and analysis make clear, however, that the ripe moment did not spring up of its own accord. It had to be cultivated by a variety of third parties, all of which showed determination, perseverance, and staying power in face of the formidable obstacles to a peace settlement and its implementation. The fact that many third parties were involved allowed the costs and risks of mediation and implementation to be widely shared. At the same time, the availability of different third-party mediators lent momentum to the peace process, particularly in the negotiation phase, because new parties could take over from previous intermediaries who had had limited success.

During the implementation phase of the peace settlement, there were many occasions when the process could have been derailed by the actions of the Khmer Rouge and the high degree of mistrust that characterized relations among all the Cambodian factions. UNTAC's ability to address successfully a number of major unanticipated issues that emerged during implementation—such as the problems of Vietnamese immigrants and the urgent need for mine clearing—contributed to peace building. Other contributions were made by the UN volunteers engaged in electoral preparation, voter registration, and electoral supervision and monitoring, who carried out their duties with professionalism.

The various roles undertaken by the United Nations were performed with widely varying degrees of success. The military component came close to being a complete failure. Although three of the four parties cooperated with UNTAC in beginning the cantonment and disarmament process, the Khmer Rouge refused to cooperate, and therefore only 5 percent of the approximately 200,000 troops were cantonized. Indeed, just prior to the May 1993 elections the Khmer Rouge's military strength was reported to have increased by some 50 percent. How this strength was measured is not known, although it may have been based on territorial control.

The eventual suspension of the provision regarding disarmament and cantonment resulted in a redeployment of UNTAC forces to protect the voter registration activities; this action would have been unnecessary had the cantonment proceeded as planned. Moreover, repeated attempts to bring the Khmer Rouge into the peace process failed. But one success in this area is that the other three Cambodian factions did provide UNTAC with the necessary information on the size and location of their forces in preparation for the cantonment process. The UN military may have also had some beneficial effect when, following redeployments in March 1993, they were willing to show more force in each district. This action may have deterred the Khmer Rouge from launching attacks during the elections.

The UN civil police component was also a failure. One of its main tasks was to investigate human rights abuses and then either charge the violators itself or persuade the local police to lay charges. But this task was performed poorly overall and in some regions of the country not at all.

The civil administration component met with mixed results because UNTAC's control over five governmental bodies was hampered by the deficiencies of those structures. The public security of Cambodia deteriorated, with politicians of opposing parties (particularly FUNCINPEC) suffering many attacks. Indeed, the existing administrative structures were accused of not providing adequate protection to some political parties, as required. Because the police and SOC soldiers were not under UNTAC's control, banditry, corruption, and political intimidation continued. At the same time, Vietnamese settlers were often the objects of military attacks initiated by the Khmer Rouge. UNTAC personnel and volunteers also became targets of military attacks. This lack of security failed to create a completely free and neutral environment. Moreover, UNTAC did not assume control of the administrative structures in areas controlled by the Khmer Rouge because UNTAC did not have access to those locations. Legal reform met with limited success, also because UNTAC was denied access to areas controlled by the Khmer Rouge.

The electoral component of the peace settlement process was, however, very successful; UNTAC registered 4.2 million voters and oversaw the adoption of an electoral law. Although the election campaign was conducted in an atmosphere of extremely fragile neutrality, in general it was a success in that all parties were given the opportunity for free expression and the electorate was not subjected to serious forms of intimidation. The elections were held on time despite concern that they would be delayed by repeated violations of the cease-fire. Almost 90 percent of eligible voters participated in the elections. The registration of political parties was a qualified success, marred only by the refusal of the Khmer Rouge to register its political party, the National Unity of Cambodia Party. As a result, one of the four Cambodian signatories to the Paris accords did not appear on the ballot. At the same time, because UNTAC was denied access to register voters in those locations controlled by the Khmer Rouge, the elections were not completely successful. The fact that UNTAC performed the electoral component of its job so well helped to strengthen the commitment of key factions in Cambodia to a political settlement and free elections.

UNHCR was largely responsible for the repatriation component, which succeeded to the extent that only 40,000 eligible voters remained in the refugee camps when registration ended. Almost 220,000 refugees were repatriated—no mean feat given the formidable obstacles that stood in the way of repatriation. However, there were difficulties in locating land and homes for the returnees because the mine-awareness and mine-clearance program was less successful. The program took longer than expected because not all the Cambodian parties cooperated in marking mines. As a result, many returnees became displaced persons within Cambodia. It was expected that the repatriation program would occur over a nine-month period; instead, it took more than ten months.

The rehabilitation component was relatively successful in attempting to establish a basic level of infrastructure, water provision, health, agriculture, and education. Two rehabilitation programs under the auspices of the United Nations Children's Fund (UNICEF) and the Asian Development Bank targeted drinking water, schools, support for women and children, transportation projects, power projects, agricultural programs, and education programs.

Monitoring of the cease-fire proved futile beyond noting when the cease-fire was violated by the various factions. The two parties responsible for violations were the Khmer Rouge and the CPP. The CPP claimed it was using military force to prevent the Khmer Rouge from consolidating its territorial victories, although the escalatory nature of CPP retaliations indicated that it was acting not in self-defense but for its own military gains. The mandate of UNTAC did not allow any punitive actions in response to violations. UNTAC action to restrict petroleum in areas controlled by the Khmer Rouge and to restrict gem and timber exports, the major source of funding for the Khmer Rouge, was not taken until late November 1992, almost a year after the first cease-fire violations. The failure of UNTAC to maintain the cease-fire did not enhance its credibility with the Cambodian people. UNTAC military personnel were also reported to be participating in corrupt behavior. UNTAC's weakness was exploited by the different factions struggling for control in Cambodia. In particular, the CPP attempted to undermine UNTAC in order to win more votes by showing that only it, the CPP, could provide peace and stability to the Cambodian people and protect them from the Khmer Rouge.

Financial constraints on the United Nations and UNTAC affected the degree of success of the implementation process. Given that UNTAC's mission was known in advance to be comprehensive and the most expensive UN operation to date, the inability or unwillingness of the international community to finance the operation as required was regrettable. The slow deployment of the military component of UNTAC was ultimately affected. Had it occurred more quickly, this deployment might have impressed upon the Cambodian factions that UNTAC could not be undermined. A stronger showing of financial disbursements would have strengthened the infrastructure and the rehabilitation elements of the settlement earlier, thus eliminating the isolation of Khmer Rouge–controlled areas. At the same time, UNTAC's determination to proceed with the implementation of the settlement regardless of such financial obstacles provided some measure of stability to a country that had been riven by conflict for almost two decades.

Unfortunately, it was the military side of the peace-building process that suffered most. As noted, UNTAC's cantonment and disarmament functions were hampered by the Khmer Rouge, as well as by poor planning and a lack of funds. UNTAC could have done a better job of supervising and monitoring the cease-fire had the resources been available. Nevertheless, UNTAC succeeded in spite of these limitations, largely because the electoral and other components of the peace plan were so well executed and because the United Nations refused to listen to pleas that it withdraw or that it postpone elections.

This chapter concludes the case studies in this volume. In the next and final chapter we look to the broader lessons about third-party involvement, not only in the negotiation and mediation of regional and civil conflicts but also in the implementation of peace settlements once they have been concluded.

THE NEED TO NURTURE PEACE

The failings of humanitarian interventions and various international mediation efforts in Rwanda, Somalia, and until quite recently Bosnia-Hercegovina have tarnished the reputation of the United Nations and jeopardized public support for peacekeeping and third-party involvement in the settlement of intrastate disputes. If there is "new" conventional wisdom in some circles, it is that outside third parties have little to contribute to the peaceful settlement and resolution of such disputes, and that intervention is desirable only when a conflict has reached a "hurting stalemate" and the parties themselves are sufficiently wearied by war to begin a search for alternatives to the use of force.[1]

Consider the following admonition by *New York Times* columnist Thomas L. Friedman: "There is no such thing as a peacekeeper or neutral force in an ethnic conflict. The very meaning of an ethnic conflict is that a society has been torn asunder, every community has grabbed a slice and there is no neutral ground left." Friedman says that "to try to extinguish one of these ethnic conflicts when it is raging at full force is futile. . . . No amount of rational argument can tone it down, and if you try to smother it with your own body, or army, it will burn a hole right through you."[2]

The same pessimistic outlook is echoed by historian and foreign policy analyst Benjamin Schwarz in the *Atlantic*. "Stability within divided societies is normally based on some form of domination," Schwarz writes, "and once internal differences become violent, usually only the logic of force can lay them to rest." He believes that the United States really has only two options in dealing with ethnic, nationalist, and separatist conflicts: "Adopting a passive role once violence has erupted in a failed state, Washington can await the time when mutual exhaustion or the triumph of one group over another will create an opening for intervention in a purely peacekeeping capacity. Alternatively, the United States can effectively intervene, not only by building civil societies or pacifying such conflicts but by helping one side impose its will on the other, as Turkey did in Cyprus."[3]

This refrain, which has become all too familiar, construes too narrowly the options and potential role of outside third parties in the peaceful settlement of civil disputes. There are other options beyond "doing nothing," or the other extreme, intervening with large-scale military force. Not all civil conflicts necessarily have to end with the victor and the vanquished. It is possible to construct power-sharing arrangements between dissatisfied minorities and intransigent majorities through third-party–assisted negotiations. By sustaining a process of mediation, negotiation, and assistance with the subsequent implementation of the peace settlement, third parties can help to bring an end to military conflict and lay the basis for a durable settlement that advances the process of national reconciliation in divided societies.

One of the main lessons that emerges from the cases in this book is that you cannot have successful peacekeeping without a successful peace process. Peacekeeping and peace-building activities cannot exist in a vacuum; they are adjuncts to a process of negotiation during which the parties to the conflict come to redefine their interests and develop a real commitment to a political settlement. The fact that the most successful settlements examined here were the result of a prolonged process of negotiation, of trial-and-error learning, is no accident. Third-party–assisted negotiations played a critical role in helping the parties realize that there were options other than a continued campaign of military violence and bitter civil conflict. Although the wars in question went on for a long time, the cases illustrate that it is better to take the time to get the details of a settlement right than to initiate a peace process that is flawed and polarizes the conflict even further, making it harder to bring the parties back to the negotiating table later.

Another major lesson is that it takes strong support and unified political direction from outside actors to help the parties realize their desire for peace. Third parties can play a critical role in nurturing the conditions that lead to a negotiated settlement, as well as in advancing the peace process once a settlement has been reached so that it can take root. In the five cases of negotiated peace settlements examined in this volume, outside third parties played crucial, though varying roles in bringing about a negotiated end to violent civil conflict and the subsequent implementation of the settlement. In some instances, the third party was confined to a limited, intermediary role during the negotiation phase of the peace settlement. In others, third-party involvement was far more extensive and involved not only the mediation of a negotiated agreement between warring parties, but also assistance with a wide range of functions during the implementation phase of the settlement. These went well beyond peacekeeping to include verification of and assistance with the demobilization of forces, refugee assistance, electoral monitoring and observation, promotion of human rights, and assistance with political, social, and economic reforms. Where there was unified and sustained third-party involvement in both the negotiation and implementation of the agreement, settlements were more durable than in those cases where settlements were orphaned and third-party intervention was sporadic or limited to a few poorly defined roles.

In the context of this study, the durability or success of the peace process is defined in terms of (1) whether violence came to an end, and (2) the extent to which the parties fulfilled the specific commitments and obligations they agreed to under the terms of the settlement. By these standards, no settlement was a complete success, but some were clearly more successful than others. At one end of the spectrum are the most successful peace settlements, those that were negotiated to end the conflicts in El Salvador and Namibia. In both countries, the fighting came to an end, demobilization of forces was complete, and key provisions of the accords providing for a restructuring of the armed forces and police, and the holding of free and fair elections, were implemented. Implementation of the Paris Peace Agreements to end the conflict in Cambodia was less successful by these standards. Although free and fair elections were held to elect a new government for the country, demobilization was only partial, fighting continued, and the Khmer Rouge, one of the key factions in the conflict, opted out of the peace process and reneged on its negotiated commitments, even though it could not stop the process.

In contrast, the settlements that were negotiated to end civil conflicts in Angola and Cyprus were almost complete failures. The MPLA government and opposition forces of UNITA[4] failed to abide by the provisions of the Gbadolite and Bicesse Accords in Angola, and the brutal civil war continued for several more years. In Cyprus, the London-Zurich Accords and the constitutional settlement of 1960 proved to be unimplementable because the power-sharing elements of the accords violated the principles of majoritarian rule favored by the Greek Cypriot leadership. As intercommunal tensions mounted, conflict broke out, leading to the de facto partition of the island between Greek and Turkish Cypriots and the permanent deployment of UN peacekeeping forces between the two sides. In spite of continual international efforts to mediate an end to the dispute, a lasting political settlement remains elusive.

The two most successful cases—Namibia and El Salvador—witnessed extensive third-party involvement and support not just in the negotiation of the peace accords but also during their implementation. Various third parties, including the United Nations, were called upon to perform a wide range of functions, including peacekeeping; assistance with demobilization of forces, civil administration, and political and judicial reform; electoral monitoring and observation; human rights verification and monitoring; and the provision of mediation services on issues where there continued to be major disagreements between the parties. Implementation of the Paris Peace Agreements in Cambodia was also undertaken with extensive third-party support and involvement, again with the United Nations playing a key role. However, in this case the United Nations was unable successfully to carry out the peacekeeping elements of its mandate; its rapid withdrawal from Cambodia following the elections left the young government to deal with the Khmer Rouge insurgency on its own.

Third-party involvement in the negotiation and implementation of the peace accords in Angola and Cyprus was much more limited than was the case in Namibia, Cambodia, and El Salvador. In Angola, although third parties helped to mediate the Gbadolite and Bicesse Accords, assistance with implementation of the latter was limited to a small UN observer force whose mission was given low priority. The Bicesse Accords were overly ambitious without any thought given to implementation; the UN contingent was clearly overwhelmed by the size of its task and its lack of available resources. In the case of Cyprus, the London-Zurich Accords and subsequent constitutional agreement of 1960 contained no provisions for third-party involvement or assistance with implementation. The Constitution almost immediately became a bitter point of contention between the two communities and the conflict quickly escalated into a violent one.

Explaining Success and Failure: Alternative Hypotheses

Are success and failure intimately related to the presence or absence and the strengths or shortcomings of third parties that can assist with not only the negotiation of a settlement but also its implementation? Or is "success" achieved more by accident than design? Three alternative hypotheses were considered in order to test whether the variation in the outcomes of the case studies can be explained by the presence or lack of effective third-party involvement in the settlement process, or by other factors and conditions. The first hypothesis is that implementation failure or success has less to do with third-party intervention and more to do with the fundamental dynamics of the conflict itself—what is sometimes called "ripeness." A conflict can be said to be ripe for resolution when it has reached a hurting stalemate on the battlefield and the parties are sufficiently exhausted to consider political options that will lead to a negotiated settlement. Ripeness therefore is seen as a key ingredient to sustaining the peace process, and it is hypothesized that those agreements that fail do so because the conditions associated with ripeness were not met at the time the peace agreement was signed.

A second alternative hypothesis or explanatory condition associates ripeness less with the motivations of the parties to the conflict and more with external pressures and influences that are exerted on them at the regional and international levels. The stability of the peace process can be a function of the withdrawal of outside military support for one or more of the parties as a result of the changing dynamics of superpower competition and/or competition between regional powers. Greater levels of cooperation between great power and/or regional interests can help promote the peace process, whereas a deterioration in relations or a lack of cooperation can serve to undermine it. According to this view, the success (or failure) of the peace process in different regions is more a function of changing patterns of amity and enmity at the regional and/or system level. The end of the Cold War may therefore have been the key contributing factor in the resolution of some conflicts. Failure, however, is associated with the presence of great powers and/or regional interests who, through their actions, have undermined settlements that they consider inimical to their interests.

A third explanation focuses on the substantive provisions of the peace accords themselves. According to the functional assessment offered by some scholars, a well-designed peace settlement is one that is based inter alia on shared principles of justice, assimilation, and consensus, and that contains appropriate conflict-resolving procedures and institutions to address current and future problems. The success of a settlement is thus intimately linked to its design and its ability to anticipate or deter new challenges to the political order that has been created. Failure is the result of ambiguity and omission in the fundamental terms of the agreement, or an inability by the parties to agree to a common set of power-sharing principles, which subsequently become bitter points of contention during the agreement's implementation.

Each hypothesis has been explored systematically in each of the case studies. In general, our findings lend support to the proposition that external third-party involvement in all phases of the peace process does indeed matter to political outcomes, and that success and failure are indeed linked to the quality and level of support given by third parties to the peace process, especially during implementation of an agreement. Success in ending civil strife is also linked to a supportive regional and international environment. If key regional actors or outside great powers are hostile to the peace process, third parties will find themselves in an uphill battle in their efforts to make a settlement succeed. At a minimum, peaceful intervention by third parties in a civil conflict requires the support of a country's neighbors and outside great powers that are involved directly or indirectly in the conflict. The evidence also suggests that we should reformulate the notion of ripeness by explicitly taking into account the role of third parties in fostering ripeness. Ripeness is a cultivated, not inherited, condition. If the peace process is to succeed and newly created political institutions are to take root, outside third parties must help former combatants in the conflict in their own efforts to nurture and sustain the ripe moment. The conditions for a durable peace settlement and the findings that emerge from the individual case studies are explored at greater length below.

Ripeness

The concept that conflicts must be ripe for resolution before a durable peace settlement can be negotiated and implemented is inherently problematic. The concept is tied to the idea of a hurting stalemate, in which the parties to the dispute eventually come to perceive the costs of a negotiated settlement as being less than the costs of continuing or escalating the conflict. As Licklider observes, "The concept is difficult to operationalize without being tautological; we want to know if a hurting stalemate exists in order to predict whether or not the parties will alter their policies, but we only know if it exists if the parties alter their policies."[5]

Although scholars and policymakers have developed various indicators to operationalize the concept in order to avoid its more tautological connotations,[6] it remains problematic for other reasons. Does ripeness really exist if the potential for renewed violence remains high throughout the course of negotiations and even after a settlement has been reached? The concept of ripeness suggests that a conflict has reached a new equilibrium in which the parties are seriously committed to laying down their arms because they are exhausted by war. It also implies that the process is irreversible. Yet, as illustrated by the case studies in this volume, in low-intensity conflict situations the ability and willingness of the parties to sustain an ongoing campaign of violence is formidable even after negotiations have begun. Moreover, the fact that absolute victory is unattainable does not mean that the parties are willing to lay down their arms; rather, the existence of a stalemate may in fact be viewed by the protagonists as a strong reason to keep on fighting because neither side is in imminent danger of defeat. Not only does this make initiating a dialogue difficult, but it also means that once negotiations are under way the parties will attempt to exploit tactical gains on the battlefield for strategic gains at the negotiating table. Paradoxically, the negotiation process can set in motion a search for military gains that tends to drive the parties further apart instead of narrowing their political differences. Thus, even with the onset of formal negotiations the potential for "unripening" remains high because parties have not completely abandoned the military option.

This proved to be true in four out of the five cases examined here. In Namibia, the conflict was beginning to approach the conditions of ripeness in 1987. The SADF was able neither to bring SWAPO to a decisive conventional battle nor to eradicate the effects of continuing bush war without a major commitment of additional forces and an escalation of the war that the South African government was unwilling to undertake. Similarly, Cuban and Angolan defense forces were having limited success in conducting offensive operations against the SADF and UNITA. Although both sides were in the midst of negotiations, the buildup of Cuban forces in Angola in 1987 raised serious questions in Pretoria and Washington about the depth of Cuba's commitment to a negotiated settlement. Only the active intervention of the U.S. mediator, who realized that Castro was keen on a settlement if a face-saving formula could be found for a Cuban troop withdrawal, kept the negotiations on track. This enabled the theoretical "ripe moment" to be exploited successfully. Once a negotiated settlement was reached, implementation was threatened by a renewed outbreak of fighting when SWAPO launched a surprise military offensive against South African security forces on April 1, 1989. Although the situation may have been ripe for resolution, the risks of a resumption of violence and armed confrontation were very real, and it took active intervention by third parties, particularly the United States, to ensure that the settlement remained on course.

In Angola, that the military situation was ostensibly at a stalemate during the negotiation of Bicesse Accords did little to advance the peace process and enhance the possibilities of achieving a durable settlement. In the period 1988–91 the military situation had remained largely balanced; neither side had been able to gain a sufficient strategic advantage despite repeated offensives by the MPLA and UNITA. Military and civilian casualties were enormous; the war had exacted a huge toll on the country's economy. One might have thought that the stalemate would have enhanced the prospects of achieving a durable settlement; in fact, it had quite the opposite effect. Almost immediately after a settlement was reached, each side took advantage of the weak monitoring provisions in the accords to cheat on its commitment to demobilize its forces. Few of UNITA's troops were disarmed and very few were actually demobilized. There was also poor government attendance in assembly and demobilization areas. Cease-fires were recklessly broken by UNITA and the MPLA. When Savimbi lost the election, he had little incentive to accept the results because he believed that there were widespread irregularities and felt that the MPLA-dominated government had little interest in seeking a modus vivendi with its political rivals. In this case, a hurting military stalemate apparently had little impact on the prospects of achieving a workable peace settlement.

The relationship between ripeness and the peace process in Cambodia is also problematic. On the one hand, a hurting stalemate existed at the time of the signing of the Paris Peace Agreements in 1991 in the sense that the different Cambodian factions had lost their principal external sources of support in a civil war that had exacted an enormous price on the Cambodian people. The Vietnamese were pulling out, leaving the government without its principal backer. China and the Soviet Union were ending military assistance to their proxies, as was the United States. The Khmer Rouge was unable to establish permanent control of its territories and was suffering from desertions. Once the Paris accords were signed, however, it became clear that this stalemate was not sufficient to lay the foundations for a durable settlement. The Khmer Rouge refused to cooperate with UNTAC in implementing provisions regarding cantonment, disarmament, and demobilization, and repeatedly violated the cease-fire. The Khmer Rouge also refused to participate in the elections and has remained a thorn in the government's side ever since. There were also other disputes among Cambodia's various factions that helped to undermine the military elements of the peace process and that eventually led to the suspension of UNTAC's peacekeeping component. While there may have been enough ripeness to pursue negotiations and reach a political settlement, there clearly was not enough to keep the Khmer Rouge from defecting from the peace process and resuming its armed struggle against the government afterwards.

Although the government of El Salvador and the FMLN were deadlocked for years in a costly confrontation that had all the features of hurting stalemate, the stalemate was not sufficient to get the parties to engage in serious peace negotiations. Several efforts to initiate negotiations between the government and the FMLN—in 1984, 1986, and 1987—all failed. When UN-mediated negotiations began in 1989, the fighting still had not stopped. The reduction of U.S. aid to the Salvadoran military lent new momentum to the peace process, as did the election of Alfredo Cristiani, a moderate conservative, to the Salvadoran presidency. Still, the fact that the government and the FMLN brought fundamentally conflicting objectives to the negotiating table meant that a settlement was not foreordained. And even when a formal agreement was reached, the great mistrust and suspicion that characterized relations between the two parties meant that the potential for violence and a resumption of military hostilities remained elevated. Ripeness, by itself, cannot explain why a negotiated agreement was concluded in 1992 and why the agreement was implemented as successfully as it was.

The failure of repeated mediation efforts to resolve the dispute in Cyprus, following the outbreak of civil war in 1964, is perhaps best explained by a lack of ripeness—that is, the absence of a hurting stalemate that would help to break the impasse. In part this is due to the presence on the island of UN peacekeeping forces that have kept tensions at a moderate level and reduced the incentive for the Turkish and Greek Cypriot communities to seek a negotiated political settlement. At the same time, however, the regional and extraregional dimensions of the conflict have been a key source of difficulty in reaching political accommodation. An improvement in Greco-Turkish relations that would bring about a withdrawal of Turkish forces from the island is a clear precondition for a resolution of the conflict. The absence of a hurting stalemate is only one aspect of the continuing difficulties of reaching a political accommodation in Cyprus. Its importance in explaining the lack of progress therefore should not be overstated.

The concept of ripeness does not fully explain why the peace process stayed on track once a negotiated settlement was reached in Namibia, El Salvador, and to lesser extent Cambodia. Nor is it helpful in explaining why successive agreements unraveled in Angola. It is a potential source of explanation for the lack of progress in negotiations in Cyprus, but, even then, the argument merits serious qualification. Implementation successes and failures were clearly affected by conditions other than ripeness (or a lack thereof). It is to these other factors that we now turn.

Systemic and Regional Power Balances

Systemic Influences

Is there a link between improving East-West relations in the 1980s and those settlements that succeeded? According to some analysts, civil and regional conflicts in the Third World were essentially proxy wars between the two superpowers; the prospects of achieving negotiated and durable settlements dramatically improved with the end of the Cold War. To the extent that the two superpowers were willing to exert joint pressure on their clients to stop fighting, so the argument goes, the prospects of achieving lasting peace settlements in many regions were greatly enhanced.

In spite of the intuitive appeal of the argument that "détente mattered," there is no systematic causal link between superpower détente and the successful settlements. This is not to say that détente did not matter to the negotiation of peace agreements in some cases. But the direct causal link between détente and the successful implementation of those agreements, according to the terms defined here, is more nebulous.

The evidence is weak that the negotiation of the Angola-Namibia peace accords was facilitated by détente or was the result of direct pressure applied by the superpowers. Moscow did not play a major role in the negotiations and only began to distance itself from Cuba well after the accords were negotiated and implemented. U.S. influence in the negotiations also had less to do with American power projection capabilities or economic or military leverage in the region (which were limited), than with its diplomatic skills in mediation. Moreover, once a settlement was reached, what kept the peace process on track was the joint commission backed by U.S. support and mediation skills. To be sure, the United Nations could not have acted without the support of the five permanent members of the Security Council, but Soviet involvement in the peace process was essentially limited to passive acquiescence.

The evidence is stronger that the peace process in Cambodia was the direct beneficiary of superpower détente, as well as improved relations between China and the Soviet Union under Gorbachev. Agreement among the United States, the Soviet Union, and China on a framework agreement affected the long-term cost-benefit analyses of the Cambodian parties those powers supported. The different factions in the Cambodian conflict could no longer rely on their foreign allies for assistance to continue the conflict, and they were under strong pressure to reach a settlement. This pressure, which mounted after Vietnamese troops withdrew from Cambodia, was clearly a key factor in reaching an agreement. Once a settlement was achieved, however, the ability of outside parties to exert pressure on the Khmer Rouge was limited because of its independent sources of wealth from trade in timber and gems. The Khmer Rouge also had sufficient arms and ammunition, as well as secret sources of supply, to carry on its guerrilla campaign against the new government.

In a general sense the peace process in El Salvador was also a direct beneficiary of the end of the Cold War between the two superpowers. With the election of George Bush to the presidency, the United States began to reduce its aid to the Salvadoran military and supported efforts to find a negotiated settlement to the conflict. In this case, however, the United States was not officially involved in the negotiations, even though it played an important behind-the-scenes role. Soviet influence over the FMLN, by comparison, was limited; the Soviets were not a key player in the negotiations. The ability of both superpowers to exercise leverage on the negotiations and peace process was also constrained by the fact that civil war in El Salvador was just that: a civil war with a self-sustaining dynamic. Internal conditions had to change before a lasting settlement could be reached.

The two cases of failure to end civil strife, Angola and Cyprus, have clearly not been significantly influenced by the end of the Cold War. This casts further doubt on the proposition that the effects of détente and the end of the Cold War were universal, or that those settlements that succeeded did so as a result of *combined* great-power pressure on the parties to negotiate and maintain a settlement. With some exceptions, the pressure was negative rather than positive; by withdrawing military support the superpowers made it more difficult for some of their clients to sustain a policy of armed struggle. But these same clients had other means of procuring arms, and the loss of superpower support was not by itself a sufficient condition to bring them to the peace table and to engage them in a serious process of peace building.

Regional Influences

The proposition that the ultimate success of a peace settlement hinges on a stable regional environment and neighbors who support the peace process has greater merit. In Cyprus, the attempts by successive third parties to bring about a negotiated settlement to the twenty-year-old conflict have been hampered by Turkey's refusal to withdraw its forces from the island. An improvement in Greco-Turkish relations that could bring about such a withdrawal is clearly a precondition for a lasting settlement. The experience in El Salvador underscores the positive role that regional interests can play if they are supportive of the peace process. The Contadora initiative, which was followed by the Esquipulas II accords, not only helped bring an end to the civil war in Nicaragua but also lent momentum to the peace process in El Salvador. The strong support for a negotiated settlement by the "four friends"—Colombia, Mexico, Spain, and Venezuela—also helped to prevent a breakdown of talks.

Similarly, the negotiation and implementation of the Angola-Namibia peace accords could not have taken place without Cuban and South African commitment to the peace process and the withdrawal of their forces from Angola and Namibia, respectively. In Cambodia, Vietnam's withdrawal of forces was obviously key to the peace process, and Cambodia's ASEAN neighbors were instrumental in helping to get negotiations started. However, the continuing insurgency in Cambodia is due, in part, to the continuing support the Khmer Rouge receives from the Thai military, which is heavily involved in the secret trade in the timber and gems the Khmer Rouge uses to finance its operations. Unless Thailand suspends its contacts with the Khmer Rouge, the civil war in the north-western part of Cambodia is likely to continue.

The experience in all five cases underscores the proposition that a combination of international and regional intervention strategies is the prerequisite for conflict termination, and that the success of a peace settlement is inextricably tied to the interests of neighboring regional powers and their overall commitment to the peace process. Where such a commitment is lacking, the risk of failure is higher.

Terms of Settlement

How do the design and terms of a peace settlement affect the prospects of achieving peace? Are some settlements better designed than others, and does this factor best explain the variation in success and failure across our five cases? The answer is that some settlements are indeed better crafted than others. The design of an agreement, particularly with regard to its provisions for reconstituting political authority in a country that has been wracked by civil war, can significantly affect the prospects of achieving a viable peace process and a durable settlement. A solid document is a key element for peacekeeping operations and the establishment of a viable political settlement. Without it there are high costs, delays, and real risk that the settlement will fail.

What are the specific requirements for a settlement? First, it is absolutely essential that all the warring parties have a seat at the negotiating table and are directly involved in discussions about the new constitutional and political order that will be created after the fighting stops. A "good" agreement is one that has been crafted by all parties to the conflict. If parties are excluded from these negotiations, or if their interests are not represented at the bargaining table, they will have a much stronger incentive to defect from the peace process and resort to violence to achieve their aims. One of the problems with the settlement following the 1960 Constitutional Accord in Cyprus was that it was seen as being imposed on the parties—the Greek and Turkish Cypriot communities—by the British and other outside powers. This contributed to the agreement's failure during the implementation phase. Even if parties decide to defect from the political process later on, as did the Khmer Rouge in Cambodia after it had signed the Paris accords, their legitimacy will be undermined if they are perceived as breaking commitments they agreed to previously. It is difficult to garner outside allies and build domestic political support if you defect from a process that you earlier endorsed.

Second, a good agreement is one that contains power-sharing provisions for winners and losers in the aftermath of elections. The context in which elections take place is crucial to the peace process. There need to be positions for both winners and losers in a new government. Winner-take-all elections are seen as zero-sum contests. Unless there is some form of compensation, the loser will have strong incentives to take up arms and turn to a renewed campaign of violence in pursuit of political objectives. A lack of power-sharing arrangements is one reason the 1992 agreements in Angola fell apart. In contrast, the elections in Cambodia resulted in a coalition government between the ruling CPP and FUNCINPEC, which had won the popular vote. The parties recognized early on that a coalition government was necessary to appease rival factions and advance the process of national reconciliation. This followed a pattern of power sharing set up during the Paris peace negotiations with the establishment of the Supreme National Council in 1989. Electoral mechanisms such as proportional representation may also be required so that minorities feel they have adequate representation in parliament.

In the absence of power-sharing mechanisms or provisions for the development of inclusive coalitions, a settlement must at a minimum establish a level playing field and allow equal and fair access to the political process by formerly excluded groups. Everybody must have a sense that they can participate and that political life is not zero-sum. The new rules about political competition must also be seen as fair and just. In the Salvadoran case, the FMLN was less interested in power sharing than in securing free elections and the right to form a political party. The FMLN was also keen to see wholesale reform of the country's military, police, and judicial institutions, which were seen as corrupt and subversive of the democratic process. The peace settlement allowed the FMLN to compete alongside ARENA in national elections for the presidency, the National Assembly, and municipal offices.

Another important element of peace agreements is provisions for third-party mediation and renegotiation during the implementation phase of the settlement process. A settlement is an imperfect road map to the future. As some of the cases in this volume illustrate, key provisions of a settlement had to be renegotiated because they were ambiguous or unimplementable. In others, new problems emerged and had to be accommodated within the framework of the settlement. In all cases, major issues unresolved at the time an agreement was reached remained the subject of ongoing negotiation and discussion. Poorly negotiated and badly designed agreements are a sure prescription for disaster. However, this does not mean that the converse is true. A well-negotiated, well-crafted agreement is no guarantee of success because, as experience shows, there are always ambiguities, differences of interpretation about key provisions, and important, unresolved issues (or new ones) that can scuttle the peace process after an agreement has been signed.

The Angola-Namibia peace accords were, by the standards of assessment applied here, a success. However, a number of problems, some minor and some more serious, surfaced during the implementation of the agreement. One set of issues concerned how the new Constitution would be ratified, whether the Constituent Assembly would be legally bound to new constitutional principles, and how the new government would be chosen. Mechanisms for demobilization and disbandment of local forces proved to be a source of contention after the agreement was signed. The status of Walvis Bay, an issue that could not be resolved during the negotiations, was deferred to future talks. Other continuing disputes concerned electoral laws and management of elections during implementation of the agreement. None of these issues derailed the peace process, largely because institutional mechanisms had been created beforehand to allow for continuing consultation and negotiations among the parties. The joint commission, in particular, was a critical dispute-resolution mechanism, as evidenced by the key role it played in defusing tensions following the SWAPO incursion into Namibia after the agreements were signed.

The Chapultepec Accords, which ended the civil war in El Salvador, were also well crafted, but nonetheless suffered from ambiguities and problems of omission. The land-for-arms exchange to ex-combatants in the agreement was hastily negotiated and became the most contentious issue during the implementation process. The resulting impasse threatened to bring a halt to the demobilization of the FMLN and government reform of the armed forces. Only when the United Nations intervened with a new proposal for an agreement on land transfers was the peace process salvaged. The overly ambitious schedule for demobilization of forces and reform of the military in the accords also had to be renegotiated—again with UN assistance—to secure the commitment of the parties to the peace process.

Major, unanticipated problems arose during the implementation of the Paris Peace Agreements in Cambodia. These included the problems of verifying the complete withdrawal of Vietnamese troops along the Vietnam-Cambodia border; dealing with large numbers of Vietnamese immigrants who had come into Cambodia in search of jobs; the need for a massive mine-clearing program; and inadequate infrastructure to support cantonment, disarmament, and demobilization provisions in the accords. Most of these problems were addressed on an ad hoc basis and with varying degrees of success by the United Nations. The most serious problem, however, was the Khmer Rouge's refusal to comply with its commitments under the accords. This problem had less to do with the structure of the agreement and more with the Khmer Rouge's defection from the peace process.

The experience of Angola in the early 1990s underscores the proposition that badly designed agreements are prone to failure. But it also suggests that hasty, ill-conceived peace proposals offered by third parties may actually be counterproductive if they contribute to feelings of bad faith and make later resumption of negotiations more difficult. The Gbadolite Accords did just that. They quickly broke down because there was no formal written accord and the substance of the agreement was left to the interpretations of the individual parties. Ambiguities in the agreement were immediately contested by the parties and tensions mounted. The residue of bad faith and mistrust made it difficult to restart negotiations and discredited any future regional role in the peace process. In contrast, the Bicesse Accords, which were negotiated under Portuguese and U.S. auspices, were a much better set of agreements. The agreements provided for a staged cease-fire, a phased schedule for demobilization of forces, and passage of enabling electoral laws that would culminate in national elections for a new government. However, the Achilles' heel of the agreement was the lack of an adequate and effective third-party presence and monitoring mechanism to supervise and assist with implementation. In some respects, the accords were far too elaborate for the implementation mechanism, so cheating and discrediting were inevitable. As a consequence, disputes over assembly points and demobilization procedures outlined in the agreement, the electoral timetable, and other issues were not properly addressed and contributed to an escalation of tensions and resumption of interfactional fighting.

If ambiguity is one potential source of error in the design of a peace agreement, inflexibility and overly restrictive provisions are another. Early efforts to establish a bicommunal structure for the government of Cyprus, which grew out of the London-Zurich Accords, failed because the settlement was too rigid and led to constitutional arrangements that were unacceptable to the island's Greek community. The Constitution contained 196 articles and 6 annexes. It mandated specific ratios between Greek and Turkish Cypriots for jobs in the public service, the legislature, and the courts. The cumbersome and politically unwieldy nature of the Constitution, rather than bringing the two communities together, quickly drove them apart, as efforts to implement it proved unworkable. Successive constitutional crises paralyzed the government and eventually spilled over into intercommunal fighting. Since the Turkish intervention of 1974, numerous efforts have been made with the assistance of third parties to negotiate a new federal, bicommunal structure for Cyprus. None has succeeded because agreement between the parties over the actual details of new set of constitutional arrangements has proven elusive, in spite of the fact the parties have been able to agree on general principles. The constitutional ghost of 1960 still haunts the process insofar as both parties continue to point to various elements in the Constitution they consider fundamental to any future settlement.

All peace agreements are prone to failure regardless of how well structured and designed they appear at first blush. Parties will exploit ambiguity in an agreement to advance their interests. Unresolved issues can easily become bitter points of contention later on. If the parties fail to abide by rigidly established timetables for demobilization of forces, the peace process can quickly become unhinged. Badly designed agreements clearly need some other force—namely, a third-party presence during implementation—to sustain the peace process and keep it on track. But so too do well-designed, properly structured agreements. In this regard, Holsti's requirement that a peace settlement "include procedures and institutions for identifying, monitoring, managing, and resolving major conflicts"[7] is critical. Namibia's and El Salvador's successes in implementing their peace accords illustrate the utility of such mechanisms.

Why Third Parties Make a Difference

A negotiated peace agreement is little more than a road map to the peace process. A settlement indicates the direction the parties must move if they are to consolidate the peace, but it usually does not tell them how to get there, except in very general terms. There is usually plenty of ambiguity in an agreement because "ambiguity is the mother of compromise." Intractable issues that are left out of the agreement for subsequent negotiation can quickly come back to haunt those elements of the peace process on which there is widespread agreement. Although there may be a will for peace when the accords are signed, this does not mean that the parties necessarily wish to fulfill all of their commitments under the agreement. Furthermore, the act of signing an agreement does not mean the parties will immediately lay down their arms, stop fighting, and return to civilian life. Although most settlements typically include a timetable for a cease-fire and the subsequent demobilization of armed combatants, the details usually have to be worked out on the ground as the agreement is being implemented. This is fertile ground for misunderstandings and delays, as each side jockeys for advantage in the tense political atmosphere that follows the signing of a peace settlement. The risk of sliding back into armed confrontation is therefore high in the early stages of the peace process. And even after a modicum of trust is built up between the parties, it can be undermined by perceived violations and failures of compliance. Thus one of the key functions of third parties is to help foster trust between different warring factions by monitoring compliance and holding them to their negotiated commitments.

Third parties can provide much-needed political status and legitimacy to the interests of warring factions by creating instruments that allow the parties to work as equal partners during both the negotiation and implementation of an agreement. In the Salvadoran case, for example, the New York Accords led to the creation of a National Commission for the Consolidation of Peace (COPAZ), which had a membership of two government and two FMLN members, as well as one representative from each party in the National Assembly. The commission was responsible for overseeing the implementation of the accords and discussing both the progress and problems with the peace process. Although COPAZ did not function particularly well and lacked proper compliance and enforcement mechanisms, it accorded the FMLN political status and the opportunity to be seen as an equal and legitimate partner in the peace process.

The role of third parties in nurturing and sustaining the peace process goes well beyond the legitimizing and monitoring functions envisaged in traditional notions about peacekeeping, however. Some of these roles represent a continuation of functions, such as mediation, carried out during the negotiations that led to the agreement. Others, however, are new and different contributions to the peace process, such as the promotion of new norms and what might be termed proxy governance functions. In the following pages we describe how the peace process was advanced in the five cases examined here when third parties carried out these functions, and why it failed when third parties were not available or performed these functions poorly or inadequately.

Peacekeeping and Demobilization

Peacekeeping is defined by Gareth Evans as "the deployment of military or police, and frequently civilian, personnel to assist in the implementation of agreements reached between governments or parties who have been engaged in conflict." He goes on to note that "peacekeeping presumes cooperation, and its methods are inherently peaceful: the use of military force other than in self-defense, is incompatible with the concept."[8] Useful as this definition is, it is important to note that the actual form and functions of peacekeeping vary considerably in the five cases examined here. Cyprus is generally viewed as the classic model of a peacekeeping operation. UNFICYP forces are deployed in a neutral buffer zone that separates the island's two communities. Through its presence, UNFICYP has helped deter major military operations and promote an uneasy truce between the two communities. Maintenance of the buffer zone has been an important confidence-building measure and has served to prevent accidental confrontations from escalating to greater levels of conflict. However, UNFICYP has also been involved in activities that go beyond "traditional" peacekeeping, including assistance with food distribution, transportation, and restoration of basic government services.

Although monitoring cease-fire provisions is a key element in any peacekeeping operation, another function, which is just as important, is assistance with the demobilization of forces. Demobilization is "the process by which the armed forces (government and/or opposition factional forces such as guerrilla armies) either downsize or completely disband." A restructuring of the armed forces, to include "an ethnically and/ or political balanced 'national army,'"[9] may also accompany demobilization. Demobilization, disarmament, and restructuring of armed forces are politically sensitive and challenging tasks. If demobilization of forces and restructuring of the state's security institutions are completed within the general time frame allotted by an agreement, the peace process has a much greater chance of succeeding than if there are major delays and commitments are honored in the breach. Outside monitors can facilitate the demobilization process if they are seen as neutral by the parties and if they have sufficiently broad mandates and adequate resources (financial and human) to do the job.[10]

The experience in Namibia and El Salvador bears this out. In Namibia the peace plan (UN Resolution 435) called for the complete demobilization of forces prior to the holding of free elections. UNTAG was tasked with monitoring the cease-fire; confining South African and SWAPO forces to their bases; assisting in the withdrawal of South African forces; confining the remaining South African forces until elections were completed; and monitoring the disbandment of citizen forces, commandos, and relevant command structures. Although there were some delays in meeting the demobilization schedule, demobilization was completed in time for the UN-supervised elections.

Similarly, in El Salvador demobilization of the FMLN and a downsizing and restructuring of the armed forces were also concluded before elections were held. To be sure, there were delays in implementing the original schedule, which had to be renegotiated several times. There were also violations: the FMLN failed to provide a complete inventory of the weapons it had in its possession, and the government failed to carry out fully the demobilization of its forces in the countryside. These violations were investigated by the local UN observer mission, ONUSAL, but they were not serious enough to upset the peace process or undermine the elections.

In Angola, UNAVEM's assistance with the partial demobilization of government (MPLA) and UNITA forces, as called for in the Bicesse Accords, was hampered by a lack of resources and personnel to carry out effective monitoring operations on the scale that was necessary for such a large country. Compared to the Namibia operation where UNTAG enjoyed a contingency of 7,500 personnel, the UNAVEM operation comprised only 425 military and police observers, who were overwhelmed by the size of their task. The demobilization of the two forces in Angola fell far behind schedule. "By the election date, 40,000 troops had yet to be demobilized, the two opposition forces were nearly intact, and the new, integrated army barely formed. When the UNITA leader, Savimbi, was dissatisfied with the election results, the continued existence of the two armies contributed to a rapid resurgence of the conflict."[11] Without doubt, the unrealistic timetable, along with a lack of cooperation by both parties, contributed to the failure of demobilization efforts in Angola, but UNAVEM's lack of resources also affected the poor result.

Under the terms of the Paris peace accords for Cambodia, the United Nations was to demobilize and disarm 70 percent of each of the four factional armies and supervise the activities of the remainder prior to elections for a new constituent assembly. To help with this task, UNTAC deployed 15,738 military personnel. However, the Khmer Rouge's refusal to participate in the peace process and repeated delays in meeting cantonment, demobilization, and disarmament schedules led to the eventual suspension of the second phase of the demobilization program, leaving more than half a million Cambodians still armed. Although legitimate national elections were held in an atmosphere that was generally free of violence and intimidation, UNTAC's inability to properly carry out the demobilization plan mandated in the Paris Agreements has plagued the restoration of civilian rule in Cambodia ever since.

Demobilization of forces is a key element in any political settlement, and experience suggests that demobilization plans, even if they are only partial, need to be carried out before elections are held; otherwise, fighting is likely to resume afterward if various parties are unhappy with the election results. Third parties have an important role to play in assisting with demobilization efforts, and the success of peace processes partly hinges on how well they are able to perform this task. In Namibia and El Salvador, they did the job well; in Angola and Cambodia, if for different reasons, they did not, and the result had a negative impact on the peace process.

Demobilization plans must be linked to a realistic timetable. As experiences in El Salvador and Cambodia suggest, an unrealistic timetable can weaken the ability of the parties to achieve the political objectives of the accord. Synchronizing demobilization with refugee resettlement, economic reconstruction, military and security provisions, and the advancement of human rights is a daunting task. When deadlines are threatened by foot-dragging and broken promises, third parties must use whatever pressure is necessary to sustain the linkage between political and military benchmarks, regain the political momentum, and recalibrate timetables as appropriate. It is critical to develop a rhythm to the peace process so that elections can be held in an environment free of violence and intimidation and other elements of the peace process can move forward.

The Role of Force

When should force be used by third parties to stabilize the political process and bring into line those elements intent on wrecking the peace process? There is no easy answer to this question. A number of recent cases illustrate that for each case where the use of force failed to achieve political aims (for example, in Somalia), one can also point to instances where, arguably, decisive force used early in the conflict might have prevented tragedy (as in Rwanda).

In cases examined here, the dilemmas were just as stark. UN officials in Cambodia were faced with the difficult decision of whether or not to use force against Khmer Rouge forces and rout them from their guerrilla hideouts, once the Khmer Rouge decided to fight with guns rather than for votes. The United Nations decided not to use force, fearing military action would jeopardize its "neutrality" and tie down UN forces in a costly counterinsurgency campaign they were ill equipped to handle. Such action would have delayed elections as well as implementation of the peace plan. Critics charge that UN failure to take more decisive action against the Khmer Rouge created serious problems later on. But they fail to address the prior question of whether a preventive use of force by the United Nations would have worked anyway, given that UN forces were neither equipped nor trained to carry out peace enforcement operations.

Timely military interventions can make a difference and help bring parties to the negotiating table, as we have seen in the case of NATO air strikes in Bosnia. But much depends upon who that third party is and whether the requisite forces are available to it. Unlike NATO, the United Nations is not an effective instrument of coercive diplomacy. It is handicapped by its inability to deploy forces quickly to arenas of conflict and by domestic opposition to enforcement actions where peacekeeping forces are put in the direct line of fire. Enforcement is therefore best left to others. The United Nations is most successful when it confines itself to peacekeeping, policing, and peace-building functions conducted under a carefully defined mandate that possesses a clear entry as well as exit strategy.

Effective mediation, however, is possible without resort to force. In Namibia and El Salvador third-party mediators were able to get warring sides to the negotiating table and to persuade them, without making military threats, that the benefits of a political settlement outweighed the costs of continued confrontation. The most successful agreements are self-enforcing; the parties have come to recognize the benefits of the peace process for themselves. Where such recognition and commitment are lacking, enforcement operations are likely to be ineffective at best and counterproductive and self-defeating at worst. It is better to lay the political groundwork before committing forces to a peacekeeping operation. Reversing this sequence is a prescription for failure. That said, the dilemma of responding to defections (as opposed to minor infractions or violations) from the terms of the settlement after a peace agreement has been signed and the peace process set in motion remains real. There is no simple answer to this problem. One approach, tried in Cambodia, is to isolate the defectors through the political process so that the peace process does not lose its momentum. The government of Cambodia is undeniably in a stronger position today to deal with the Khmer Rouge than it was at the time of elections. The Khmer Rouge has not been eliminated, but it is a thorn rather than a sword in the side of the government. The challenge is to ensure that the thorn does not grow.

Mediation and Renegotiation

The demand for mediators does not end once a deal is reached, because negotiations between the parties typically do not end. The terms of a settlement are constantly being renegotiated during its implementation, and new problems can emerge that have the potential, if left unresolved, to jeopardize the peace process. Because the parties are unable to resolve these problems on their own through direct negotiations, they may be forced to turn to outside mediators for assistance. There is a need for ongoing dispute resolution between parties throughout the duration of the peace process and implementation of a settlement.

All five cases witnessed extensive third-party involvement and assistance with negotiation of a peace settlement. In the case of the Angola-Namibia peace accords, negotiations were assisted first by the Western Contact Group and then by the Reagan administration, which played a key role in sustaining the negotiation process and ripening the possibilities of an agreement by defining the critical elements that would have to go into a settlement package. In El Salvador, UN mediators played a similar role. Although the conflict had reached a stalemate, fighting had not stopped. A political settlement was by no means inevitable, because the parties brought competing political objectives to the negotiating table. As mediator, the United Nations played a key role by being a constant source of new ideas that narrowed differences and moved the parties toward a negotiated settlement. The Permanent Five likewise sustained the negotiation process among the factions fighting to seize control of Cambodia; the final settlement package could not have been reached without the active intervention of France and the United States, in particular, in the negotiations. Agreements in Cyprus and

Angola were also reached via third-party mediation in peace talks, although in the case of Cyprus the agreement was imposed by Britain, Greece, and Turkey without the active involvement of the Greek and Turkish Cypriot communities.

The active contribution of third parties to a negotiated peace settlement in all five cases underscores the centrality of the argument that ripeness is simultaneously an intrinsically and extrinsically generated condition. Third parties proved critical to engaging the conflicting parties in a process of negotiation that strengthened their interest in a politically negotiated settlement. In the early stages of negotiation, the commitment of warring factions to a negotiated settlement was weak to nonexistent. Negotiations were seen as a way to deflect international criticism, enhance legitimacy, and build outside support for military objectives rather than to achieve a political settlement. By sustaining the negotiation process and getting the parties to view their options in political instead of military terms, third parties helped build momentum toward a negotiated settlement.

Once a settlement was reached, however, the need for third-party assistance in negotiating new political arrangements and implementation timetables remained strong. In Namibia, the United States and United Nations helped negotiate follow-up agreements at Mount Etjo, after the SWAPO incursion into Namibia on April 1, 1989. In El Salvador, UN mediation was crucial to resolving outstanding differences over land tenure and reform issues involving former combatants. UN mediation was required to negotiate a new timetable for implementation of key provisions of the peace accords, following repeated delays and failures of compliance. UN mediation among Cambodia's factions also helped with various difficulties that arose during implementation of the Paris peace accords, although much of the brokering of rival and competing interests was conducted by Prince Sihanouk, who appeared to enjoy a special position of trust and legitimacy among his coalition partners. There was clearly less mediation and brokerage in Angola because the settlement came apart so quickly, and the United Nations found itself both overextended and overwhelmed by the situation on the ground. In Cyprus, in the period following the implementation of the London-Zurich Accords and the new Constitution, there was also no mediation; perhaps the outcome might have been different had there been outside third-party mediation to help the parties resolve their constitutional differences before fighting broke out.

Viewed this way, the negotiation and implementation phases of the peace process are overlapping, intertwined, and mutually interdependent. Furthermore, the need for continuing third-party mediation during all phases of the peace process, including implementation, is obvious. It is therefore more accurate to view ripeness as a *cultivated* condition that has to be sustained, even after a settlement has been reached, to prevent the peace process from sliding back into violence.

Establishing New Norms

Third parties also have a key role to play in promoting new norms and codes of conduct, particularly in the area of human rights. Atrocities and violations of human rights are unfortunately all too characteristic of civil wars. The security institutions of the state—the armed forces and police—are usually suspect because they are seen as instruments of coercion by the state against its people. Reform of these institutions can be fundamental to the peace process and the consolidation of democratic reforms, but the dismantling and/or reform of these institutions can lead to an increase in anarchy and violence in a society that is unaccustomed to the rule of law. Similar problems face reform of the judicial and legal systems, which are viewed as instruments of repression and state-sponsored violence and whose overhaul is essential. Yet, if a new social order based on the rule of law and accepted principles of justice is to be fashioned, respect for human rights and due process must be nurtured.

The deployment of ONUSAL's human rights monitoring team before the fighting had ended and the final accords were signed helped instill in El Salvador's warring parties a sense of confidence in the nascent peace process. ONUSAL investigated cases and situations involving human rights violations and followed up these investigations with relevant bodies in the government. It also developed regional and local contacts with the main political, judicial, and military authorities and maintained ongoing contact with FMLN leaders inside the country. By working closely with local human rights organizations, ONUSAL was able to design a human rights program for the armed forces, a group responsible for some of the worst human rights abuses in the country.

By putting parties on notice that certain actions and behaviors will not be tolerated and that human rights violators will be dealt with accordingly, third parties can help advance the cause of justice. The El Salvador experience illustrates that the early promotion of human rights can also

serve as an important confidence-building measure before a formal
negotiated settlement is reached.

There is an obvious tension between conflict resolution and the promotion of human rights, judicial reform, and the development of legal
systems governed by due process. Peace and justice do not always work
in tandem. The need to establish power-sharing structures that accommodate rival factions and interests may well clash with the desires of some
to root out the perpetrators of human rights abuses. Similarly, the need
to reform the security institutions of the state, including the police and
military, may be at odds with the practical need to bring into the peace
process those groups that wield power and have a monopoly on the
instruments of coercion in a society. Without peace there can be no justice. Without justice, democratic institutions, and the development of the
rule of law, the peace itself will not last. But the political requirements
for reaching a peace settlement may well conflict with the desire to lay
the foundations for long-term democratic stability. Which model works
best when and where: the conflict managers' power-sharing model or the
democratizers' political justice model? The evidence suggests that a concern for justice must be tempered by the realities of negotiation and the
parties' interests in reaching a political settlement.

In Cambodia, for example, implementation of the human rights provisions in the Paris Peace Agreements was weak not only because of the
practical difficulties of implementation, but also because "more vigorous
pursuit of human rights goals ran the risk of upsetting the delicate political balance that was necessary for election to take place." Moreover, in "a
country with a history of human rights abuses that approached genocide,
it was going to be an uphill task to educate the population, to develop
indigenous human rights organizations, and most important, to develop
mechanisms that would truly protect the people from human rights
abuses."[12] Yet by opting out of the elections, the Khmer Rouge, which
was guilty of the worst human rights abuses in Cambodia, isolated itself
and ironically has facilitated the task of developing democratic institutions and the rule of law because it does not have the power or political
legitimacy to block judicial and democratic reform.

In El Salvador all parties were sensitive to the need to address human
rights problems at the outset of the peace process. The success of the
process is largely attributable to the fact that political reform was linked
to the promotion of human rights and the principle of accountability for
those guilty of the worst human rights abuses. However, given the

volatile conditions in El Salvador and the fact that local efforts to investigate human rights abuses were neither feasible nor credible, international authorities were relied on to evaluate and assess the evidence assembled by local interests. The Commission on the Truth helped develop greater confidence in the peace process and in efforts to reform the judicial and security institutions of the state, even though not all of its recommendations were implemented. The slow pace of continuing judicial reform reflects the fact that significant obstacles remain.

In Namibia all parties recognized the need to develop strong democratic institutions based on the rule of law—institutions that simultaneously entrenched minority rights in the Constitution. In El Salvador human rights problems were initially addressed by the truth commission, which identified the perpetrators of the most egregious abuses. In Angola all three recent political agreements have focused on the need for power sharing, while displaying little regard for justice, moral accountability, or the need to address past human rights abuses. In Cambodia the question of accountability and how to prosecute those responsible for war crimes under the Pol Pot regime remains difficult and controversial. It is not clear whether an attempt to try Khmer Rouge leaders for war crimes, genocide, and crimes against humanity would advance the process of national reconciliation or further radicalize the Khmer Rouge and jeopardize political stability.

The problem in any settlement is not how to resolve a theoretical tension among human rights, democracy, and power sharing, but how to work with the parties themselves who may be reluctant to push the frontiers of human rights too far. The challenge for third parties is to advance the cause of human rights without undermining the settlement itself and to foster institutional mechanisms that will advance human rights and democratic development once the political situation has stabilized. Third parties can play a critical role in investigating human rights abuses and other war crimes and in evaluating evidence collected by local authorities before arrests are made. In the fragile political climate that prevails following agreement on a settlement, the temptation to exact retribution and revenge is considerable. International tribunals and commissions bring the element of impartiality necessary to restore faith in the judicial process and the rule of law. It is both unwise and unreasonable to expect parties to be able to reestablish the rule of law and due process on their own.

Proxy Governance

Proxy governance is another potential area for third-party involvement in the peace process. Civil conflicts usually take a severe toll on the administrative and fiscal capacity of state institutions. Not only do such institutions lack political legitimacy in the form of trust and support from the people, but they often have difficulty performing key administrative tasks such as the provision of basic services. By taking over some of these administrative functions until local authorities are able to perform them themselves, international governmental and nongovernmental actors can help with the administration and governance of the state, thus contributing to the development of a more stable social, political, and economic order. They can also play a critical role in observing and monitoring elections to ensure that they are free and fair and that the results are accepted by the electorate and the formerly warring parties. The term "proxy" is used to describe these governance functions because third parties are temporary stand-ins for local authorities that are unable or unwilling to perform these activities themselves. These functional contributions to the reestablishment of local political and administrative authority should not be confused with "nation building" in the larger sense. The assumption is that within a relatively short period of time third parties will turn over full responsibility and authority for these administrative activities to local officials.

In Cambodia the proxy governance functions undertaken by UNTAC were extensive. The elections for a new Cambodian government were organized by UNTAC with the assistance of many nongovernmental organizations. UNTAC's civil administration unit also took over those government bodies or agencies perceived to be vulnerable to outside manipulation and therefore able to influence the election process. These included offices for foreign affairs, national defense, finance, information, and public security. UNTAC relinquished its control over these bodies once the new government had been formed. In Namibia the UN special representative had extensive review powers over the activities of the local South African administrator-general and helped draft electoral laws and plans for a constituent assembly. ONUSAL's assistance with reform of the judiciary, political institutions, armed forces, and police in El Salvador was also quite extensive, going well beyond its initial mandate. Various UN agencies (such as United Nations Development Programme, the Food and Agriculture Organization, and the UN High Commission for Refugees), along with many nongovernmental organizations, also played key roles in helping El Salvador with its social, political, and economic reforms.

As the problems experienced by UNTAC's civil administration component in Cambodia suggest, proxy governance is a difficult undertaking. Successful implementation can be hindered by delays in deployment; a third party's lack of familiarity with local conditions, culture, and forms of government; and the lack of a cease-fire, which can upset timetables and thwart cooperation among the parties at other levels. There is also the danger that a third party that becomes too involved will leave itself open to charges of neocolonialism by local critics. The situation in El Salvador illustrates some of these risks. Furthermore, if third parties become too intrusive, they may actually weaken rather than strengthen local infrastructure and rehabilitation elements. It is important to set clear and realistic peacekeeping mandates that are sensitive to local conditions and to limit external intervention to functional areas where the need is compelling and mandates can be properly executed. Otherwise third-party efforts to develop local governance structures will be counterproductive and ultimately self-defeating.

Why Third Parties Need Other Third Parties

In instances where a workable settlement was reached, as in the cases of El Salvador and Namibia, third parties made a critical contribution to the peace process by helping with not only the negotiation but also the implementation of the agreement. In instances where the peace process clearly failed, as in Angola, failure was associated with a lack of adequate third-party support and involvement during the peace process.

Another lesson emerges from cases examined in this volume: third parties need other third parties if they are to work efficiently and effectively in nurturing the conditions for peace. No single third party alone had the resources or leverage to make the peace process work. In those settlements that did succeed, many different laborers tilled the soil so that the peace process could bear fruit. The United Nations required the backing of great powers. Great powers needed the local support of a country's neighbors. Regional actors and groups needed the assistance of subregional groups. Governments and international organizations also required the active assistance and involvement of nongovernmental organizations and agencies, particularly during implementation of the agreement.

In El Salvador, for example, UN mediation efforts were assisted by the "four friends" and the United States, which played a useful behind-the-scenes role during negotiations. Earlier, the Contadora and Esquipulas II group of states drew up a general proposal for a regional peace plan that paved the way for the initiation of the peace process in El Salvador. Once the agreement was in place, ONUSAL's efforts were complemented by the work of other UN agencies and nongovernmental organizations in development assistance, repatriation of refugees, monitoring and observation of elections, and a host of other activities.

Similarly, although the Permanent Five were the principal agents in bringing the different Cambodian factions to the peace table (with the United States as the central figure), the Permanent Five received crucial support from ASEAN and individual states in the region such as Australia and Indonesia. The United States was obviously the primary player in the negotiation of the Angola-Namibia peace accords, but much of the groundwork was laid by the Western Contact Group, which earlier had defined some of the critical elements for a settlement. Once the United Nations assumed direct responsibility for managing the implementation of the peace settlement in Namibia, it had to work closely with the U.S. mediator to make sure that the peace process was not scuttled by SWAPO's incursion into Namibia in direct violation of the accords. Nongovernmental organizations also worked closely with the United Nations in helping with voter registration and electoral observation and monitoring in the run-up to the elections. In Portugal's efforts to mediate an end to the civil war in Angola, the American and Soviet presences were keenly evident in negotiations. Although the agreement subsequently failed, failure had more to do with the lack of adequate third-party involvement in implementation than with the lack of third-party support for negotiations. The lesson for Cyprus is that ongoing UN mediation efforts to reconcile the island's two communities are unlikely to bear much fruit unless other third parties, especially the allies of Greece and Turkey, become involved and help reach an accommodation that will effect the removal of foreign forces from the island.

Peacemaking and peace building are a nurturing process. As we have seen, negotiated settlements are unlikely to endure if left unattended; they must be cultivated by skillful, committed people able to manage the problems that inevitably arise as the terms of a settlement negotiated at a given point in time are translated over time into practice. By entrenching their roles and remaining fully engaged, third parties can help settlements take root.

NOTES

1. What Makes a Peace Settlement Stick?

1. Kalevi J. Holsti, *Peace and War: Armed Conflicts and International Order, 1648–1989* (Cambridge: Cambridge University Press, 1991), 353.

2. Ibid., 24.

3. This assistance can include diverse activities such as election monitoring, refugee resettlement, or the monitoring of cease-fires.

4. Boutros Boutros-Ghali, *Agenda for Peace* (New York: United Nations, 1992), 11.

5. There is an extensive literature on both the causes and the consequences of what are here called protracted social conflicts. See, for example, Ted Robert Gurr, *Minorities at Risk: A Global View of Ethnopolitical Conflicts* (Washington, D.C.: United States Institute of Peace Press, 1993); Milton J. Easman, *Ethnic Politics* (Ithaca: Cornell University Press, 1994); Michael E. Brown, ed., *Ethnic Conflict and International Security* (Princeton: Princeton University Press, 1993); Walker Connor, *Ethnonationalism: The Quest for Understanding* (Princeton: Princeton University Press, 1994); and Ernest Gellner, *Nations and Nationalism* (Ithaca: Cornell University Press, 1993).

6. Barry Buzan, "Third World Regional Security in Structural Perspective," in Brian L. Job, ed., *The Insecurity Dilemma: National Security of Third World States* (Boulder, Colo.: Lynne Rienner, 1992), 187.

7. See, for example, Thomas G. Weiss and James G. Blight, eds., *The Suffering Grass: Superpowers and Regional Conflict in Southern Africa and the Caribbean* (Boulder, Colo.: Lynne Rienner, 1992).

8. See, for example, Morton Deutsch, *The Resolution of Conflict: Constructive and Deconstructive Processes* (New Haven: Yale University Press, 1979); C. R. Mitchell and K. Webb, "Mediation in International Relations: An Evolving Tradition," and John B. Stephens, "Acceptance of Mediation Initiatives: A Preliminary Framework," both in C. R. Mitchell and K. Webb, eds., *New Approaches to International Mediation* (Westport, Conn.: Greenwood Press, 1988), 1–15 and 52–74; and Kumar Rupesinghe, "Theories of Conflict Resolution and Their Applicability to Protracted Ethnic Conflicts," *Bulletin of Peace Proposals* 18, no. 4 (winter 1987): 527–539.

9. Brian L. Job, "The Insecurity Dilemma: National, Regime, and State Securities in the Third World," in Job, *Insecurity Dilemma*, 17–18.

10. Stephen John Stedman, *Peacemaking in Civil War: International Mediation in Zimbabwe, 1974–1980* (Boulder, Colo.: Lynne Rienner, 1988), 9.

11. Roy Licklider, "The Consequences of Negotiated Settlements in Civil Wars, 1945–1993," *American Political Science Review* 89, no. 3 (September 1995): 685–687.

12. See, for example, John Burton, *Conflict: Resolution and Provention* (New York: St. Martin's, 1990); John Burton, *Resolving Deep-Rooted Conflict: A Handbook* (Lanham, Md.: University Press of America, 1987); and Edward E. Azar and John W. Burton, eds., *International Conflict Resolution: Theory and Practice* (Sussex, England: Wheatsheaf Books, 1986).

13. Christopher R. Mitchell, "Conflict Resolution and Civil War: Reflections on the Sudanese Settlement of 1972," working paper no. 3, Center for Conflict Analysis and Resolution, George Mason University, August 1989, 32.

14. Boutros-Ghali, *Agenda for Peace,* 32.

15. This list of tasks was suggested by Patricia Weiss Fagen, Chief of Mission, United Nations High Commission for Refugees, El Salvador, at an academic workshop on "Resolving Civil Conflicts: The Lessons of El Salvador," held at Stanford University, May 5–7, 1993.

16. This point is made by Saadia Touval in *The Peace Brokers: Mediators in the Arab-Israeli Conflict, 1948–1979* (Princeton: Princeton University Press, 1982).

17. John Burton quoted in Jacob Bercovitch, *Social Conflicts and Third Parties: Strategies of Conflict Resolution* (Boulder, Colo.: Westview, 1984), 26.

18. See, for example, Husch Hanning, ed., *Peacekeeping and Confidence-Building Measures in the Third World* (New York: International Peace Academy, 1985); Louis Kriesberg, "Transforming Conflicts in the Middle East and Central Europe," in Louis Kriesberg, Terrell A. Northrup, and Stuart J. Thorson, eds., *Intractable Conflicts and Their Transformation* (Syracuse, N.Y.: Syracuse University Press, 1989), 109–131; and Brian S. Mandell, *The Sinai Experience: Lessons in Multimethod Arms Control, Verification, and Risk Management,* Arms Control and Verification Studies no. 3 (Ottawa: Arms Control and Disarmament Division, Department of External Affairs, 1987).

19. See, for example, National Democratic Institute for International Affairs, *Nation Building: The U.N. and Namibia* (Washington, D.C.: National Democratic Institute for International Affairs, 1990).

20. Brian S. Mandell, "Anatomy of a Confidence-Building Regime: Egyptian-Israeli Security Cooperation," *International Journal* 45, no. 2 (spring 1990): 218.

21. See Jacob Bercovitch, "Third Parties in Conflict Management: The Structure and the Conditions of Effective Mediation in International Relations," *International Journal* 37, no. 4 (autumn 1985): 736–752; Loraleigh Keashly and Ronald J. Fisher, "Towards a Contingency Approach to Third-Party Intervention in Regional Conflict: A Cyprus Illustration," *International Journal* 45, no. 2 (spring 1990): 424–453; and Fen Osler Hampson, "Building a Stable Peace: Opportunities and Limits to Security Cooperation in Third World Regional Conflicts," *International Journal* 45, no. 2 (spring 1990): 454–489.

22. Paul Diehl, "When Peacekeeping Does Not Lead to Peace: Some Notes on Conflict Resolution," *Bulletin of Peace Proposals* 18, no. 1 (winter 1987): 47–53; and Paul F. Diehl, "Peace-Keeping Operations and the Quest for Peace," *Political Science Quarterly* 103, no. 3 (autumn 1988): 485–507.

23. Keashly and Fisher, "Towards a Contingency Approach," 424.

24. See, for example, Edward E. Azar, *The Management of Protracted Social Conflict: Theory and Cases* (Hampshire, England: Dartmouth Publishing, 1990); Sydney D. Bailey, *Peaceful Settlement of International Disputes* (New York: UNITAR, 1969); Alan James, *The Politics of Peacekeeping* (New York: Praeger, 1969); Johan Kaufman and Nico Schrijver, *Changing Global Needs: Expanding Roles for the United Nations System* (New Hampshire: Dartmouth College, Academic Council of the United Nations System, 1990); Anthony Lake, ed., *After the Wars* (New Brunswick, N.J.: Transaction Books, 1990); and Henry Wiseman, *Peacekeeping and the Management of International Conflict* (Ottawa: Canadian Institute for International Peace and Security, 1987).

25. See I. William Zartman, *Ripe for Resolution: Conflict and Intervention in Africa* (Oxford: Oxford University Press, 1985).

26. I. William Zartman, "Ripening Conflict, Ripe Moment, Formula, and Mediation," in Diane B. Bendahmane and John W. McDonald, Jr., eds., *Perspectives on Negotiation* (Washington, D.C.: Foreign Service Institute, U.S. Department of State, 1986), 217–218.

27. Richard N. Haass, *Conflicts Unending: The United States and Regional Disputes* (New Haven: Yale University Press, 1990), 6, 27–28.

28. See Janice Gross Stein, "Getting to the Table: Triggers, Stages, Functions, and Consequences of Pre-negotiation," *International Journal* 42, no. 2 (spring 1989): 475–502; and Brian Tomlin and Brian S. Mandell, "Mediation in the Development of Norms to Manage Conflict: Kissinger in the Middle East," *Journal of Peace Research* 28, no. 1 (February 1991): 43–55.

29. Haass, *Conflicts Unending*, 138–139.

30. In contrast, some situations may be overripe for resolution. See Douglas G. Anglin, "Ripe, Ripening, or Overripe? Sanctions as an Inducement to Negotiations: The South African Case," *International Journal* 45, no. 2 (spring 1990): 360–385.

31. See, for example, Roger E. Kanet and Edward A. Kolodziej, eds., *The Cold War as Cooperation: Superpower Cooperation in Regional Conflict Management* (Baltimore: Johns Hopkins University Press, 1991).

32. These viewpoints are discussed in Hampson, "Building a Stable Peace."

33. For a theoretical discussion of these views, see Robert Keohane, ed., *Neorealism and Its Critics* (New York: Columbia University Press, 1986), 1–97, 322–346; and Joseph F. Grieco, "Anarchy and the Limits of Cooperation: A Realist Critique of the New Liberal Institutionalism," *International Organization* 42, no. 3 (summer 1988): 485–507. For a useful review of some of the most recent work in international security in the realist tradition, see Fareed Zakaria, "Realism and Domestic Politics," *International Security* 17, no. 1 (summer 1992): 177–198.

34. The most forceful exposition of this viewpoint is found in John Mearsheimer, "Back to the Future: Instability in Europe after the Cold War," *International Security* 15, no. 1 (summer 1990): 5–56.

35. Buzan, "Third World Regional Security," 168. See also Barry Buzan, *People, States, and Fear: The National Security Problem in International Relations* (Chapel Hill: University of North Carolina Press, 1993); Edward E. Azar and Chung-In Moon, eds., *National Security in the Third World: The Management of International and External Threats* (Aldershot, England: Edward Elgar Publishing, 1988); and Mohammed Ayoob, *Regional Security in the Third World* (London: Croom Helm, 1986).

36. Buzan, "Third World Regional Security," 169.

37. Ibid., 170.

38. Is this not identical to Jervis's "security dilemma" in international politics? See Robert Jervis, *Perception and Misperception in International Politics* (Princeton: Princeton University Press, 1979), 58–116.

39. Is this not the functional equivalent to Walt's notion of "balance of threats" as opposed to "balance of power"? See Stephen M. Walt, *The Origins of Alliances* (Ithaca: Cornell University Press, 1987).

40. Buzan, "Third World Regional Security," 171.

41. Shmuel Sandler, "The Protracted Arab-Israeli Conflict: A Temporal-Spatial Analysis," *Jerusalem Journal of International Affairs* 10, no. 4 (December 1988): 54–78.

42. Holsti, *Peace and War,* 337.

43. Ibid., 337–339.

44. We might also want to add to the list the presence (or absence) of ambiguities in the agreement that subsequently become (1) major points of contention or (2) a pretext for the parties, including third parties, to shirk their responsibilities and obligations.

45. Arend Lijphart, "The Power Sharing Approach," in Joseph V. Montville, ed., *Conflict and Peacemaking in Multiethnic Societies* (New York: Lexington Books, 1991), 494.

46. See Donald L. Horowitz, "Making Moderation Pay: The Comparative Politics for Ethnic Conflict Management," in Montville, *Conflict and Peacemaking in Multiethnic Societies,* 451–476.

47. Zartman, "Ripening Conflict," 205–228; Richard N. Haass, "Ripeness and the Settlement of International Disputes," *Survival* 30, no. 3 (May/June 1988): 232–251; and Haass, *Conflicts Unending.*

2. Cyprus

1. Richard N. Haass, *Conflicts Unending: The United States and Regional Disputes* (New Haven: Yale University Press, 1990), 77.

2. Brian S. Mandell, "The Cyprus Conflict: Explaining Resistance to Resolution," in Norma Salem, ed., *Cyprus: A Regional Conflict and Its Resolution* (New York: St. Martin's, 1992), 221.

3. Cultivated ripeness, unlike an imposed settlement, involves the active involvement and cooperation of the disputing parties in negotiations undertaken with the assistance of third parties.

4. Former U.S. ambassador to Greece Monteagle Stearns adds further proof of this Greco-Turkish intrusion into the affairs and decisions of the two ethnic communities in Cyprus. See Monteagle Stearns, *Entangled Allies: U.S. Policy toward Greece, Turkey, and Cyprus* (New York: Council on Foreign Relations, 1992), 107–116.

5. For various accounts of the history of Cyprus and the evolution of the dispute, see Evangelos Averoff-Tossizza, *Lost Opportunities: The Cyprus Question, 1950–1963* (New Rochelle, N.Y.: Aristide D. Caratzas, 1968); Dimitri S. Bitsios, *Cyprus: The Vulnerable Republic* (Thessaloniki, Greece: Institute for Balkan Studies, 1975); Nancy Crawshaw, *The Cyprus Revolt: An Account of the Struggle for Union with Greece* (London: George Allen and Unwin, 1978); Thomas Ehrlich, *Cyprus: 1958–1967* (London: Oxford University Press, 1974); Charles Foley and W. I. Scobie, *The Struggle for Cyprus* (Stanford, Calif.: Hoover Institution, 1975); Christopher Hitchens, *Hostage to History: Cyprus from the Ottomans to Kissinger* (New York: Noonday, 1989); Linda B. Miller, *Cyprus: The Law and Politics of Civil Strife* (Cambridge, Mass.: Center for International Affairs, Harvard University, 1968); Van Coufoudakis, ed., *Essays on the Cyprus Conflict* (New York: Pella, 1976); Stephen G. Xydis, *Cyprus: Reluctant Republic* (The Hague: Mouton, 1973); and Tozun Bahcheli, *Greek-Turkish Relations since 1955* (Boulder, Colo.: Westview, 1990).

6. On Britain's relationship with Cyprus, see John Reddaway, *Burdened with Cyprus* (London: Weidenfeld and Nicolson, 1986).

7. Stanley Kyriakides, *Cyprus: Constitutionalism and Crisis Government* (Philadelphia: University of Pennsylvania Press, 1968), 51.

8. For discussions on the 1960 Constitution of Cyprus, see Kyriakides, *Cyprus*, 53–162; Zaim M. Necatigil, *The Cyprus Question in International Law* (New York: Oxford University Press, 1993), 14–25, 56–64; and Polyvios G. Polyviou, *Cyprus in Search of a Constitution: Constitutional Negotiations and Proposals, 1960–1975* (Washington, D.C.: American Hellenic Institute, 1976).

9. This discussion draws upon the analysis by Norma Salem in "The Constitution of 1960 and Its Failure," in Salem, *Cyprus*, 117–125.

10. Kyriakides, *Cyprus*, 76.

11. Reportedly, Turkish aircraft flew over the island and Turkish military and naval concentrations were positioned off the coast. See Robert McDonald, *The Problem of Cyprus*, Adelphi Papers no. 234 (London: International Institute of Strategic Studies, 1989), 12–13.

12. United Nations, *The Blue Helmets: A Review of United Nations Peace-Keeping*, 2d ed. (New York: United Nations, 1990), 285–288.

13. By 1974, UNFICYP forces had been reduced to 2,200 as the situation stabilized.

14. The largest contribution came from NATO countries.

15. Indar Jit Rikhye, *The Theory and Practice of Peacekeeping* (London: C. Hurst, 1984), 91–93.

16. For an in-depth treatment of the Greco-Turkish relationship, see Bahcheli, *Greek-Turkish Relations since 1955*.

17. Paschallis Kitromilidis, "Greek Irredentism in Asia Minor and Cyprus," *Middle Eastern Studies* 26, no. 1 (1990): 13.

18. On the broader ramifications of the Cyprus dispute for NATO, see Stearns, *Entangled Allies*; Parker T. Hart, *Two NATO Allies at the Threshold of War: Cyprus, A Firsthand Account of Crisis Management, 1965–1968* (Durham, N.C.: Duke University Press, 1990); Theodore A. Couloumbis, *The United States, Greece, and Turkey: The Troubled Triangle* (New York: Praeger, 1983); and Laurence Stern, *The Wrong Horse: The Politics of Intervention and the Failure of American Diplomacy* (New York: Times, 1977).

19. Mandell, "The Cyprus Conflict," 222.

20. Quoted in Ronald J. Fisher, "Introduction: Understanding the Tragedy of Cyprus," in Salem, *Cyprus*, 5.

21. "Efforts to Resolve the Cyprus Dispute," in Diane B. Bendahmane and John W. McDonald, eds., *Perspectives on Negotiations: Four Case Studies and Interpretations* (Washington, D.C.: Foreign Service Institute, U.S. Department of State, 1986), 111.

22. Mandell, "The Cyprus Conflict," 212.

23. Polyvios Polyviou, *Cyprus: Conflict and Negotiation, 1960–1980* (London: Gerald Duckworth, 1980), 186.

24. Pierre Oberling, *The Road to Bellapais: The Turkish Cypriot Exodus to Northern Cyprus* (New York: Columbia University Press, 1982), 176.

25. See R. R. Denktash, *The Cyprus Triangle* (New York: Office of the Turkish Republic of Northern Cyprus, 1988), 118–141.

26. McDonald, *The Problem of Cyprus,* 25.

27. The High-Level Agreement containing the Four Guidelines and the Ten-Point Agreement is reproduced in full in Republic of Cyprus, *The Cyprus Problem: Historical Review and Latest Developments* (Nicosia: Republic of Cyprus, 1993), 100–101.

28. Mandell, "The Cyprus Conflict," 215.

29. "Efforts to Resolve the Cyprus Dispute," 118.

30. Ibid., 129; Mandell, "The Cyprus Conflict," 215–216.

31. "Efforts to Resolve the Cyprus Dispute," 131.

32. Mandell, "The Cyprus Conflict," 216.

33. United Nations Security Council, "Report of the Secretary-General on His Mission of Good Offices in Cyprus," S/21183, March 8, 1990.

34. United Nations Security Council, "Report of the Secretary-General on His Mission of Good Offices in Cyprus," S/21393, July 12, 1993; and United Nations Security Council, "Report of the Secretary-General on His Mission of Good Offices in Cyprus," S/21932, November 7, 1993.

35. United Nations Security Council, "Report of the Secretary-General on His Mission of Good Offices in Cyprus," S/23121, October 8, 1991.

36. United Nations Security Council, "Report of the Secretary-General on His Mission of Good Offices in Cyprus," S/23780, April 3, 1992.

37. United Nations Security Council, "Report of the Secretary-General on His Mission of Good Offices in Cyprus," S/24472, August 21, 1992.

38. United Nations Security Council, "Report of the Secretary-General on His Mission of Good Offices in Cyprus," S/24830, November 19, 1992.

39. United Nations Security Council, "Report of the Secretary-General on His Mission of Good Offices in Cyprus," S/26026, July 1, 1993; and United Nations Security Council, "Report of the Secretary-General in Connection with the Security Council's Comprehensive Reassessment of the United Nations Operation in Cyprus," S/2677, November 22, 1993.

40. United Nations Security Council, "Report of the Secretary-General on His Mission of Good Offices in Cyprus," S/1994/629, May 30, 1994.

41. Mandell, "The Cyprus Conflict," 230.

42. McDonald, *The Problem of Cyprus,* 74.

43. For a fascinating discussion of the role of perceptions, misperceptions, and history in the conflict, see Vamik D. Volkan, *Cyprus—War and Adaptation: A Psychoanalytic History of Two Ethnic Groups in Conflict* (Charlottesville: University of Virginia Press, 1979).

44. McDonald, *The Problem of Cyprus,* 76.

45. Quoted in Reed Coughlan, "Stalemate in Cyprus: Negotiations between the Greek and Turkish Cypriot Leadership," in K. M. de Silva and S. W. R. de A. Samarasinghe, eds., *Peace Accords and Ethnic Conflict* (London: Frances Pinter, 1993), 49.

46. Ibid., 51.

47. Ibid., 55.

48. Stearns, *Entangled Allies,* 127.

49. McDonald, *The Problem of Cyprus,* 80.

50. Canada announced the withdrawal of its peacekeeping forces from Cyprus in 1993, after a twenty-seven-year commitment.

51. Mandell, "The Cyprus Conflict," 221.

3. Namibia

1. See Alexandra Bugaliskis, "Implementation of the Namibian Settlement Plan" (master's thesis, Norman Paterson School of International Affairs, Carleton University, July 1992), 109.

2. See Chester A. Crocker, *High Noon in Southern Africa: Making Peace in a Rough Neighborhood* (New York: W. W. Norton, 1992), 67–70.

3. For treatments of the history of this conflict, see Robert S. Jaster, *South Africa and Its Neighbours: The Dynamics of Regional Conflict,* Adelphi Papers no. 209 (London: International Institute of Strategic Studies, summer 1986); and John A. Marcum et al., "Regional Security in Southern Africa," *Survival* 30, no. 1 (January/ February 1988): 3–58.

4.. Opposition parties likewise received some support from the Ovambo.

5. The seven members of the "alliance" of frontline states—Angola, Botswana, Mozambique, Namibia, Tanzania, Zambia, and Zimbabwe—saw themselves as victims of aggression by South Africa during the years in which South Africa was trying to defend its apartheid system against its neighbors.

6. The following discussion is based on these sources: Robert S. Jaster, *The 1988 Peace Accords and the Future of South-Western Africa,* Adelphi Papers no. 253 (London: International Institute of Strategic Studies, autumn 1990); Vivienne Jabri, "The Western Contact Group as Intermediary in the Conflict over Namibia," in C. R. Mitchell and K. Webb, eds., *New Approaches to International Mediation*

(Westport, Conn.: Greenwood Press, 1988), 102–130; Pamela S. Falk, "Namibian Independence and the Cuban Presence in Angola: Third-Party Involvement in Southern African Conflict Resolution," in International Peace Academy, *Southern Africa in Crisis: Regional and International Responses* (Dordrecht: Martinus Nijhoff, 1988), 91–102; Gerald Bender and Witney Schneidman, "The Namibia Negotiations: Multilateral versus Bilateral Approaches to International Mediation," Pew Program in Case Teaching and Writing, case no. 422, Pittsburgh, 1988; Pamela S. Falk, "The U.S., USSR, Cuba, and South Africa in Angola, 1974–88: Negotiators' Nightmare, Diplomats' Dilemma," Pew Program in Case Teaching and Writing, case no. 405, Pittsburgh, 1988; and Pamela S. Falk and Kurt M. Campbell, "The U.S., USSR, Cuba, and South Africa in Angola, 1974–88: The Quagmire of Four-Party Negotiations, 1981–1988," Pew Program in Case Teaching and Writing, case no. 429, Pittsburgh, 1988.

7. The United States offered to try to get reference to SWAPO as the "sole and authentic representative of the people of Namibia" withdrawn if South Africa would agree to a date to implement UN Security Council Resolution 435. Dirk Mudge turned down the offer, however.

8. Crocker, *High Noon in Southern Africa,* 75.

9. Ibid., 77. For other discussions of U.S. policies toward Southern Africa under the Reagan administration, see Ben L. Martin, "American Policy towards Southern Africa in the 1980s," *Journal of Modern African Studies* 27, no. 1 (1989): 23–46; Davidson Nicol, "United States Foreign Policy in Southern Africa: Third World Perspectives," *Journal of Modern African Studies* 21, no. 4 (1983): 587–603; Michael Clough, "Southern Africa: Challenges and Choices," *Foreign Affairs* 66, no. 5 (summer 1988): 1067–1090; Howard Wolpe, "Seizing Southern African Opportunities," *Foreign Policy* 73 (winter 1988–89): 60–75; and Robert E. Clute, "The American-Soviet Confrontation in Africa: Its Impact on the Politics of Africa," *Journal of Asian and African Studies* 24, nos. 3–4 (1989): 159–169.

10. Quoted in Ronald Dreyer, *Namibia and Angola: The Search for Independence and Regional Security, 1966–1988,* PSIS Occasional Papers no. 3/1988 (Geneva: Programme for Strategic and International Security Studies, Graduate Institute of International Studies, 1988), 31.

11. Crocker, *High Noon in Southern Africa,* 195.

12. Ibid., 370.

13. The final settlement phase of the peacemaking process was preceded by a range of agreements reached during 1988, including (1) the Governor's Island Agreement on "Principles for a Peaceful Settlement in South-Western Africa" (July 13), accepted by the governments of South Africa, Cuba, and Angola on July 20; (2) the Protocol of Geneva (August 5), which reaffirmed the Governor's Island principles and sought to formalize the then current de facto cease-fire, with Cuba and Angola using their good offices to get SWAPO to withdraw above the 16th

parallel following a South African troop withdrawal, in accordance with the general negotiations on South African-Cuban-Angolan troop withdrawals then in progress; (3) the Protocol of Brazzaville (December 13), which recommended that implementation of the peace plan as outlined in UN Security Council Resolution 435 (1978) should begin on April 1, 1989, with the parties meeting on December 22 in New York for the signing of the Tripartite Agreement, upon which signature parties agree to exchange prisoners of war (a joint commission was also established in the annex to the agreement, comprising representatives from Cuba, Angola, and South Africa, along with the United States and Soviet Union; Namibian representatives would attain membership upon independence, so that Namibia could oversee the implementation of the Tripartite Agreement); and (4) the Tripartite Agreement (December 22), which reaffirmed the provisions of UN Security Council Resolution 435 and previous agreements on principles for the implementation period, with a beginning implementation date of April 1 being reaffirmed and linked to bilateral accords on Cuban troop withdrawal being signed.

Subsequent to these agreements, UN Security Council Resolutions 628 and 629 of January 1989 confirmed April 1, 1989, as the starting date for the implementation of UN Security Council Resolution 435.

14. All documents in this period refer to the implementation of UN Security Council Resolution 435 of September 29, 1978, which by itself was not an independently cohesive plan for Namibian independence. Instead, UN Security Council Resolution 435 references several earlier resolutions, reports, and letters that give expression to the general principles and guidelines contained in the resolution. Specifically, these included UN Security Council Resolutions 385 (1976), 431 (1978), and 432 (1978), and also the following: "Report of the Secretary-General Submitted Pursuant to Paragraph 2 of Security Council Resolution 431 (1978) Concerning the Situation in Namibia" (United Nations Document S/12827); "Letter Dated 10 April 1978 from the Representatives of Canada, France, the Federal Republic of Germany, the United Kingdom of Great Britain and Northern Ireland and the United States of America to the President of the Security Council" (United Nations Document S/12636); "Explanatory Statement by the Secretary-General Regarding His Report Submitted Pursuant to Paragraph 2 of Security Council Resolution 431 (1978) Concerning the Situation in Namibia" (United Nations Document S/12869); and "Letter Dated 8 September 1978 from the Representatives of Tanzania and Zambia to the Secretary-General" (United Nations Document S/12841).

These documents, along with the subsequent 1982 Constitutional Principles and the "Impartiality Agreements" of September 1982, formed the principal guidelines for the creation of UNTAG and the implementation of the peace settlement. See "Letter Dated 12 July 1982 from the Representatives of Canada, France, the Federal Republic of Germany, the United Kingdom of Great Britain and Northern Ireland and the United States of America to the Secretary-General" (United Nations Document S/15287/Annex) for the list of Constitutional Principles. Further significant documents concluded prior to the actual implementation included the more contemporary and expansive "Further Report of the Secretary-General Concerning the Implementation of Security Council Resolutions 435 (1978) and 439 (1978) Concerning the Question of Namibia" (United Nations Document S/20412, January 23, 1989), which updated the earlier proposals set forth in United Nations Document S/12827, and the Status of Forces agreement (contained in United Nations Document S/20412/Add.1) concluded on March 16, 1989.

15. Douglas G. Anglin, "Ripe, Ripening, or Overripe? Sanctions as an Inducement to Negotiations: The South African Case," *International Journal* 45, no. 2 (spring 1990): 368. Anglin points out, however, that the international banking community had taken the sting out of sanctions on the South African economy by repeatedly bailing out the South African regime when foreign exchange crises forced it to default on its debts.

16. For discussions of Soviet foreign policies toward the region, see Kurt M. Campbell, *Southern Africa in Soviet Foreign Policy*, Adelphi Papers no. 227 (London: International Institute of Strategic Studies, winter 1987–88); Chi Su, "Moscow's Ideology and Policy in Southern Africa," *Issues and Studies* 22, no. 2 (February 1986): 99–110; Christopher Coker, "Moscow and Pretoria: A Possible Alignment," *World Today* 44, no. 1 (January 1988): 6–9; Peter Clement, "Moscow and Southern Africa," *Problems of Communism* 34, no. 2 (March–April 1985): 29–50; Keith Somerville, "The USSR and Southern Africa since 1976," *Journal of Modern African Studies* 22, no. 1 (1984): 73–108; Peter Shearman, "Soviet Foreign Policy in Africa and Latin America: A Comparative Case Study," *Millennium: Journal of International Studies* 15, no. 3 (winter 1986): 339–359; and Sam C. Nolutshungu, "Soviet Involvement in Southern Africa," *Annals AAPSS*, no. 481 (September 1985): 138–146.

17. Mark Owen Lombardi, "The Angolan-Namibian Peace Agreement and Superpower Foreign Policy: A Regionalist or Globalist Solution?" (paper presented at the annual meeting of the International Studies Association, Washington, D.C., 1990).

18. Neil S. MacFarlane, "The Soviet Union and Southern African Security," *Problems of Communism* 38, nos. 2–3 (March–June 1989): 85–86.

19. Crocker, *High Noon in Southern Africa,* 423.

20. Ibid., 451.

21. Jorge I. Dominguez, "Pipsqueak Power: The Centrality and Anamoly of Cuba," in James G. Blight and Thomas G. Weiss, eds., *The Suffering Grass: The Superpowers and Regional Conflict in Southern Africa and the Caribbean* (Boulder, Colo.: Lynne Rienner, 1992), 70.

22. United Nations Document S/12636.

23. United Nations Document S/12827.

24. United Nations Document S/12869.

25. United Nations Document S/12827.

26. United Nations Document S/12841.

27. United Nations Document S/15287/Annex.

28. "Agreement between the United Nations and the Republic of South Africa Concerning the Status of the United Nations Transition Assistance Group in Namibia" (United Nations Document S/20412/Add.1).

29. "Further Report of the Secretary-General Concerning the Implementation of Security Council Resolutions 435 (1978) and 439 (1978) Concerning the Question of Namibia" (United Nations Document S/15776).

30. "Report of the Secretary-General" (United Nations Document S/20338).

31. "Letter Dated 26 November 1985 from the Secretary-General Addressed to the Minister of Foreign Affairs of South Africa" (United Nations Document S/17658).

32. United Nations Document S/12827.

33. Jaster, *1988 Peace Accords,* 34–35.

34. Donald L. Sparks and December Green, *Namibia: The Nation after Independence* (Boulder, Colo.: Westview, 1992), 41, 106.

35. National Democratic Institute for International Affairs, *Nation Building: The UN and Namibia* (Washington, D.C.: National Democratic Institute for International Affairs, 1990), 35 (hereafter cited as NDIIA).

36. See "Letter Dated 13 October 1989 from the Permanent Representative of South Africa to the United Nations Addressed to the Secretary-General" (United Nations Document S/20899/Annex I).

37. Jaster, *1988 Peace Accords,* 40–41.

38. NDIIA, 26–27.

39. Ibid., 33.

40. NDIIA, 31–34; "Report of the Secretary-General on the Implementation of Security Council Resolution 640 (1989) Concerning the Question of Namibia" (United Nations Document S/20883); and "Further Report of the Secretary-General on the Implementation of Security Council Resolution 435 (1978) Concerning the Question of Namibia" (United Nations Document S/20967/Annex I).

41. NDIIA, 35–36.

42. "Report of the Secretary-General on the Implementation of Security Council Resolution 643 (1989) Concerning the Question of Namibia" (United Nations Document S/20943); United Nations Document S/20967/Add.1; and NDIIA, 36.

43. See NDIIA, appendix IX.

44. United Nations Document S/20412/Add. 1.

45. United Nations Document S/20883/Add.1.

46. "Letter Dated 13 October 1989 from the Permanent Representative of South Africa to the United Nations Addressed to the Secretary-General" (United Nations Document S/20899/Annex II).

47. United Nations Document S/20943.

48. NDIIA, 39–40.

49. Crocker, *High Noon in Southern Africa,* 417.

50. "Letter Dated 7 April 1989 from the Permanent Representative of South Africa to the United Nations Addressed to the Secretary-General" (United Nations Document S/20576).

51. Jaster, *1988 Peace Accords,* 38–39; and NDIIA, 24–25.

52. Jaster, *1988 Peace Accords,* 38–39; NDIIA, 24–25; and Sparks and Green, *Namibia,* 50.

53. NDIIA, 24–25.

54. Ibid., 38–39.

55. Crocker, *High Noon in Southern Africa,* 420.

56. Ibid., 420–421.

57. Ibid., 422.

58. "Note by the Secretary-General" (United Nations Document S/20579/Annex).

59. United Nations, *The Blue Helmets* (New York: UN Department of Public Information, 1990), 381.

60. Bugaliskis, "Implementation of the Namibian Settlement Plan," 109–110.

61. Ibid., 136–138.

62. *Africa Research Bulletin* 28, no. 12 (December 1–31, 1991): 10387.

63. *Africa Research Bulletin* 29, no. 9 (September 1–30,1992): 10714.

64. *Africa Research Bulletin* 29, no. 12 (December 1–31, 1992): 10818.

65. NDIIA, 75; and Jaster, *1988 Peace Accords,* 39.

66. NDIIA, 78.

67. Ibid., 79.

68. Ibid.

69. Ibid., 76–77.

4. Angola

1. Cuba had 2,000 troops in the country by mid-November, with the number rising to an estimated 14,000 by February 1976.

2. Angola is potentially one of the richest nations in Southern Africa because of its oil reserves and other bountiful natural resources.

3. Chester A. Crocker, "Angola: 'Can This Outrageous Spectacle Be Stopped?'" *Washington Post*, November 13, 1993. UNAVEM II stands for United Nations Angola Verification Mission II.

4. Chester A. Crocker, *High Noon in Southern Africa: Making Peace in a Rough Neighborhood* (New York: W. W. Norton, 1992), 198.

5. Ibid., 194–196.

6. Ibid., 231.

7. Ibid., 348.

8. Ibid., 393.

9. "Angola/Namibia Accords," *Department of State Bulletin* 89 (February 1989): 11. The positive role played in the peace process by President Denis Sassou-Nguesso of Congo, who invited the parties in April 1987 to meet at Brazzaville while he was still chairman of the OAU, was specifically mentioned in the text of the protocol. Furthermore, Crocker observed at the end of the Brazzaville talks that Sassou-Nguesso's role "served as a catalyst to restore and reinvigorate contact and dialogue" between the United States and Angola. Ibid., 10.

10. Robert C. R. Siekmann, *Basic Documents on United Nations and Related Peace-Keeping Forces* (London: Martinus Nijhoff, 1989), 386–390, 392.

11. In statements made to the delegations, U.S. secretary of state George Shultz specifically welcomed the presence of Soviet deputy foreign minister Adamishin and members of the Soviet delegation, focusing on the "important and constructive" role the Soviets had played in the peace process. See "Angola/ Namibia Accords," 11–12.

12. Ibid., 13.

13. United Nations, *The Blue Helmets: A Review of United Nations Peace-Keeping* (New York: United Nations, 1990), 337.

14. "Angola/Namibia Accords," 15–16.

15. Robert S. Jaster, *The 1988 Peace Accords and the Future of South-Western Africa*, Adelphi Papers no. 253 (London: International Institute of Strategic Studies, autumn 1990), 38–39.

16. James Brooke, "South African Insurgents Agree to Shut Their Bases, Angola Says," *New York Times*, January 6, 1989.

17. *Africa Research Bulletin* 27, no. 4 (May 15, 1990): 9659.

18. *Africa Research Bulletin* 27, no. 5 (June 15, 1990): 9692.

19. Ibid., 9675.

20. *Africa Research Bulletin* 27, no. 6 (July 15, 1990): 9730.

21. Ibid.

22. *Africa Research Bulletin* 27, no. 7 (July 1–31, 1990): 9759.

23. Ibid., 9767.

24. Ibid., 9768.

25. *Africa Research Bulletin* 27, no. 8 (August 1–31, 1990): 9798.

26. Ibid.

27. *Africa Research Bulletin* 27, no. 9 (September 1–30, 1990): 9834.

28. *Africa Research Bulletin* 27, no. 8 (August 1–31, 1990): 9798.

29. *Africa Research Bulletin* 27, no. 9 (September 1–30, 1990): 9834.

30. Ibid.

31. *Africa Research Bulletin* 27, no. 10 (October 1–31, 1990): 9869.

32. *Africa Research Bulletin* 27, no. 11 (November 1–30, 1990): 9908.

33. *Africa Research Bulletin* 27, no. 12 (December 1–31, 1990): 9934.

34. Ibid., 9944.

35. Ibid., 9944–9945.

36. *Africa Research Bulletin* 28, no. 1 (January 1–31, 1991): 9717.

37. *Africa Research Bulletin* 28, no. 2 (February 1–28, 1991): 10018.

38. Ibid., 10018–10019.

39. Ibid., 10002.

40. Ibid., 10019.

41. *Africa Research Bulletin* 28, no. 3 (March 1–31, 1991): 10053.

42. *Africa Research Bulletin* 28, no. 4 (April 1–30, 1991): 10090–10091.

43. Ibid., 10091.

44. Ibid.

45. Ibid.

46. The different portions of the Bicesse Accords are attached to "Letter Dated 17 May 1991 from the Chargé d'Affaires a.i. of the Permanent Mission of Angola to the United Nations Addressed to the Secretary-General" (United Nations Document S/22609).

47. "Report of the Secretary-General on the United Nations Angola Verification Mission" (United Nations Document S/22627).

48. "Letter Dated 29 May 1991 from the Permanent Representative of Angola to the United Nations Addressed to the Secretary-General" (United Nations Document S/22644).

49. "Report of the Secretary-General in Pursuance of Security Council Resolution 696 (1991)" (United Nations Document S/22672).

50. "Letter Dated 13 June 1991 from the Secretary-General Addressed to the President of the Security Council" (United Nations Document S/22716); and "Letter Dated 18 June 1991 from the President of the Security Council Addressed to the Secretary-General" (United Nations Document S/22717). Of the countries composing UNAVEM II, Algeria, Argentina, Brazil, Congo, India, Jordan, Spain, and Yugoslavia were already contributing to the observer mission.

51. *Africa Research Bulletin.* 28, no. 7 (July 1–31, 1991): 10206.

52. *Africa Research Bulletin* 28, no. 9 (September 1–30, 1991): 10271.

53. "Report of the Secretary-General on the United Nations Angola Verification Mission II (UNAVEM II)" (United Nations Document S/23191).

54. *Africa Research Bulletin* 28, no. 11 (November 1–30, 1991): 10345.

55. *Africa Research Bulletin* 28, no. 12 (December 1–31, 1991): 10383.

56. Ibid., 10391.

57. *Africa Research Bulletin* 29, no. 1 (January 1–31, 1992): 10424.

58. "Letter Dated 6 February 1992 from the Secretary-General Addressed to the President of the Security Council" (United Nations Document S/23556); and "Letter Dated 7 February 1992 from the President of the Security Council Addressed to the Secretary-General" (United Nations Document S/23557).

59. *Africa Research Bulletin* 29, no. 3 (March 1–31, 1992): 10517.

60. "Further Report of the Secretary-General on the United Nations Angola Verification Mission II (UNAVEM II)" (United Nations Document S/23671).

61. *Africa Research Bulletin* 29, no. 3 (March 1–31, 1992): 10505.

62. *Africa Research Bulletin* 29, no. 4 (April 1–30, 1992): 10539.

63. Ibid., 10656.

64. *Africa Research Bulletin* 29, no. 8 (August 1–31, 1992): 10684.

65. *Africa Research Bulletin* 29, no. 9 (September 1–30, 1992): 10712.

66. John A. Marcum, "Angola: War Again," *Current History* 92, no. 574 (May 1993): 221.

67. *Africa Research Bulletin* 29, no. 10 (October 1–31, 1992): 10743.

68. Ibid., 10742–10744.

69. Marcum, "Angola," 221–222.

70. *Africa Research Bulletin* 29, no. 11 (November 1–30, 1992): 10788–10789.

71. Ibid., 10789.

72. Ibid.

73. Ibid., 10790.

74. *Africa Research Bulletin* 29, no. 12 (December 1–31, 1992): 10810.

75. *South West Africa*, no. 3928 (December 29, 1992–January 10, 1993): 253.

76. *South West Africa,* no. 3929 (January 11–17, 1993): 30.

77. *South West Africa*, no. 3930 (January 18–24, 1993): 61, 74.

78. Steven A. Holmes, "U.S. Accuses Angolan Rebel of Inciting Civil War," *New York Times*, January 23, 1993.

79. *Secretariat News* (January–February 1993).

80. *South West Africa*, no. 3932 (February 1–7, 1993): 167.

81. *South West Africa*, no. 3933 (February 8–14, 1993): 188–189.

82. *South West Africa*, no. 3934 (February 15–21, 1993): 259.

83. *South West Africa*, no. 3935 (February 22–28, 1993): 291.

84. "Letter Dated 29 May 1991 from the Permanent Representative of Angola to the United Nations Addressed to the President of the Security Council" (United Nations Document S/25496).

85. Kenneth B. Noble, "Angolan Rebels Rebound within Reach of a Victory," *New York Times*, April 13, 1993.

86. Barbara Crosette, "UN to Send 7,000 Peacekeepers to Monitor Accord in Angola," *New York Times*, February 9, 1995, A8; and Paul Taylor, "Angola Civil War Rivals Embrace," *Washington Post*, May 7, 1995, A32.

5. El Salvador

1. For accounts of that struggle, see Peter Sollis, "Displaced Persons and Human Rights: The Crisis in El Salvador," *Bulletin of Latin American Research* 11 (January 1992): 49–67; Linda Robinson, "The End of El Salvador's War," *Survival* 33 (September/October 1991): 387–400; Peter Frisk, "Displaced Persons and Human Rights: The Crisis in El Salvador," *Third World Quarterly* 12, nos. 3–4 (1990–91): 40–63; William M. LeoGrande, "After the Battle of San Salvador," *World Policy Journal* 7 (spring 1990): 321–356; Frank Smyth, "Consensus or Crisis: Without Duarte in El Salvador," *Journal of Interamerican Studies and World Affairs* 30 (winter 1988/89): 29–52; Cynthia J. Aronson, *Crossroads: Congress, the Reagan Administration, and Central America* (New York: Pantheon, 1989); Morris J. Blachman and Kenneth E. Sharpe, "Things Fall Apart: Trouble Ahead in El Salvador," *World Policy Journal* 6 (winter 1988/89): 107–139; Robert S. Leiken and Barry Rubin, *The Central American Crisis Reader* (New York: Summit Books, 1987); Martin Diskin and Kenneth E. Sharpe, "El Salvador," in Morris J. Blachman, William M. LeoGrande, and Kenneth E. Sharpe, eds., *Confronting Revolution: Security through Diplomacy in Central America* (New York: Pantheon, 1986): 88–124; United States House Committee on Foreign Affairs, *El Salvador at the Crossroads: Peace or Another Decade of War: Hearings, January 24–February 6, 1990, before the Subcommittee on Human Rights and International Organizations, and on Western Hemisphere Affairs,* 101st Cong., 2d sess. SD cat. no. Y4.F76/1:Sa3/11, 1990; and United States House Committee on Foreign Affairs, Subcommittee on Western Hemisphere Affairs, "From Duarte to Cristiani: Where Is El Salvador Headed? Hearing, July 13, 1989," 101st Cong., 1st sess, SD cat. no. Y4.F76/1:D85, 1989.

2. See United Nations Security Council, "Letter Dated 28 March 1994 from the Secretary-General Addressed to the President of the Security Council," S/1994/361, March 30, 1994.

3. David Browning, "El Salvador: History," in *South America, Central America, and the Caribbean* (London: Europa Publications, 1995), 310.

4. Ibid.

5. Terry Lynn Karl, "El Salvador's Negotiated Revolution," *Foreign Affairs* 71, no. 2 (spring 1992): 149.

6. Joseph G. Sullivan, "How Peace Came to El Salvador," *Orbis* (winter 1994): 84–85.

7. William LeoGrande, "After the Battle of San Salvador: Breaking the Deadlock," *World Policy Journal* 7, no. 2 (spring 1990): 350.

8. Comment by senior UN official at an academic workshop, "Resolving Civil Conflicts: The Lessons of El Salvador," hosted by the Center for Latin American Studies and the Center for International Security and Arms Control, Stanford University, May 5–7, 1993 (hereafter referred to as Stanford Workshop). Participants at the high-level workshop organized by Professor Terry Karl, Stanford University, included senior officials from the government of El Salvador, the FMLN, and the United Nations who were directly involved in the negotiations that led to the peace accords.

9. Observation by a senior official of the government of El Salvador, Stanford Workshop.

10. The Esquipulas II agreements (or Guatemala Procedure) were signed by the presidents of the five Central American nations on August 7, 1987. They agreed to launch a process of democratization in their countries, promote a national dialogue, decree general amnesty, bring about a genuine cease-fire, and promote the holding of free, pluralistic, and fair elections. They also requested all governments concerned to terminate support for irregular forces or insurrectional movements and reiterated their commitment to prevent the use of their own territory for destabilization of other countries in the region. To help achieve these objectives, the presidents also set up an International Verification and Follow-Up Commission (CIVS) composed of the foreign ministers of the Contadora and Support Groups and of the Central American countries, as well as the secretaries-general of the United Nations and the Organization of American States (OAS). Steps toward implementation of the Esquipulas II accords were taken by the five presidents on February 14, 1989, when they signed the Costa del Sol Declaration requesting their foreign ministers to arrange technical meetings to establish verification mechanisms with UN assistance. On July 27, 1989, in Resolution 637, the Security Council welcomed the Esquipulas II and other agreements made by the five Central American presidents and indicated its full support to the secretary-general in his mission of good offices to the region.

11. "Peace for El Salvador," *Christian Science Monitor,* January 6, 1992.

12. Observation by senior FMLN member, Stanford Workshop.

13. Observation by senior FMLN member, Stanford Workshop.

14. Comment by senior UN official, Stanford Workshop.

15. Comment by Salvadoran government official, Stanford Workshop.

16. Comment by senior Salvadoran government official, Stanford Workshop.

17. Comment by Salvadoran government official, Stanford Workshop.

18. United Nations General Assembly, "Report of the Economic and Social Council: Situation of Human Rights in El Salvador: Note by the Secretary-General," A/45/630, October 22, 1990, 3–5.

19. "The Agreement on Human Rights," ONUSAL Fact Sheet no. 5, DPI/1149E, July 1991.

20. United Nations Observer Mission in El Salvador, "Central America: Efforts toward Peace," S/22031, December 21, 1990.

21. United Nations Observer Mission in El Salvador, "Central America: Efforts toward Peace," Report of the Secretary-General, S/22494, d. 16 April 1991.

22. This was because amendments had to be ratified by two successive National Assemblies; a delay would have run up against the first deadline, the expiry of the current National Assembly. It would have taken three more years to get any amendment passed.

23. United Nations Observer Mission in El Salvador, "Mexico Agreements," ONUSAL/El Salvador, DPL/1149D-40697, July 1991.

24. United Nations General Assembly, Security Council, "Letter Dated 26 September 1991 from the Permanent Representative of El Salvador to the United Nations Addressed to the Secretary-General," A/46/502, S/23082, September 26, 1991, 3.

25. Ibid., 5.

26. United Nations General Assembly, Security Council, "Letter Dated 4 October 1991 from the Permanent Representative of El Salvador to the United Nations Addressed to the Secretary-General," A/46/502 Add.1, S/23082/Add.1, October 7, 1991, 2–5.

27. United Nations Security Council, "Central America: Efforts toward Peace: Report by the Secretary-General," S/23402, January 10, 1992, 2–3.

28. Observations by Professor Condolezza Rice, Stanford Workshop.

29. According to UN negotiator Alvaro de Soto, this issue never came up in the negotiations. Personal communication, November 28, 1994.

30. Knut Walter and Philip J. Williams, "The Military and Democratization in El Salvador," *Journal of Interamerican Studies and World Affairs* 35, no. 1 (spring 1993): 67.

31. Ibid., 69.

32. David Holiday and William Stanley, "Building the Peace: Preliminary Lessons from El Salvador," *Journal of International Affairs* 46, no. 2 (winter 1993): 424.

33. Ibid., 429.

34. Ibid.

35. Alvaro de Soto and Graciana del Castillo, "An Integrated International Approach to Human Security: El Salvador: A Case Study" (unpublished paper, United Nations, New York, April 1993), 11.

36. Ibid., 12–13.

37. Ibid., 15.

38. Ibid., 31.

39. Comment by senior Salvadoran government official, Stanford Workshop.

40. United Nations General Assembly, Security Council, "The Situation in Central America: Threats to International Peace and Security and Peace Initiatives: Note by the Secretary-General," A/45/1055, S/23037, September 16, 1991.

41. "First Report of the Director of the Human Rights Division" (A/45/1055), in ibid., 11.

42. United Nations General Assembly, Security Council, "Second Report of the United Nations Observer Mission in El Salvador, Annex, Report of the Director of the Human Rights Division," A/46/658, S/2322, November 15, 1991, 38.

43. United Nations General Assembly, Security Council, "Second Report of the United Nations Observer Mission in El Salvador," A/46/658, S/23222, November 15, 1991, 2.

44. A useful account of some of the early problems of implementation of the peace accords is to be found in George Vickers and Jack Spence, *Endgame: A Progress Report on Implementation of the Salvadoran Peace Accords* (Cambridge, Mass.: Hemisphere Initiatives, December 3, 1992).

45. United Nations Security Council, "United Nations Observer Mission in El Salvador: Report of the Secretary-General," S/23642, February 25, 1992.

46. United Nations General Assembly, Security Council, "The Situation in Central America: Threats to International Peace and Security and Peace Initiatives: Annex: Report of the Director of the Human Rights Division," A/46/935, S/24066, June 5, 1992.

47. United Nations Security Council, "Report of the Secretary-General on the United Nations Observer Mission in El Salvador," S/24833, November 23, 1992, 16.

48. Ibid., 3.

49. Ibid., 10.

50. United Nations Security Council, "Report of the Secretary-General on the United Nations Observer Mission in El Salvador (ONUSAL)," S/25006, December 23, 1992.

51. Ibid., 9–10.

52. William Stanley, *Risking Failure: The Problems and Promise of the New Civilian Police Force in El Salvador* (Washington, D.C.: Hemisphere Initiatives and Washington Office on Latin America, September 1993), 7–8.

53. Alvaro de Soto and Graciana del Castillo, "El Salvador: Still Not a Success Story" (unpublished manuscript, June 1994), 11–12.

54. United Nations Security Council, "Report of the Secretary-General on the United Nations Observer Mission in El Salvador," S/23999, May 26, 1992, 15.

55. The proposal provided that the total number of beneficiaries should not exceed 47,500, consisting of 15,000 ex-combatants from the armed forces, 7,500 FMLN ex-combatants, and approximately 25,000 landholders in the former zones of conflict. The proposal established a three-phased program of land transfer because of financing difficulties and the complexity of the transactions involved. Operational aspects of the land-transfer activity were to be worked out by a supervisory committee established under the secretary-general's proposal. Because a large portion of the land to be transferred was under private ownership, international and regional organizations and bilateral donors would have to supplement limited financing available for the purchase of land. On October 31 the land transfer officially started with the signing by the government and the FMLN, in the presence of ONUSAL, of an agreement to transfer to state properties to FMLN ex-combatants and current landholders on these properties. See "Report of the Secretary-General on the United Nations Observer Mission in El Salvador," S/24833, November 23, 1992, 12–13.

56. S/23130, 5 and 16–18.

57. See Secretary-General's remarks, "Presentation of the Report of the Commission on the Truth," United Nations, New York, March 15, 1993.

58. Lauren Weiner, "El Salvador Confronts the Truth Commission Report," *Freedom Review* 24, no. 6 (November–December 1993): 36.

59. Ibid., 37.

60. United Nations Security Council, "Further Report of the Secretary-General on the United Nations Observer Mission in El Salvador," Annex 1, S/26581, October 14, 1993, 6–7.

61. UN Security Council Resolution, 3223d meeting, S/RES/832, May 23, 1993.

62. United Nations Security Council, "Report of the Secretary-General on the United Nations Observer Mission in El Salvador," S/1994/304, 1–2.

63. United Nations Security Council, "Report of the Secretary-General on the United Nations Observer Mission in El Salvador," S/25812, May 21, 1993, 21–22.

64. "Note by the President of the Security Council," S/26695, November 5, 1993.

65. United Nations Security Council, "Report of the Secretary-General on the United Nations Observer Mission in El Salvador," S/26606, October 20, 1993; and United Nations Security Council, "Report of the Secretary-General on the United Nations Observer Mission in El Salvador," S/1994/179, February 16, 1994.

66. On the election process, see Jack Spence and George Vickers, *Toward a Level Playing Field? A Report on the Post-War Salvadoran Electoral Process* (Washington, D.C.; Cambridge, Mass.: Hemisphere Initiatives, January 1994).

67. "Report of the Secretary-General on the United Nations Observer Mission in El Salvador," S/1994/179, 5.

68. United Nations Security Council, "Further Report of the Secretary-General on the United Nations Observer Mission in El Salvador," S/26790, November 23, 1993, 19.

69. Ibid., 2.

70. Ibid.

71. Washington Office on Latin America (WOLA), *El Salvador Peace Plan Update no. 3: Recent Setbacks in the Police Transition* (Washington, D.C.: WOLA, February 4, 1994), 6.

72. United Nations Security Council, "Report of the Secretary-General on the United Nations Observer Mission in El Salvador," S/1994/536, May 4, 1994, 4.

73. See United Nations Security Council, "Report of the Secretary-General on the United Nations Observer Mission in El Salvador," S/1994/375, March 31, 1994.

74. Ibid., 2–4.

75. "Report of the Secretary-General on the United Nations Observer Mission in El Salvador," S/1994/536, May 4, 1994, 3–4.

76. See United Nations Security Council, "Letter Dated 6 February from the Secretary-General Addressed to the President of the Security Council," S/1995/143, February 17, 1995; United Nations Security Council, "Report of the Secretary-General on the United Nations Observer Mission in El Salvador," S/1995/220, March 24, 1995; and United Nations Security Council, "Letter Dated 18 May 1995 from the Secretary-General Addressed to the President of the Security Council," S/1995/407, May 18, 1995.

77. Holiday and Stanley, "Building the Peace," 430.

78. Ibid., 437.

79. Alvaro de Soto and Graciana del Castillo, "Obstacles to Peacebuilding," *Foreign Policy* 94 (spring 1994): 74.

80. De Soto and del Castillo, "El Salvador," 9

81. Ibid., 17.

82. Ibid., 12.

83. Douglas Farah, "Salvadorans Complain Postwar Crime Defeating Rebuilt Police Force," *Washington Post,* March 15, 1995, A24.

84. De Soto and del Castillo, "El Salvador," 20.

6. Cambodia

1. Patrick Brogan, *World Conflicts: Why and Where They Are Happening,* 2d ed. (London: Bloomsbury, 1992), 67.

2. Ibid., 158–160.

3. The following discussion is drawn from Wayne Bert, "Cambodia: Who Will Rule?" *Defense and Diplomacy,* no. 8 (January/February 1990): 20; Martin Wright, *Cambodia: A Matter of Survival* (Essex, England: Longman, 1989), 20, 22–38; and Brogan, *World Conflicts,* 160–164.

4. Michael Vickery, *Cambodia: 1975–82* (Boston: South End Press, 1989), 28–30.

5. Nayan Chandra, "Civil War in Cambodia?" *Foreign Policy,* no. 76 (fall 1989), 28.

6. Vickery, *Cambodia,* 30–31.

7. Ibid. 225.

8. Frank Frost, "The Cambodian Conflict: The Path towards Peace," *Contemporary Southeast Asia* 13 (September 1991).

9. Muthiah Alagappa, "Regionalism and the Quest for Security: ASEAN and the Cambodian Conflict," *Journal of International Affairs* 46 (winter 1993): 455–456.

10. John McAuliff and Mary Byrne McDonnell, "Ending the Cambodian Stalemate," *World Policy Journal* (winter 1989): 38; Wright, *Cambodia,* 51.

11. Michael Leifer, "Power-Sharing and Peacemaking in Cambodia?" *SAIS Review* 12 (winter–spring 1992): 141.

12. Ulrich Fuesser and Gerhard Will, "Cambodia: No Peace in Sight," *Aussenpolitik* 42, no. 2 (1991): 201.

13. Leifer, "Power-Sharing and Peacemaking in Cambodia?" 142.

14. Alagappa, "Regionalism and the Quest for Security," 459.

15. Frost, "The Cambodian Conflict," 155; *UN Chronicle,* June 1991, 26–27.

16. Leifer, "Power-Sharing and Peacemaking in Cambodia?" 144.

17. Wright, *Cambodia,* 53–54; Chandra, "Civil War in Cambodia?" 31.

18. Lewis Stern, "Cambodia: Diplomacy Falters," *Current History* (March 1990): 135.

19. Brogan, *World Conflicts,* 166.

20. Wright, *Cambodia,* 73, 101; Chandra, "Civil War in Cambodia?" 31.

21. William S. Turley, "The Khmer War: Cambodia after Paris," *Survival* 33 (September/October 1990): 444–447.

22. Feusser and Will, "Cambodia," 202; McAuliff and McDonnell, "Ending the Cambodia Stalemate," 78; Wright, *Cambodia*, 55.

23. Frost, "The Cambodian Conflict," 40; Stern, "Cambodia," 136; Wright, *Cambodia,* 55–57.

24. Frost, "The Cambodian Conflict," 141; Leifer, "Power-Sharing and Peacemaking in Cambodia?" 144.

25. On these and subsequent negotiations, see McAuliff and McDonnell, "Ending the Cambodian Stalemate," 80–84; Alagappa, "The Cambodian Conflict," 460; Stern, "Cambodia," 137; Frost, "The Cambodian Conflict," 142; Feusser and Will, "Cambodia," 204–205; and Turley, "The Khmer War," 442–449.

26. Fuesser and Will, "Cambodia," 203–208.

27. United Nations General Assembly, "Letter Dated 15 March 1990 from the Representatives of China, France, the Union of Soviet Socialist Republics, the United Kingdom of Great Britain and Northern Ireland, and the United States of America to the United Nations Addressed to the Secretary-General," A/45/167, S/21196, March 16, 1990.

28. Abdulgaffar Pean-Meth, "The United Nations Plan, the Cambodian Conflict, and the Future of Cambodia," *Contemporary Southeast Asia* 14 (June 1992): 37.

29. "Gist: A Comprehensive Political Settlement in Cambodia," *U.S. Department of State Dispatch,* October 21, 1991, 776.

30. Fuesser and Will, "Cambodia," 205–206; Frost, "The Cambodian Conflict," 143.

31. Leifer, "Power-Sharing and Peacemaking in Cambodia," 145.

32. "Gist: Cambodia Settlement Agreement," *U.S. Department of State Dispatch,* June 8, 1992, 455.

33. United Nations General Assembly, "Letter Dated 8 January 1991 from the Permanent Representatives of France and Indonesia to the United Nations Addressed to the Secretary-General," A/46/61, S/22059, January 11, 1991.

34. "Secretary-General Recommends Establishment of UN Advance Mission in Cambodia (UNAMIC)," *UN Chronicle,* December 1991, 26.

35. Brogan, *World Conflicts,* 167.

36. Secretary of State James Baker, "Cambodia Conference Intervention: Remarks at the Paris Conference on Cambodia, Paris," *U.S. Department of State Dispatch,* October 28, 1991, 792.

37. See text of UN Security Council Resolution 718, *UN Chronicle,* March 1992, 53.

38. *U.S. Department of State Dispatch,* October 21, 1991, 781.

39. Some thirty-two countries contributed military personnel to UNTAC: Algeria, Argentina, Australia, Austria, Bangladesh, Belgium, Bulgaria, Cameroon, Canada, Chile, China, France, Germany, Ghana, India, Indonesia, Ireland, Japan, Malaysia, the Netherlands, New Zealand, Pakistan, the Philippines, Poland, Russia, Senegal, Thailand, Tunisia, the United Kingdom, the United States, and Uruguay. See "Gist: Cambodia Settlement Agreement," *U.S. Department of State Dispatch,* June 8, 1992; "UNclear," *Economist,* February 29, 1992, 38; and UN Security Council, "First Report of the Secretary-General on the United Nations Transitional Authority in Cambodia," S/23870, May 1, 1992.

40. United Nations Security Council, "Report of the Secretary-General on Cambodia," S/23613, February 19, 1992, and Add.1, February 26, 1992.

41. "Urge Full Deployment of UN Transitional Authority in Cambodia," *UN Chronicle,* September 1992, 19.

42. United Nations Security Council, "Special Report of the Secretary-General on the United Nations Transitional Authority in Cambodia," S/24090, June 12, 1992.

43. "Cambodia's Cause for Concern," *Economist,* June 20, 1992, 31; "Deep Concern Expressed over Implementation of Paris Agreements in Cambodia," *UN Chronicle,* December 1992, 31–32.

44. United Nations Security Council, "Second Special Report of the Secretary-General on the United Nations Transitional Authority in Cambodia," S/24286, July 14, 1992.

45. "Trusting Pol Pot," *Economist,* September 5, 1992; UN Security Council, "Second Progress Report of the Secretary-General on the United Nations Transitional Authority in Cambodia," S/24578, September 21, 1992.

46. "From Paris to Phnom Penh" and "Sihanouk for President," *Economist,* November 14, 1992, 16–18 and 36–37.

47. "The Road to Cambodia's Peace," *Economist,* November 21, 1992, 37; "Shattered Land," *Far Eastern Economic Review,* May 27, 1993, 12.

48. United Nations Security Council, "Third Progress Report of the Secretary-General on the United Nations Transitional Authority in Cambodia," S/25124, January 25, 1993.

49. "Memories of Paris," *Economist,* January 23, 1993, 34; United Nations Security Council, "Report of the Secretary-General on the Implementation of Security Council Resolution 792 (1992)," S/25289, February 13, 1993.

50. "The Unwanted," *Economist,* March 20, 1993, 45; "Black Clouds," *Economist,* April 3, 1993, 40; "Khmer Blues," *Economist,* February 20, 1993, 36.

51. "Best They Can Do," *Economist,* April 10, 1993, 36.

52. "The Missionaries' Position," *Economist,* April 24, 1993, 36.

53. "Vote for Cambodia," *Economist,* April 10, 1993, 19.

54. "Shattered Land," *Far Eastern Economic Review,* May 27, 1993, 12.

55. "Khmer Rouge Won't Halt Insurrection," *Globe and Mail,* May 31, 1993, A6.

56. "Cambodian Vote Great Success," *Globe and Mail,* May 26, 1993, A7.

57. "Guerrillas Join Trek to Polls in Free Election," *Ottawa Citizen,* May 25, 1993, A6.

7. The Need to Nurture Peace

1. David C. Unger, for example, argues that "historically [the United Nations] has done best by intervening only after contending parties reach a mutually acknowledged stalemate. It can then play the role of neutral peacekeeper, monitoring agreements the parties have already reached." See his article, "U.N. Troops Cannot Stop Genocide, Pretending They Can Invites Failures," *New York Times,* July 31, 1994, E14.

2. Thomas L. Friedman, "Lift, Lift, Contain," *New York Times,* June 4, 1995, E15.

3. Benjamin Schwarz, "The Diversity Myth: America's Leading Export," *Atlantic* 275, no. 5 (May 1995): 66, 67.

4. For the full names of organizations (like MPLA and UNITA) referred to in this chapter by their acronyms, see the appropriate case-study chapter or the index.

5. Roy Licklider, "What Have We Learned and Where Do We Go from Here?" in Roy Licklider, ed., *Stopping the Killing: How Civil Wars End* (New York: New York University Press, 1993), 309.

6. Ripeness is associated with such factors as a change in leadership, a leader who stakes his or her position on attaining a negotiated settlement, factional changes, a reversal in the military fortunes of competing sides (see Stephen John Stedman, *Peacemaking in Civil War: International Mediation in Zimbabwe, 1974–1980* [Boulder, Colo.: Lynne Rienner, 1991], 240–241), and/or a change in *expectations* about future battlefield outcomes (see Roy Licklider, "How Civil Wars End," in Licklider, *Stopping the Killing,* 310).

7. Kalevi J. Holsti, *Peace and War: Armed Conflicts and International Order, 1648–1989* (Cambridge: Cambridge University Press, 1991), 338.

8. Gareth Evans, *Cooperating for Peace: The Global Agenda for the 1990s and Beyond* (London: Allen and Unwin, 1993), 11.

9. World Bank, *Demobilization and Reintegration of Military Personnel in Africa: The Evidence from Seven Country Case Studies,* report no. IDP-130 (Washington, D.C.: World Bank, 1993), vi.

10. This observation follows from ibid., viii.

11. Ibid., 26.

12. Janet E. Heininger, *Peacekeeping Transition: The United Nations in Cambodia* (New York: Twentieth Century Fund Press, 1994), 39.

INDEX

Jennings Randolph Program for International Peace

As part of the statute establishing the United States Institute of Peace, Congress envisioned a fellowship program that would appoint "scholars and leaders of peace from the United States and abroad to pursue scholarly inquiry and other appropriate forms of communication on international peace and conflict resolution." The program was named after Senator Jennings Randolph of West Virginia, whose efforts over four decades helped to establish the Institute.

Since it began in 1987, the Jennings Randolph Program has played a key role in the Institute's effort to build a national center of research, dialogue, and education on critical problems of conflict and peace. Through a rigorous annual competition, outstanding men and women from diverse nations and fields are selected to carry out projects designed to expand and disseminate knowledge on violent international conflict and the wide range of ways it can be peacefully managed or resolved.

The Institute's Distinguished Fellows and Peace Fellows are individuals from a wide variety of academic and other professional backgrounds who work at the Institute on research and education projects they have proposed and participate in the Institute's collegial and public outreach activities. The Institute's Peace Scholars are doctoral candidates at American universities who are working on their dissertations.

Institute fellows and scholars have worked on such varied subjects as international negotiation, regional security arrangements, conflict resolution techniques, international legal systems, ethnic and religious conflict, arms control, and the protection of human rights, and these issues have been examined in settings throughout the world.

As part of its effort to disseminate original and useful analyses of peace and conflict to policymakers and the public, the Institute publishes book manuscripts and other written products that result from the fellowship work and meet the Institute's high standards of quality.

Joseph Klaits
Director

NURTURING PEACE

This book is set in Garamond Light. Hasten Design Studio designed the book's cover, and Joan Engelhardt and Day W. Dosch designed the interior. Helene Y. Redmond of HYR Graphics did the page makeup. Nigel Quinney was the book's editor.